IN
BED
WITH THE
ANCIENT
GREEKS

SEX & SEXUALITY
IN ANCIENT GREECE

*Sexual intercourse never did anyone any good; we should be glad
if it does us no actual harm.*

Epicurus, fragment 62

Sexual intercourse is a brief attack of apoplexy.

Democritus, fragment 32

IN
BED
WITH THE
ANCIENT
GREEKS

SEX & SEXUALITY IN
ANCIENT GREECE

PAUL CHRYSTAL

AMBERLEY

*For Ian Dickson, for no particular reason other than that
he has been a constant friend for more than forty years*

Books by the same author:

Women in Ancient Rome (2013)
Roman Women: The Women Who Influenced Roman History (2015)
In Bed with the Romans: Sex and Sexuality in Ancient Rome (2015)
*Wars and Battles of the Roman Republic: The Bloody Road to
Empire* (2015)
Roman Military Disasters: Dark Days and Lost Legions (2015)
Ancient Greece in 100 Facts (2016)
Women in Ancient Greece (2016)
When in Rome: Everyday Life in Ancient Rome (2016)
Women and War in Greece and Rome (2016)

First published 2016

Amberley Publishing
The Hill, Stroud
Gloucestershire, GL5 4EP

www.amberley-books.com

British Library Cataloguing in Publication Data.
A catalogue record for this book is available from the British Library.

ISBN 978 1 4456 5412 6 (hardback)
ISBN 978 1 4456 5413 3 (ebook)

Typesetting and Origination by Amberley Publishing.
Printed in the UK.

Contents

Preface

This is a companion volume to the author's *In Bed with the Romans*, published in 2015. *In Bed with the Ancient Greeks* provides a balanced, comprehensive and well-researched survey of sex and sexuality in the various ancient Greek societies – from the Minoan civilisation, through Athens and Sparta, to Macedon and Hellenistic Greece. Along the way we examine attitudes towards and the practice of sex in Greek society; sexuality in myth, literature and in real life; prostitution; love, marriage, divorce and adultery; sex in religion and philosophy; sex in the visual arts; sexual medicine; sex as magic; and the vocabulary of sex. Primary sources are used extensively to support findings and provide evidence.

In Bed with the Ancient Greeks is an important and much-needed book which will shine light on sex and sexuality in ancient Greece, highlighting the part it played in one of the world's most influential civilisations and the contribution it made to subsequent cultures and societies.

Introduction

For one reason or another, to the ancient Greeks bed was an important place to be. For a man it was where he discharged his important duty as a citizen to replenish and increase the citizenry of his *polis,* his city state, by having many children – ideally boys. It was also where he might commit adultery with impunity when he entertained his female slaves, prostitutes or concubines in pursuit of sexual gratification, or when his wife was heavily pregnant or had just given birth, or if she was being unadventurous or just not interested. Alternatively, he might take his boy lovers there in his role as a pederast, or he might consort there with an effeminate adult male or two. For a woman, it was where she had sex with her husband in order to mother as many children as possible – again ideally boys – in order to fulfil her responsibility to provide citizens to populate the army and the state machinery. Doctors, poets and philosophers had all ordained that sex, and therefore bed, was neither a thing nor a place of pleasure for the average woman.

As the title hints, *In Bed with the Ancient Greeks* surveys the sex and sexuality of ancient Greek men and women. It opens with a survey of the Minoan civilisation's sexuality, noting the relative freedom enjoyed there by women and girls as relatively full and active members of Cretan society. Then we move on to sex and sexuality in Greek mythology, where the templates for social and sexual conduct in real-world Greece were established: male power and dominance, double standards relating to adultery, and the misogynist view of woman as the worst of all things and the source of all man's troubles. The chapter on sex in literature takes this forward and reveals the prevalent attitudes to women in society, again demonising them to some extent, although we do get a picture of what the typical Greek male thought might constitute the ideal Greek wife.

A chapter dealing with social aspects of sex follows with coverage of love, marriage, adultery and sexual violence. Sexual deviance and strange practices are then examined, followed by chapters on male and female homoeroticism, and the important role of prostitution. Differences in attitudes towards sex and sexuality are exposed in Sparta and Macedon – the one proving relatively liberal and reminiscent of the Minoans, the other using sex as a political weapon to cement alliances and save dynasties. How Greek historians, mainly Herodotus, deal with sex, particularly sex in other countries, is followed by a chapter on sexuality in the visual arts. Sex was always prominent and evident in Greek religion and a major subject for discussion by philosophers: both are covered next. The dark arts would not be nearly so dark were it not for their erotic element – the subject of the following chapter describing witches and violent sexual cursing. Gynaecology, obstetrics and male sexual medicine then precede a much-needed survey of sex manuals and the Greek sexual vocabulary.

1

In Bed with the Minoans

Despite the scant surviving evidence, we are still able to piece together with some considerable accuracy a reasonable picture of sex and sexuality in the world of the Minoans.

Minoan society predated the male-dominated norm found elsewhere in ancient Greece. It seems to have been more egalitarian, with archaeological evidence suggesting that women played a relatively prominent role in public life. Women were priestesses, officials, administrators, skilled artisans and entrepreneurs; women took part in athletics – all functions which in other parts of Greece would be dominated exclusively by males. The kings in the palaces were male, but Minoan society was not necessarily patriarchal and indeed may have been matrilineal. Chelsea O'Toole puts it well in her *Aegean Gender: Minoans, Mycenaeans, and Classical Greeks:*

> Because we have not deciphered the language of the Minoans, our information about gender roles comes from the depictions of women in these frescoes and figurines. However, from these works of art, archaeologists have been able to discover that women played an important role in Minoan society. The lifestyle of the Minoan women seems more similar to gender in ancient Egypt than in later mainland Greece. Mycenaean-ruled Greece shows the start of a period of transition in which gender roles became more clearly defined and in which women started becoming more and more associated with domestic duties. By the time of the Classical Greeks, there was an established history of great gender inequality, as evidenced by property laws, house constructions, and social roles. In the archaeological and historical evidence in

the Aegean, there seems to be a clear pattern of increasing repression of women over time.[1]

Barbara Olsen has further argued that Minoan women did not have the main responsibility for rearing children, as in other cultures such as the Mycenaean and later Greek societies.[2]

On the Greek mainland, archaeologists have unearthed numerous *kourotrophoi* or child nurturers. These figurines in the form of women and children are the only depictions of mothers and children on the mainland; there is nothing to be found dating from the late Bronze age. *Kourotrophoi* may have been children's toys, grave offerings or simply everyday domestic objects; whatever they are, they signify the importance of motherhood, domesticity and family life in Mycenaean Greece. In Minoan Crete there are no such figures or anything else depicting a human mother and child. Instead, Crete women feature in public assemblies, dancing, chatting, and participating in religious ceremonies, all suggesting a high and active public profile which did not limit them to maternal or domestic duties. Therefore Mycenaean and Minoan women fulfilled very different roles in their respective societies: the domesticity evident in the former can be seen as an important stage in the transition toward the stricter gender roles we see in later urbanised Greek culture, typified in the classical era by women who, for the most part, did not participate in public life. After the eighth century BC, mothers and children appear frequently on artefacts found on Crete, reflecting the fact that that classical Greek culture embraced a domestic, maternal role for women which had only become the historical norm in post-Minoan Crete.

Some scholars have argued that Minoan Crete did not fight wars and was not at all warlike – an aspect that might have contributed to the elevated status of women in Minoan culture. Recent research, however, shows that this was not the case: 'Research reveals that war was in fact a defining characteristic of the Minoan society, and that warrior identity was one of the dominant expressions of male identity.'[3] So, far from long-term peace providing an environment which allowed women to thrive socially, it might be argued that war and combat were in fact drivers of women's status, imbuing women with militaristic purpose.

The principal Minoan goddess, Potnia (meaning lady or mistress), exhibited a number of characteristics which elsewhere are associated with male divinities: she is a veritable multitasker – shown with the sword, with the double-axe, as a huntress, as a goddess of sports, as an armed goddess. The name often occurs with some defining qualification such as Potnia of Grain, Potnia of Horses, or Potnia of the Labyrinth. Whether they are derivatives of Potnia or goddesses in their own right, Minoan goddesses far outnumber gods: female deities presided over dances, ruled over the mountains, the earth, the sky and the sea; they held dominion over life and over death. Potnia was a household goddess, a vegetation goddess, a mother and a maid. She was a lunar goddess and a fertility goddess. During early Minoan civilisation, only the goddesses seemed to exhibit military characteristics and no sign of any men with weapons. There was a Mother Goddess of fertility, a Mistress of the Animals, a protectress of cities, the household, the harvest, and the underworld. To complement this in concrete experience, women played a vital role in Minoan religion, sacrificing goats, pigs, doves and hares. Women far outnumber priests and male attendants, for example, in the paintings on the four sides of the Aghia Triadha sarcophagus.

It is only with the post-palatial period that we meet the first divine male counterpart, a male deity who eventually becomes associated with weapons and is depicted with a bow, a spear, and a shield. At roughly the same time, a festival heavy with sexual significance emerges where both the men and women dance, wearing bull and cow masks: the festival of the solar bull (the new male god) and the lunar cow (the female goddess). Zeus and Hera emerged from this: Hera was originally a cow goddess; Zeus was the sun disguised as a bull, or a solar bull.

Boxing and bull-jumping – *taurokathapsia*, from ταυροκαθάψια – were the two most popular sports in Crete, and women as well as men participated. A common theme found in Minoan wall paintings and vases, the illustrations of these events emphasise grace, fluidity and gymnastic skill more than bravery. Female bull leapers feature in the famous Taureador Fresco, where, interestingly, they are wearing men's clothing and do not appear to have breasts – Minoan artists often did not include breasts on female figures.

Minoan men wore little except loincloths or a codpiece, a belt, shoes, and the occasional jewellery; these loincloths were made from materials such as linen, leather, or wool, and were sometimes highly decorated with bright colours and patterns. Many had a decorative pagne or sheath that covered and protected the penis, and some had long aprons in the front and back with tassels or a fringe.

Women wore more clothing and were covered up, with only their breasts and forearms bare. The main items were short-sleeved robes that had layered, flounced skirts; these were open to the navel, leaving the breasts exposed. They also wore a strapless fitted bodice, the first fitted garments known in history. Women were typically depicted as having a tiny waist, full breasts, long hair and full hips. To our eyes and ears this is sexually charged and provocative, but to a Minoan probably not so. In contrast, the voluptuous figure may have been a means by which women, and their artists, expressed their gender and status rather than male artists simply idealising their sexuality for their own delectation, satisfying a prurient male voyeurism. Moreover, when women inhabit the lower positions within a society they are often obliged to cover the body and wear a veil; the openly glamorous Minoan woman would suggest quite the opposite: that women occupied a high position in society. Women in Minoan Crete, it seems, were able to celebrate their femininity. The body shape described above re-emerged during the late 1800s AD, when women laced themselves into tight corsets to make their waists small and wore hoops under their skirts to exaggerate the proportions of their lower body. Some scholars believe that Minoan women too must have had some sort of framework under their skirts to support the bell shape. Indeed, so similar were Minoan fashions to French fashions of the 1800s that one of the women in an ancient Minoan painting was nicknamed 'La Parisienne' by those who discovered her.

The so-called 'snake goddesses' are figurines depicting a women holding a snake in each hand and date to the neo-palatial period of Minoan civilisation. They are important because they clearly demonstrate what we assume is the typical Minoan female body and the clothing described above. The serpent is often associated with the renewal of life and with reproduction because it sloughs its skin; it is also the protector of the house – two functions closely connected with women's role in society.

The Minoans may have practiced human sacrifice. At the temple at Anemospilia four human skeletons have been discovered. One, by its contracted position, suggests that the man had been trussed up for sacrifice, and the discoloration of the bones on one side of his body reveals that he died through blood loss. The skeleton of a twenty-eight-year-old woman was found spreadeagled on the ground in the same room as the male. Next to them was the skeleton of a man in his late thirties, with broken legs. At Fournou

Korifi, fragments of a human skull are thought to have been the remains of a sacrificed victim. In the North House at Knossos, the bones of at least four healthy children have been discovered with signs that they were butchered, sacrificed and eaten.

Cretan pederasty was an early form of paedophilia dating from the Minoan period, around 1650 to 1500 BC, that involved the ritual kidnapping (*harpagmos*) of a boy from an elite background by an aristocratic adult male, with the consent of the boy's father. This male was known as *philetor*, befriender; the boy was *kleinos*, glorious. The man took the boy out into the wilderness, where they spent two months hunting and feasting with friends. If the boy was pleased with how this went he changed his status from *kleinos* to *parastates,* or comrade, signifying that he had metaphorically fought in battle alongside his *philetor* and went back and lived with him. The *philetor* showered the boy with expensive gifts, including an army uniform, an ox for sacrifice to Zeus, and a drinking goblet – a symbol of spiritual accomplishment. At the same time, according to Strabo, the boy must choose between continuing with or putting an end to the relationship with his abductor, and whether to denounce the man if he had misbehaved in any way.

The Roman historian Cornelius Nepos claims that Cretan youths had more than one lover.[4] Apart from teaching the boy essential adult skills, pederasty allegedly also demonstrated who the best men were. We learn from Aristotle that it was originally instituted as a form of population control:

[They] segregated the women and set up sexual relations among the males so that women would not have children. [5]

Strabo gives us more detail:

[The Cretans] have a strange custom regarding love affairs, for they win the objects of their love, not by persuasion, but by abduction; the lover tells the friends of the boy three or four days beforehand that he is going to make the abduction; if the friends hide the boy, or restrain him, it is indeed a most disgraceful thing, a confession, as it were, that the boy is unworthy to obtain such a lover; and when they meet, if the abductor is the boy's equal or superior in rank or other respects, the friends pursue him and lay hold of him, though only in a very gentle way, thus satisfying the custom; and after that they cheerfully turn the boy over to him to lead away; if, however, the abductor is unworthy, they take the boy away from him.[6]

Failure to attract a *philetor* was stigmatic for a good-looking or noble boy; on the other hand, *parastates* are honoured and are given privileged positions in dances. Once they have grown into manhood, they wear a special dress which shows them to have been a distinguished *kleinos*. According to Strabo:

> The most desirable youths, according to Cretan conventions, are not the really handsome ones, but rather those who are distinguished for manly courage and discipline.

There is ample archaeological evidence for pederasty. At a shrine dedicated to Hermes and Aphrodite on Mount. Dikte numerous bronze objects and the remains of animal sacrifices have been unearthed. They include bronze figures of youths from the Minoan period. One set, from the eighth or seventh century BC, now in the Louvre, shows a male couple: an older bearded male and a younger male with long hair and curls at the front. The older partner is carrying a horn bow and is grasping the younger by the arm and drawing him close. The boy carries a slain goat on his shoulders for sacrifice. They are gazing at each other, their legs and feet touch, the younger male exposes his genitals.

A number of bronze figures, dated about 750 BC, can be seen in the Heraklion Museum: two helmeted but otherwise naked youths sport erections and stand next to each other holding hands. Yet another, dated to the seventh century BC, shows a boy, nude except for a long, ornate cape and sandals, holding a bow and quiver. The Chieftain Cup, found in 1903 in the male dining club of the palace at Hagia Triada, and dated around 1650 BC to 1500 BC, is carved out of serpentinite and shows two beardless youths, one older than the other, dressed in kilts and high boots and wearing jewellery. The older is giving the younger a sword and a javelin, while on the reverse of the cup, other youths, presumably the lover's friends, bring three pressed ox hides for making a shield.

Two Cretan pederastic folktales have survived in fragments, both featuring boys called Leucocomas, a name meaning *leukos*, bright and *kóme*, hair. In the first, Leucocomas tests his lover by setting him a number of challenging tasks, known as *athlon*, and reminiscent of the twelve Labours of Heracles – *dodekathlos*. Euxinthetus the lover must retrieve the boy's dog from Prasus (twenty-eight kilometres away). In the second, that of Promachus, 'forward fighter', Leucocomas also sets his lover a number of difficult challenges, culminating in the retrieval of a priceless helmet. Promachus, however, angered by his lover's interminable and unreasonable demands, procures the helmet but provocatively places it on the head of another boy, leading Leucocomas to kill himself in a jealous rage.[7]

It comes as no surprise that this pederasty was seen as the origin of the myth of Zeus kidnapping Ganymede as his lover on Olympus; Plato, however, rejects this interpretation.[8]

2

Mythical Sex: Rape, Incest and Homoeroticism

In the beginning was sex. To the ancient Greek mythologisers sexuality, love and sex were inextricably connected with the creation of the Earth, the heavens, and the Underworld. Greek myth was a panoply of incest, murder, polygamy and intermarriage in which eroticism and fertility were elemental; they were there right from the start, demonstrating woman's essential reproductive role in securing the cosmos, extending the human race and ensuring the fecundity of nature. Simultaneously, Zeus wasted no time in asserting his dominance – not just over the other gods, male and female – but over all things. His cavalier attitude towards female sexuality, as manifested in serial rape and seduction, set the tone for centuries of male domination and female subservience; the depiction of Hera as a distracting, duplicitous and deceptive woman opened the door for years of male mistrust, insecurity and misogyny. Down on earth, hapless Pandora was soon doomed to open the box and slam the door for evermore on any hope women had for equality or due recognition in the grand scheme of things.

The Creation

Chaos, the first Greek deity, was a goddess who gave birth to 'Gaia, the broad-breasted' and 'Eros, the fairest of the deathless gods'. Chaos also gave birth to Erebos and dark Night, who mated and produced Ether and Day. Then Night created Doom, Fate, Death, Sleep, Dreams, Nemesis, and all the other chthonic entities that dwell in the darkness haunting mankind. Gaia gave birth to Uranus, the sky. Uranus married his mother, Gaia, enveloping her: they gave birth to the three Cyclopes, the three Hecatoncheires, and twelve Titans.

Uranus despised the Hecatoncheires and incarcerated them in Gaia's womb, much to her annoyance. She made a flint sickle and incited her children to assault Uranus; but only the youngest Titan, named Cronus, was brave enough to do so. Gaia and Cronus planned to attack Uranus while he was asleep. Cronus castrated his father with the sickle, throwing the seemingly redundant genitals into the sea. Blood was spilled on the earth, from which emerged the Giants, the Ash Tree Nymphs (the Meliae), and the Furies (the Erinyes). Aphrodite rose from the foam that was produced in the sea when Uranus' genitalia fell in there, hence her name, meaning 'foam-arisen'. Hesiod in his *Theogony* says that the genitals 'were carried over the sea for a long time, and white foam arose from the immortal flesh; with it a girl grew.' That girl, Aphrodite, floated ashore on a scallop shell: this iconic image of Aphrodite as a mature 'Venus rising from the sea', Venus Anadyomene, was made famous in a painting by Apelles, now lost, but described for us in the *Natural History* of Pliny the Elder.

Cronus took control. He imprisoned the Cyclopes and the Hecatoncheires in Tartarus and married his sister Rhea, who produced lots of children. Meanwhile, Gaia and Uranus had prophesied that Cronus would be deposed by a son; to avoid this, Cronus methodically swallowed all of his children as they were being born. Rhea, naturally, was livid at the atrocious treatment of her children and plotted against Cronus. On the birth of her sixth child, Rhea hid herself away and left the child to be raised by nymphs. To save the child she wrapped a stone in swaddling cloths and passed it off as the baby to Cronus, who promptly swallowed it as with all the rest. That sixth child was Zeus, who in time consulted Metis on how to he might defeat Cronus. She concocted a special drink for Cronus which would make him vomit up the other five children.

Zeus was concealed in a cave on Mount Ida in Crete. He was suckled by the goat Amalthea. One day, when playing with Amalthea, Zeus accidentally broke off her horn; in compensation and as a sign of gratitude, Zeus blessed the horn, so that its owner would find everything they ever desired in it. This became known as the Horn of Amalthea, or the Cornucopia, an eternal symbol of abundance.

In time, Rhea persuaded Cronus to accept Zeus, who was allowed to return to Mount Olympus as Cronus's cup-bearer, giving him the chance to serve up Metis' potion to Cronus. Cronus spewed out the other five children who, in gratitude, made him their leader, the leader of the gods.

After further conflict, known as the Titanomachy, Zeus eventually prevailed. Gaia gave birth to her last child, Typhon, the deadliest monster of all, who confronted Zeus only to be killed by Zeus' lighting bolts and buried under Mount Etna. Later, Zeus survived an invasion of Olympus by the Giants.

Who were the deities implicated in the pantheon of divine sexuality, the embodiments of typical masculine and feminine sexual qualities such as beauty, seduction and jealousy?

Hera

As wife of Zeus, Hera was the queen of heaven; she had a responsibility to protect wives and wifehood. Surprisingly, Hera was not the mother of other gods like Athena; Zeus flexed his omnipotence when he circumvented the normal biological process by having a womb in his penis, and gave birth to his progeny that way. By circumventing the normal biological process he also undermined Hera and her role as wife and mother; this led to later centuries in which the male dominance of human reproduction was enshrined in the work of such philosophers, scientists and medics as Aristotle and Galen. Usurping Hera had other implications: it was a slight from which she never recovered but bore an eternal grudge, commencing with the asexual birth of disabled Hephaestus. Her reputation as a 'difficult' woman was emphasised further when Homer shows her in the *Iliad* dressing up glamorously and provocatively to distract Zeus from the all-important business that was the Trojan War:

> There she annointed her lovely body, and she combed her hair, and braided the bright tresses, fair and divine, that flowed down from her immortal head. Then she put on a heavenly robe, which Athene had skilfully made for her with lots of embroidery; she pinned it on her breast with golden brooches of gold; her belt had a hundred tassels, and in her pierced ears she put ear-rings with three clustering drops which shone gracefully.

The conceit of woman as a disputatious and duplicitous schemer deploying sexual power was born.

Aphrodite

Aphrodite was the goddess of beauty and sexual love. Aphrodite did not have a childhood; instead she was born a mature woman, a sexually attractive and desirable one at that. Fittingly, she is often depicted nude. Some say Aphrodite was born pregnant with the twins Eros and Himeros, her constant companions and agents of her divine power. In later mythology she is vain, bad tempered, and petulant. She is a married woman and a serial adulteress. Aphrodite's great beauty unsettled the other gods, who feared that the rivalry raging over her would lead to war, so Zeus married her off to saturnine Hephaestus, who, because of his ugliness and deformity, would in theory diminish the threat she posed. However, Hephaestus achieved the very opposite when he forged her beautiful jewellery, including the *cestus*, a girdle that made her even more irresistible. Trapped in a loveless marriage, Aphrodite took many lovers – both gods, such as bellicose Ares, and mortals, like Anchises, by whom she had Aeneas. In the *Odyssey*, she is attracted to Ares because of his exciting, volatile nature.

Aphrodite also had an affair with Hermes. The couple named their beautiful, winged son Hermaphroditus. As a young man, Hermaphroditus once was peacefully bathing in a pool when the naiad Salmacis started pestering him. Hermaphroditus repelled her advances and asked her to leave. But when Hermaphroditus took his clothes off, Salmacis assaulted him, wrapping her body so tightly around his that they merged as one. Hermaphroditus now resembled a beautiful woman – with male genitals. He had serious issues with his new image and asked his parents to curse the pond so that all men who went in it thereafter would develop hermaphrodism.

Aphrodite is implicated in the Eros and Psyche legend, in which she is jealous of the ravishingly beautiful Psyche and enlists Eros to extinguish man's desire for her. Later she was both lover and surrogate mother to Adonis. Of all her lovers, Adonis is probably the greatest; he is the child of Myrrha, cursed by a jealous Aphrodite with insatiable lust for her own father, King Cinyras of Cyprus, after Myrrha's mother boasted that her daughter was more beautiful than the goddess. After becoming pregnant, Myrrha is changed into a myrrh tree, a silencing punishment, but still gives birth to Adonis. Ovid tells the story of Myrrha's incest in *Metamorphoses* 10, 300ff; he warns his readers beforehand of the enormity of the crime:

> The story I am going to tell is a horrible one: I beg that daughters and fathers should hold themselves aloof, while I sing, or if they find my songs enchanting, let them refuse to believe this

part of my tale, and suppose that it never happened: or else, if they believe that it did happen, they must believe also in the punishment that followed.

Aphrodite finds the baby Adonis and takes him to the underworld to be fostered by Persephone. She goes back to claim him when he is grown up and handsome, but Persephone is reluctant to let him go. Zeus decrees that Adonis will spend a third of the year with Aphrodite, a third with Persephone, and a third with whomsoever he wishes. Adonis chooses Aphrodite but bleeds to death after an attack by a boar; his shade is duly received in the underworld by Persephone but Aphrodite wants to return him to life. She and Persephone squabble again, and Zeus intervenes again, now decreeing that Adonis will spend six months with Aphrodite and six months with Persephone.

Aphrodite, of course, was also involved in the causes of the Trojan War when Athena, Hera and Aphrodite bickered, after Eris, the goddess of all things disputatious and discordant, mischievously gave them a golden apple, the Apple of Discord, inscribed 'for the fairest'. Eris had not been invited to the wedding of Peleus and Thetis and was somewhat resentful as a result. Zeus impatiently sent the three quarrelling goddesses to the Trojan Paris for judgement; at the time, Paris was working as a shepherd in a bid to thwart a prophecy that would see him bring about the destruction of Troy. After bathing in the spring of Ida, the three goddesses appeared before him naked, in the hope that the sight of each of them with no clothes on would help them win. An indecisive Paris, though, could not decide between them, so the goddesses resorted to yet more bribery: Athena offered Paris wisdom, skill in battle, and the ability to compete with the greatest warriors; Hera offered him political power and control over all of Asia; and Aphrodite offered him the love of the most beautiful woman in the world, Helen of Sparta no less. We have no way of knowing how long he deliberated on this but Paris gave the fateful apple to Aphrodite, and eventually returned to Troy with Helen. The result was the Trojan War.

It did not pay to be on the wrong side of Aphrodite. Aphrodite caused the death of Hippolytus, who had tactlessly scorned her in favour of Artemis. Aphrodite made his stepmother, Phaedra, fall in love with him, in full knowledge that Hippolytus would reject her. Phaedra committed suicide, and Hippolytus died. Glaucus of Corinth annoyed Aphrodite, so during the chariot race at the funeral games of King Pelias she drove his horses insane and they tore him apart.[1] Polyphonte was a young woman who chose a life of virginity with Artemis instead of getting married and having children, as recommended by Aphrodite. Aphrodite cursed her and made her have children by a bear. The offspring, Agrius and Oreius, were wild cannibals who incurred the hatred of Zeus; he transformed the whole family into birds and ill portents for mankind.[2]

By the late fifth century BC, a distinction was being made between two separate Aphrodites: Aphrodite Ourania, the Aphrodite born from the sea foam, and Aphrodite Pandemos, the common people's Aphrodite 'of all the folk', born from the union of Zeus and Dione. Amongst the neo-Platonists, Aphrodite Ourania is associated with spiritual love, and Aphrodite Pandemos with physical love. In the *Symposium*, Plato, through Pausanias (not the geographer) describes two Aphrodites; Aphrodite Ourania inspires homosexual male love; Aphrodite Pandemos, on the other hand, inspires the love of women for women. Aphrodite is also known as Areia, to show her relationship with Ares, the god of war, with whom she had an affair. Consequently, she was made into something of a war goddess, notably in Sparta.

Athena

Athena was the goddess of war; she could boast wisdom and she protected the arts and the sciences. However, in classical Greece Athena was stripped of her femininity. In the visual arts, her genital areas were robed and her breasts covered; she was sometimes depicted wearing a corset of snakes over her breasts. Elsewhere, men gave her a Medusa-like head with a garland of snakes.

The Erotes

The Erotes, plural of *eros,* were a group of winged gods and part of Aphrodite's retinue. They include Demeter, goddess of agriculture and fertility, of motherly and unconditional love. Demeter had a sexual liaison with a mortal, Iasion, in a thrice-ploughed field; the sexual imagery of the ploughed field is suggestive and in keeping with Demeter's responsibility, along with her daughter, Persephone, for world fertility, birth and abundance. The cults of Demeter and Persephone celebrated this every year, with women taking a leading part; the festivals were marked by *aischrologia* – 'dirty' jokes and sexual insults along with the display of phalluses and female genitalia.

Eros, god of love and sexual desire, was a son of Aphrodite and Ares; he is the Eros associated with athleticism, with statues erected in gymnasia, and a guardian and protector of male homosexual love. The role of Himeros, another of the sons of Ares and Aphrodite, from Ιμερος ('uncontrollable desire'), was to inspire desire and lust in people; he represented sexual desire or unrequited love. Hedylogos, god of sweet talk and flattery, can be seen depicted on vases; Hermaphroditus was god of hermaphrodites and of effeminate men; Hymenaeus was the god of weddings, the wedding hymn and the song; Pothos was god of sexual longing, yearning and desire. Anteros was another son of Ares and Aphrodite, god of requited love. He punished anyone who repudiated love or the advances of others, and was the avenger of unrequited love.

Erotes were typically mischievous, playing pranks on people; they became a popular theme in Hellenistic culture. Spells were chanted to attract or repel Erotes in order accordingly to induce love or repel it. They are often associated with homoerotic love.

Ganymede

Ganymede is the god of homosexual love. He was abducted by Zeus disguised as an eagle to serve as cup-bearer in Olympus, a highly privileged position. Homer describes Ganymede as the most beautiful of mortals:

> [Ganymede] was the loveliest born of the race of mortals, and therefore the gods took him to be Zeus' wine-pourer, for the sake of his beauty, so he might be among the immortals.[3]

Everyone on Olympus liked Ganymede, except for Hera, who regarded him as a rival for her husband's affection. Ganymede became a model for *paiderastía*, the erotic relationship between a man and a youth described above.[4] Xenophon has Socrates deny that Ganymede was the catamite of Zeus, and say that the god loved him non-sexually for his *psychē*, mind or soul, giving the etymology of his name as *ganu*, taking pleasure, and *mēd*, mind. Ganymede, he points out, was the only one of Zeus's lovers who was granted immortality.[5]

Narcissus

Narcissus is the god of self-love and vanity, also known for his prodigious beauty. Narcissus was proud and scorned anyone who admired him, a vice which did not go unnoticed by Nemesis. The deity lured him to a pool, where he saw his own reflection in the water and fell in love with it. He was transfixed and eventually lost the will to live, so besotted was he with himself. We, of course, get the term narcissism from his example, a fixation with oneself and one's physical appearance. The famous version of the myth is told in Ovid's *Metamorphoses* but there are at least three less well-known variants: one ascribed to Parthenius of Nicaea, composed around 50 BC, recently rediscovered amongst the Oxyrhynchus papyri; a version by Conon, a contemporary of Ovid, also ends in suicide;[6] and Pausanias recorded a novel variant of the story, in which Narcissus falls in love with his twin sister rather than himself.[7]

Peitho is a personification of persuasion and seduction, closely connected with Aphrodite. Philotes, daughter of Nyx, 'though she lay with none' according to Hesiod, is either goddess of affection or a daimon, a spirit of sexual intercourse. Siblings who were also symbolised as largely unpleasant personifications include:

> Hateful Moros (Doom) and black Ker (Violent Death) and Thanatos (Death), and she bore Hypnos (Sleep) and the tribe of Oneiroi (Dreams) ... Momos (Blame) and painful Oizys (Misery), and the Hesperides ... Also she bore the Moirai (Fates) and the ruthless avenging Keres (Death-Fates) ... Nemesis (Envy) to afflict mortal men, and after her, Apate (Deceit) ... and hateful Geras (Old Age) and hard-hearted Eris (Strife). [8]

Pan

Pan, god of the great outdoors, shepherds and flocks, nature, hunting and country music, and companion of the nymphs, is closely associated with sexuality and fertility. He is often depicted with an erect phallus. Diogenes the Cynic (412–323 BC) relates a myth in which Pan learns how to masturbate from his father, Hermes, and then teaches the habit to shepherds.[9] Pan's greatest conquest was that of the moon goddess, Selene, whom he seduced by wrapping himself in a sheepskin to hide his hairy, black goat-like appearance, and drew her down from the sky into the forest. Duris of Samos (*c.* 350–*c.* 281 BC), a historian, and the Vergilian commentator Servius report that Penelope slept with all 108 suitors in Odysseus' absence, and gave birth to Pan as a result.[10]

Echo was a nymph who was an accomplished singer and dancer; she scorned the love of any man, much to the chagrin of Pan, who ordered his people to kill her. Echo was torn to pieces, her body parts spread all over earth. Echo was doomed by Hera to repeat words that had been said by someone else, so she could never speak for herself.

Zeus

Zeus played the Olympian field with unbridled and endless gusto. His first lover was Metis, a Titan goddess and mother of Athena. She was unlucky: Zeus swallowed her and, while in Zeus' stomach, she gave birth to Athena, who later was evacuated from Zeus' body via his skull. He married Themis, another Titan goddess, by whom he had six children: the three Horai (Hours) and the three Moirai (Fates) and three Nymphai (Nymphs). Keeping it in the family, he later took a shine to his sister Demeter. His third wife was his aunt, Mnemosyne, who gave birth to the nine Muses. He had a liaison with cousin Leto just before his marriage to sister Hera, with whom he had Apollo and Artemis. Neither were his cousins' daughters safe from his advances, as Dione and Maia were to discover. He had an affair with his daughter Aphrodite, and was cursed by Hera who blessed them with the birth of Priapus, the phallus with a face. He also married Eurynome and Europa, seducing the latter in the guise of a bull. He tried his luck with Asteria (and failed), and had an affair with Nemesis, and in the form of a swan raped Leda; he produced a child with Hybris and two children with Selene, as well as an unspecified number of offspring with the ninth muse Calliope. He accidentally impregnated his grandmother, Gaia, twice; he pursued Persephone twice, once in the upper world and once in the underworld. He also chased Thetis but lost interest when it was prophesised that she would give birth to a son greater than his father. Zeus abducted the naiad Aigina for sex and consorted with two other Pleiades apart from Maia: Electra and Taygete. Other seductions included Aix, Deino, Himalia, Hora, Callirhoe, Carme, Othreis, Plouto, Sinope, and Thaleia, as well as an unnamed African nymph. Zeus liked his mortals too – apart from the boyish Ganymede the other nineteen victims were women: Lysithea, the Hellenics Pandora, Protogeneia, and Thyia, Antiope of Boeotia, Callisto of Arcadia, Cassiopeia of Crete, Danae of Argos, Dia of Thessalia, Elara of Orkhomenos, Eurymedousa of Phthiotis, Kalyke of Elis, Lamia of Libya, Laodemia of Lykia, Leda of Lakedaimonia, Nioba of Argolis, Olympias of Macedonia, Pyrrha (wife of Deukalion) and Phthia of Aegion. Zeus had sexual relations with at least fifty-seven others. For a helpful catalogue see Hesiod's *Theogony*, 886–929.

Sometimes, Zeus' rapacity had serious consequences for others. Danaë was the daughter and only child of King Acrisius of Argos and his wife Queen Eurydice. Acrisius was exercised by his inability to father a male heir so he asked the oracle at Delphi to divine the future prognosis of his erectile dysfunction. The bad news he received was that he would never have a son – the even worse news was that his virgin daughter would, and that this son would eventually kill him. In an attempt to prevent the inevitable, a prudent King Acrisius imprisoned Danaë in a bronze chamber under his palace – other versions say in a tall brass tower with a single richly adorned chamber, but without doors or windows, just a window in the roof for light and air. However, Zeus took a fancy to Danaë and impregnated her in the form of golden rain which poured in through the roof of the subterranean chamber and into her womb. Perseus was thus born.

A nervous Acrisius prevailed on the Furies in vain for permission to kill his grandchild, and so cast Danaë and Perseus into the sea in a wooden chest; the pair were taken in by Dictys – the brother of King Polydectes – who raised Perseus to manhood. The king took a shine to Danaë but she showed no interest; he agreed not to force her into marriage if Perseus would bring him the head of the Gorgon Medusa. Perseus cleverly avoided Medusa's gaze and decapitated her, presenting the head to Acrisius. Unfortunately, the doom-laden oracle came true when Perseus set out for Argos but, learning of the prophecy, diverted to Larissa, where athletic games were being held attended by Acrisius. At the games, Perseus accidentally struck Acrisius on the head with his javelin and killed him.

The virginal nymph Callisto was an adherent of the goddess Artemis – virginity was a prerequisite for cult membership – so Zeus disguised himself as Artemis in order to lure Callisto into the woods to rape her. Artemis discovered that her supposedly virgin follower was pregnant; she turned Callisto into a bear and set her loose in the forest, where she gave birth to Arcas. Zeus hid Arcas away and never revealed the true identity of his mother, with fatal consequences: Arcas went out hunting one day and shot a bear – his mother no less.

There is a good example of Zeus' oafish tactlessness in *Iliad* 14 when he tells Hera, as he tries to have sex with her:

Come, let us turn to lovemaking. For never did such desire for goddess or woman ever flood over me, taming the heart in my breast, not even when I loved Ixion's wife, who bore Peirithoös, the gods' equal in counsel.

According to Hesiod, Alcmene was the tallest, most beautiful and most clever mortal woman who ever lived. Her face and dark eyes were as glamorous as Aphrodite's, and she honoured her husband, Amphitryon, as no woman before her ever honoured a husband.[11] Alcmene's brothers were killed during a cattle raid and when Amphitryon, on Alcmene's bidding, sought revenge, he accidentally killed her father, Electryon. Amphitryon and Alcmene went into exile but Alcmene refused to sleep with him until he had avenged the deaths. Amphitryon set out and left for battle. For Zeus, Alcmene, his great-granddaughter, was to be his next – and last – mortal mistress. He assumed the form of Amphitryon and slept with Alcmene, but when the real Amphitryon came home from his quest for vengeance, he also had sex with his wife. Alcmene duly became pregnant with twins – Heracles (a name which ironically and annoyingly for Hera means 'the gift of Hera'), the son of Zeus, and Iphicles, Amphitryon's child. A jealous Hera contrived to delay Alcmene's delivery of Heracles so that his cousin, Eurystheus, could become king of Mycenae and Tiryns instead.[12] When Amphitryon died, Alcmene married Rhadamanthys, son of Zeus, and lived with him in exile in Boeotia. Hyllus pursued and killed Eurystheus, 'cut off his head and presented it to Alcmene; she gouged out the eyes with weaving pins'.[13] One wonders how familiar Fulvia Flacca Bambula (*c.* 83–40 BC), was with this myth when she gleefully pricked the decapitated Cicero's tongue with a hairpin.

Zeus, of course, was not the only promiscuous, immoral Olympian; as king of the gods he simply set a very poor example. Typhon or Typhoeus was the most terrible of all monsters in Greek mythology. He was Gaia's last son, his father none other than infernal Tartarus. Typhon himself, with his serpentine mate Echidna, was the father of many celebrated and scary monsters. According to the *Homeric Hymn to Apollo,* Typhon's mother was Hera who, angry at Zeus for having given birth to Athena without her involvement, prayed to Gaia to give her a son as strong as Zeus, then slapped the ground and became pregnant with Typhon.[14]

Echidna is described as having the head of a beautiful woman, with long hair and a serpent's body from the neck down.[15] Nonnus in his *Dionysiaca* describes Echidna as being 'hideous, with 'horrible poison'.[16] Herodotus tells the story of how, when Heracles was driving the cattle of Geryones, he awoke and discovered that his horses had disappeared. In his search, he 'found in a cave a creature of double form that was half maiden and half serpent; above the buttocks she was a woman, below them a snake'. This monster possessed the missing horses and promised to return them if Heracles would have sex with her. Heracles agreed and she had three sons by him: Agathyrsus, Gelonus and Scythes, who gave his name to Scythia.[17]

Ixion

Mortals in mythology could be equally promiscuous and hubristic. Ixion, king of the Lapiths of Thessaly, married Dia and, according to tradition, promised Deioneus, his father-in-law, a valuable present, the bride price. However, Ixion reneged on this offer, so Deioneus stole some of Ixion's horses as compensation. Ixion slyly invited his father-in-law to a feast at Larissa, at which Ixion pushed him into a fire of burning coals and wood. Ixion went insane, defiled by his act of violating *xenia*, hospitality to guests, and with all hopes of purification gone. Thereafter Ixion lived as an outcast, the first man to be guilty of kin-slaying in Greek mythology.

Zeus took pity on Ixion who, instead of being grateful, lusted after Hera, a further violation of guest–host relations. Zeus was having none of this and made a cloud nymph in the shape of Hera, Nephele, and duped Ixion into having sex with it. From this Centauros was born; he mated with the Magnesian mares on Mount Pelion, thus creating the Centaurs. Ixion was banished from Olympus and blasted with a thunderbolt; Zeus then ordered Hermes to bind Ixion to an eternally spinning, flaming wheel, and later transferred him to Tartarus.

Tiresias

We have Tiresias, the seer, to thank for answering an age-old question which many of us have pondered: is sex better for men or for women? When Tiresias came across a pair of snakes copulating, he killed the female with his staff. An angry Hera turned him into a woman as a result. Obviously 'she', Tiresias, learned a lot of interesting things about women in this time, but when, eight years later, 'she' happened on another pair of mating snakes, 'she' trampled on the male and promptly turned back into a man. A curious Zeus and Hera asked him which of the two sexes enjoyed sexual intercourse more: the man, as Hera claimed, or, as Zeus said, the woman. Tiresias, with the unique wisdom of having experienced both, divulged that sex was more enjoyable when he was a woman: 'Of ten parts a man enjoys one only.' This was not what Hera wanted to hear so she punished him for heresy with blindness; Zeus, however, inclined to the opposite and invested in Tiresias the power of prophecy and the gift of longevity.[18]

Poseidon

Poseidon was almost as prolifically promiscuous as Zeus, with forty-two seductions of mortal women and one man, Pelops, to his credit. Most of the women bore him at least one son, including Theseus, Orion and Bellerophon. He was not averse to affairs with goddesses, too, and can include Aphrodite, Demeter, Gaia and Hestia amongst his Olympian conquests. Demeter required some nifty shape-changing, according to Pausanias:

> When Demeter was wandering in search of [Persephone] her daughter, she was followed, it is said, by Poseidon, who lusted after her. So she turned, the story runs, into a mare, and grazed with the mares of Ogkios [in Arkadia]; realising that he was outwitted, Poseidon changed into a stallion and enjoyed Demeter. At first, they say, Demeter was angry at what had happened, but later on she laid aside her wrath.[19]

Twenty-six nymphs also succumbed, including one of the three Gorgons, the grotesquely ugly Medusa before she was so transformed. Poseidon raped her while in the shape of a bird. They had two children – the giant Khrysaor and the winged horse Pegasus – both of which sprang from her severed neck when she was slaughtered by Perseus. Hesiod describes it romantically:

> Poseidon, he of the dark hair, lay with one of these in a soft meadow and among spring flowers.

Ovid, less so:

> She [Medusa], it's said, was raped in Athena's shrine by Poseidon. Zeus' daughter turned away and covered with her shield her virgin's eyes. And then for fitting punishment [Zeus] transformed the Gorgo's lovely hair to hateful snakes.[20]

Poseidon fell for the beautiful Theophane, daughter of the Macedonian King Bisaltes, who was in turn a son of Helios and Gaia. Theophane had numerous suitors so Poseidon kidnapped her and took her to the isle of Crinissa to which the suitors pursued her. To hide her, Poseidon 'changed Theophane into a very beautiful ewe, himself into a ram, and the citizens of Curmissa into cattle'. When the suitors got hungry, they killed the cattle and roasted them; Poseidon then changed the suitors into wolves. Hyginus tells us that 'he himself had sex with Theophane in the guise of a ram' and eventually gave birth to a ram with a golden fleece – Aries Chrysomallus – which carried Phrixus to Colchis, and whose fleece, hung in the grove of Ares, waited for Jason.[21]

Hades too got off lightly when he abducted Persephone and consigned her to the underworld as his bride, as described in the *Homeric Hymn to Demeter* (4–20).

Mythical bestiality

The Greeks, of course, had a long tradition of bestiality going back to King Minos on Crete. The gods, as usual, did not set the best example, with Zeus slyly having sex with Leda, a swan, and unashamedly seducing Europa, Minos' mother, as a bull.

Minos was keen to get a sign from Poseidon which showed that he endorsed his accession as king. Poseidon duly sent a big white bull out of the sea which Minos was obliged to sacrifice to Poseidon. Minos however exchanged it for a different bull, which outraged Poseidon, who cursed Pasiphaë, Minos' queen, with zoophilia. Clever Daedalus built a wooden cow for her in which she concealed herself. The bull copulated with the wooden cow, at the same time impregnating Pasiphaë (Euripides, *Cretans* TrF5.1 472e, 4–52). She eventually gave birth to the Minotaur, half-man, half-bull, which was installed in the Labyrinth also built by Daedalus. To ensure no one would ever know about the Minotaur, or how to escape the Labyrinth, only Daedalus was privy to both secrets. Minos imprisoned Daedalus and his son, Icarus, with the monster. Nevertheless, Daedalus and Icarus flew away on wings invented by Daedalus; Icarus' wings melted because he famously flew too close to the sun. He plummeted to the sea and drowned.

Zeus was besotted with Europa and changed into a white bull, mixing with her father's herds so that he could seduce her. While Europa and her helpers were gathering flowers, she saw the bull, caressed his flanks, and eventually got onto his back. Zeus in the aspect of the bull ran to the sea and swam to the island of Crete. Europa became the first queen of Crete. This is how Ovid described it in his *Metamorphoses*:

> And gradually she lost her fear, and he
> Offered his breast for her virgin caresses,
> His horns for her to garland with chains of flowers
> Until the princess dared to mount his back
> Her pet bull's back, unwitting whom she rode.[22]

Zeus also took a shine to Leda and seduced her in the guise of a swan – he fell into her arms when being chased by an eagle. They copulated on the same night as Leda had sex with her Spartan husband Tyndareus. This pairing resulted in two eggs, from which hatched Helen of Troy, Clytemnestra, and Castor and Pollux, the Dioscuri (Διόσκουροι).

How far this divine bestiality extended into real Greek life it is impossible to say. Herodotus narrates that within his lifetime, a billy-goat had intercourse with a woman in Egypt – moreover in full view of everyone – 'a most surprising incident' (Herodotus 2, 46). Pliny records that Semiramis, the ninth-century-BC Assyrian queen, had sex with a horse (*NH* 8, 64), but having sex with an animal is probably something most people would want to keep between them and the animal. However, we do find evidence that it went on in the Roman period, so why not in ancient Greece? Martial in his *De Spectaculis* 6 (5) suggests that bestiality was re-enacted on stage at the inaugural games of the Flavian Amphitheatre in AD 80. Juvenal, bitter and misogynist, says that women are so sexed up at the Bona Dea that, if men are not available, they will fornicate with a donkey. He describes women as drunken maenads, mad with sex, which, if their desire cannot be satisfied by an adulterer, can be sated by the adulterer's son, or by slaves or the water carrier; as a last resort a donkey will take them in the arse, *inposito clunem sumittat asello* (Juvenal 6, 314–334). Apuleius, in the *Metamorphoses* (16; 17), describes how Lucius, when a donkey, has vigorous and consensual intercourse with an insatiable woman who pays Thiasus, his master, for the pleasure. Thiasus sees an opportunity here and Lucius' next celebrity engagement is in the full glare of an amphitheatre, caged up with a woman condemned to be fed to wild animals; before the bestial spectacle can begin, however, he escapes.

Attis

There is also evidence of divine castration, genital mutilation, the creation of eunuchs and impregnation by nuts. Attis was a Phrygian vegetation god, the consort of the great Mother Cybele who compelled him to castrate himself in a mad frenzy as punishment for his infidelity. Initiates into the resulting eunuch priesthood were called the Gallai, who re-enacted the myth with their ritual self-castration. Attis' mother was Nana, a woman impregnated by an almond from the tree which grew from the severed genitals of Agdistis:

> The gods, fearing Agdistis, cut off his penis from which grew an almond-tree with its fruit ripe; a daughter of the river Saggarios they say, took the fruit and laid it in her breast; it immediately disappeared leaving her pregnant. A boy [Attis] was born, and exposed, but was brought up by a he-goat. [Attis] was of such extraordinary beauty, that when he had grown up Agdistis fell in love with him. His relatives, however, destined him to become the husband of the daughter of the king of Pessinus, whither he went accordingly. But at the moment when the wedding song had begun, Agdistis appeared, and Attis was seized by a fit of madness, in which he castrated himself; the king who had given him his daughter followed suit. Agdistis now regretted her deed, and obtained from Zeus the promise that the body of Attis should not decompose or rot away.[23]

Agdistis was an hermaphrodite born of Gaia after she was accidentally impregnated by the sleeping sky-god Zeus. The gods feared the strange double-gendered creature and castrated it; it then became Cybele, the great Phrygian goddess.

Satyrs and Satyriasis

Satyrs, with their obnoxious equine or goat-like features, 'animal-like men with the tail of a horse, donkey ears, upturned pug noses, reclining hair-lines, and erect penises', have a reputation for being inveterate masturbators with a penchant for rape, sodomy and necrophilia – all of which goes some way to account for their dual form. Our Buggery Act of 1533 was designed in part to prevent such creations.[24] A satyr symbolises a state of lusty dissipation, representing the insatiable Dionysian passion for dancing, women and wine. Nonnus vividly describes one such party:

> Many of the horned Satyroi joined furiously in the festive dancing with nimble steps. One felt within him a new hot madness, a

sign of passion, and threw a hairy arm round a Bacchanal girl's waist. One shaken by the madness of mind-crazing drink laid hold of the girdle of a modest unwedded virgin, and as she was not up for sex pulled her back by the dress and fondled her rosy thighs from behind. Another dragged back a resisting mystic maiden while kindling the torch for the god's nightly dances, laid tentative fingers upon her bosom and pressed the swelling circle of her firm breast.[25]

Satyrs were experts on the *aulis*, a phallic-shaped double-reed instrument; some vase paintings show satryrs ejaculating while playing, one even shows a bee deftly avoiding the discharge in mid-flight. Another vase illustrates a hirsute satyr masturbating while shoving a dildo of sorts into his anus.

Apart from inspiring some wonderful depictions on ceramics, satyrs have left us the word *satyriasis*, hypersexuality – classified today in *ICD-10* as 'satyriasis' in men and as 'nymphomania' in women (in 1951 it was still listed as a 'sexual deviation') – which appears frequently in the medical authors of the Roman empire, who describe a condition no doubt extant centuries previously. Aretaeus denies its existence in women, saying that others believe that it manifests, as in men, as a desire for sex; Soranus adds that the 'itching' felt in the genitals which makes women 'touch themselves' increases their sexual urge and causes 'mental derangement' and an immodest desire for a man. His treatment involved bleeding, a liquid diet, refreshing poultices applied to the genitals and avoiding anything which caused flatulence or sexual desire. Galen called it 'uterine fury', *furor uterinus*. Theodorus Priscianus termed it *metromania*. The therapy recommended by Rufus of Ephesus included blood-letting, taking honeysuckle seed and the root of the water lily, hot baths and the avoidance of all things erotic. Rufus compares the treatment of female satyriasis with the therapy for spermatorrhea – an involuntary ejaculation of sperm which was thought to occur in both men and women.[26]

The Satyroi Nesioi were a tribe of wild Satyrs native to the islands known as the Satyrides, believed to be located somewhere off the coast of north Africa. According to Pausanias, when some sailors were forced to land on the island, the Satyroi captured and savagely violated one of their female passengers:

As soon as they caught sight of their visitors, they [the Satyrs] ran down to the ship without uttering a cry and assaulted the women in the ship. At last the terrified sailors sent a foreign woman on to the island [as a sacrificial decoy]. The Satyroi violated her not only in the usual way, but also in a most shocking manner as well.[27]

Satryros Argios was a satyr who frequented the Lernaean Springs of Argos and who attempted to rape King Danaus' daughter, Amymone, when she came to fetch water. Amymone had thrown a spear at a deer and hit a sleeping satyr by mistake; Poseidon, however, appeared on the scene and chased the satyr away. Once the satyr had fled, Poseidon, not wanting to miss an opportunity, made love to her.[28]

According to Athenaeus, gender was obviously not an issue for a satyr:

A Satyros in [a satyr-play of] Sophocles ... when burning with passion for Heracles: 'Would I might leap right on his neck as he lies back (sleeps) there.'[29]

The Amazons

The Amazons (Ἀμαζόνες) were fearsome woman warriors; as horse-born fighters they are also credited with inventing the cavalry. The most famous Amazons were Penthesilea who fought in the Trojan War and her sister Hippolyta, whose magic girdle, given to her by her father Ares, the god of war, formed the ninth labour which Hercules had to deal with. He was assisted in this by Theseus, who abducted princess Antiope, Hippolyta's sister; Antiope died fighting when Attica was invaded; this battle is commemorated in *amazonomachy*, marble bas-reliefs such as those featuring on the Parthenon or the sculptures of the Mausoleum of Halicarnassus.

The etymology of Amazon is hotly disputed. It may be from a Greek word meaning without men or husbands; alternatively, it has been suggested that it could be from ἀ- and μαζός, literally 'without breast', reflecting an ancient tradition that Amazons cut off their right breast.[30] Greek art does not support this mastectomy etymology, as the Amazons are always depicted with both breasts intact. Hippocrates differs but there seems little credibility in what he says in his *Airs, Waters, Places*:

They have no right breasts ... for when they are still babies their mothers make red-hot a bronze instrument constructed for this very purpose and apply it to the right breast and cauterize it, so that its growth is arrested, and all its strength and bulk are diverted to the right shoulder and right arm.

If the Amazons lived without men and they really were 'killers of men' (*androktones*), as Herodotus would have us believe, we have to ask how then did they survive? Apparently, once a year they visited the neighbouring Gargareans and had sex with them. Any resulting male children were either killed, sent back to their fathers or left to die of exposure; the girls, however, were retained as future Amazons, to be raised by their mothers with training in agriculture, hunting, and combat. Others say that when the Amazons went to war they would spare some of the men and take them as sex slaves, having sex with them to produce their girls.[31] In the *Iliad*, the Amazons are called *antianeirai*, those who fight like men.

Priapus

Priapus was a rustic fertility god, who looked after livestock, fruit plants, gardens and male genitalia. Priapus is characterised by his oversized, permanent erection, which gives us the medical term priapism and is the subject of the obscene collection of verse called the *Priapeia*. Depending on the source, Priapus was the son of Aphrodite by Dionysus, the father or son of Hermes, and the son of Zeus or Pan. Whichever was the case, he was a victim of Hera's wrath, who cursed him with impotence, ugliness and a filthy mind even while he was still in Aphrodite's womb; this act was in revenge for Paris judging Aphrodite the more beautiful than Hera. The other gods evicted him from Olympus, abandoning him on a hillside eventually to be found and raised by shepherds. Body image and self esteem must have been at an all-time low for Priapus.

Statues of Priapus were everywhere in ancient Greece, erected in gardens or at doorways and crossroads. To propitiate Priapus, the traveller would stroke the statue's penis as he or she passed. According to Ovid, Priapus tried to rape a sleeping Hestia but was thwarted by a donkey, whose braying caused him to lose his erection at the critical moment and woke Hestia. Naturally, this led to a lifelong hatred of asses.[32]

Dionysus

Given Dionysus' association with procreative power, fertility, phalluses, and wine and drug-fuelled ecstasy, it is perhaps surprising to learn that he is rarely depicted sporting an erection, unlike his

friends the satyrs and Priapus, and that he tends to keep his clothes
on, unlike many others on Olympus. His clothes are, admittedly,
often women's clothes but by and large he exhibits little of the
natural rakishness of Zeus, his father. While he is something of a
gender deviant and may well have succumbed to anal penetration,
he is at the same time a loving and affectionate husband to Ariadne.
In the *Acharnians*, Aristophanes describes the procession of the
phallus at the Dionysiac festival:

> Xanthias, walk behind the basket-bearer and hold the phallus
> erect; I will follow, singing the Phallic hymn; wife, watch from
> the top of the terrace. Forward! [259–62]

The *phallophori*, phallus carriers, were crowned with violets
and ivy; their faces were obscured with green foliage. They sang
'Phallics' redolent with obscenities and sexual double entendres.
Married women were not permitted to join the procession.

The ubiquity of phalluses reminds us that ancient society was
dominated by men and the symbols of manhood; the phallus was
also a good luck token against evil spirits. It was a defence against
the 'evil eye' and was exhibited to ward off the pernicious. It was
furthermore usually devoid of the shame or embarrassment it has
evoked in subsequent cultures.

Plutarch describes the *falloforia* staged by Ptolomy of Alexandria,
featuring a procession of celebrants carrying a fifty-metre-long
phallus covered in gold. The *falloforia* spread to Greece where
processions held in honour of Priapus and Dionysus involved large
wooden phalluses. Athenaeus ascribes it to Antiochus, King of
Syria, in a festival in Alexandria in 275 BC which was the last word
in extravagance, exoticism and sumptuousness:

> In other carts, also, were carried a Bacchic wand of gold, one
> hundred and thirty-five feet long, and a silver spear ninety feet
> long; in another was a gold phallus one hundred and eighty feet
> long, painted in various colours and bound with fillets of gold;
> it had at the extremity a gold star, the perimeter of which was
> nine feet.[33]

In Greece, the phallus was thought to have a mind of its own,
animal-like, separate from the mind and outside control of the
man.[34] Priapism today is understood as an often painful medical
condition in which the erect penis does not return to its flaccid

state, despite the absence of physical and psychological stimulation, usually within four hours. Priapism is a medical emergency. In females, continued painful erection of the clitoris is known as clitoral priapism or clitorism.

We first met mythic homoeroticism with Zeus and Ganymede. There are many other examples in the literature and on surviving ceramics. Hylas, for example, was Heracles' comrade and lover. Theocritus gives us a description of the young man:

> We are not the first mortals to see beauty in what is beautiful. No, even Amphitryon's bronze-hearted són, who defeated the savage Nemean lion, loved a boy – charming Hylas, whose hair hung down in curls. And like a father with a dear son he taught him all the things which had made him a mighty man, and famous.[35]

Pelops

Pelops got off to a bad start in life when his father, Tantalus, chopped him up and made a stew for the gods from the body parts; only a distracted Demeter, grieving over Persephone, had the misfortune to have a taste, and ate his shoulder. Things picked up, though, when the Fates restored the boy, replacing the missing shoulder with a newly constructed prosthesis in ivory. Poseidon fell in love with him and taught him to drive the divine winged chariot. Later, however, Pelops only had eyes for Hippodamia and wished for her hand in marriage; there was a problem, though, in that her father, King Oenomaus, was understandably worried about a prophecy that predicted he would be killed by his son-in-law. As a consequence, the king had already killed eighteen suitors after beating each of them in a chariot race; he had stuck their heads on the wooden columns around his palace as trophies. Pelops was naturally quite concerned so he called upon Poseidon, reminding him of their love – 'Aphrodite's sweet gifts.' Poseidon helped by magicking up a chariot drawn by untamed winged horses.[36]

Things got complicated and decidedly messy when a less-than-confident Pelops, on the eve of the race, convinced Oenomaus' charioteer, Myrtilus, to help him win. The prize for the deception was half of Oenomaus' kingdom and the first night of marriage in bed with Hippodamia. Myrtilus replaced the bronze linchpins attaching the wheels to the axle with ones made of beeswax ... just when Oenomaus was catching up to Pelops and getting ready to kill him, the wheels flew off. Myrtilus survived, but Oenomaus was dragged to death by his horses. Pelops murdered Myrtilus by throwing him off a cliff into the sea after he had attempted to rape Hippodamia.

In his youth, King Laius of Thebes abducted and raped Chrysippus, the son of his friend and host Pelops, King of Pisa in the Peloponnesus, and took him back to Thebes; this is the subject of one of the lost tragedies of Euripides, *Chrysippus*. Laius, who was Chrysippus' tutor, never recovered from this violation of the laws of hospitality. He was advised by the oracle never to have a son but, one night while drunk he had sex with his wife Jocasta who later gave birth to Oedipus – the infamous son who was to return from being abandoned to murder Laius.

Orpheus

Orpheus paid for his pederasty with his life. Ovid tells that Orpheus

> had abstained from loving women, either because things ended badly for him, or because he had sworn to do so. Yet, many desired to have sex with the poet, and many were upset when he rejected them. Indeed, he was the first of the Thracian people to give his love to young boys, and enjoy their brief springtime, and early flowering, before manhood.[37]

Spurned by Orpheus for taking only male lovers and for losing Eurydice by looking back on their return from the Underworld, the Ciconian Maenads, frenzied, drunken ravers and ecstatic followers of Dionysus, threw sticks and stones at him as he performed; but his music was so fine that even the rocks and branches were deflected. This maddened the already enraged women, who tore him limb from limb in frenzy. In Dürer's drawing of Orpheus' death, based on an original (now lost) by Andrea Mantegna, a ribbon bears the script *Orfeus der erst puseran*: 'Orpheus, the first pederast'.[38] Pausanias writes that the River Helicon sank underground when the Ciconian women who dismembered Orpheus tried to wash their blood-stained hands in its waters.[39] Orpheus' head floated down the River Hebrus, still singing, and came to rest on Lesbos.

Hyacinth

The beautiful youth Hyacinth was lover of Apollo, although he was admired by Zephyrus who also had claims on him. Apollo and Hyacinth would take it in turns throwing the discus, but one day Hyacinth was hit by the discus and died.[40] One version has it that a jealous Zephyrus blew Apollo's discus off course to kill Hyacinth.[41]

Apollo did not allow Hades to claim Hyacinth but created a flower, the eponymous hyacinth, from his blood.

Thamyris

Thamyris was reputedly a lover of Hyacinth's and was the first man to have loved another man.[42] Thamyris, a Thracian singer, was something of a chancer, hubristic and proud. He boasted he could sing better than the Muses, only to compete against them and lose. As punishment for his hubris they blinded him and removed his ability to make poetry and to play the lyre.[43] To make matters worse, Thamyris had claimed as his prize, if he should win the contest, the privilege of having sex with all the Muses or of marrying one of them. The story clearly demonstrates that what the gods give, the gods can take away, including the god-given gift of poetic inspiration.

3

Epic Sex, Tragic Sex and Comedic Sex

Epic Sex

Achilles and Patroclus

Controversy has raged for centuries over the nature of the relationship between Achilles and Patroclus. Some argue that it was homosexual, or at least pederastic, *paiderasteia*, while others contend that it was no more and no less than a manifestation of the deep camaraderie which bonds and binds comrades in war – a phenomenon which is impossible to feel or envisage unless it has been personally experienced. There is nothing in the *Iliad* to suggest that Achilles and Patroclus were lovers; Achilles is certainly affectionate towards Patroclus while he is unkind and arrogant to others – but there is no evidence of physical love.[1]

Their relationship is typical of that between a pair of *hetaeiroi*, companions or army 'buddies', brothers in arms.[2] It is a bond that can also be seen further down the years between Alexander the Great and Hephaestion, which was based directly on the one between Achilles and Patroclus, as well as the cases of Damon and Pythias, Orestes and Pylades, Harmodius and Aristogeiton, and that between Nisus and Euryalus in Virgil's *Aeneid* Book 9. When Patroclus is killed, Achilles is naturally distraught and his grief is couched in language not dissimilar from that used to describe Andromache's despair over the death of Hector. Achilles and Patroclus have heterosexual relationships:

> But Achilles slept in the innermost part of the well-built hut, and by his side lay a woman that he had brought from Lesbos, the daughter of Phorbas, called fair-faced Diomede. Patroclus lay

down opposite, and by him in the same way lay fair-girdled Iphis, whom good old Achilles had given to him when he took steep Scyrus, the city of Enyeus.[3]

The only real evidence for a physical relationship that is possibly a pederastic one is found in the line from Aeschylus' fragmentary *Myrmidons,* in which the tragedian gives Achilles the role of *erastes,* or protector, and Patroclus the role of *eromenos,* and Achilles speaks of a 'devout union of the thighs'.[4]

Achilles and Briseis

Epic gives us one of our earliest expressions of deep heterosexual love. It comes from a rather surprising source – from the battle-hardened, Homeric war hero and alpha male, Achilles. Achilles uncharacteristically wears his heart on his sleeve when he reveals how much he loves Briseis in Book 9 of the *Iliad,* referring to her as if she were his wife. Briseis returned his love even though it all originally came into being at the wrong end of a spear. To Achilles it was simply the right and decent thing to do to love your woman, an attitude, of course, which may have been at odds with some of the male audience members of Homer's epic down the years. Being at the centre of a damaging spat between Achilles and Agamemnon, Briseis is clearly important in the *Iliad;* her destiny has massive implications for the Greek army in the Trojan War. She was renowned for her beauty and intelligence; the relationship began when Achilles took her as war booty, having killed her father, mother, three brothers, and husband to eliminate any bothersome back story.

Briseis was thereby bereft of country, family, and freedom, not unlike Andromache after the death of Hector although on a very different social level, at least initially. Briseis was comforted, though, by Patroclus who promised to see that Achilles both married her and threw a wedding feast for them when they returned to Phthia after the war. Achilles and Patroclus knew that marriage, like love, was the right and proper thing to do. The course of their love, however, was derailed when Apollo forced Agamemnon to give up his concubine, Chryseis, and he selfishly and spitefully demanded Briseis as compensation. Achilles famously sulked and withdrew military support for the Greek allies when Briseis disappeared into Agamemnon's tent, comparing his relationship with Briseis with that between Menelaus and Helen, the breaching of which sparked the major war in which they were all now embroiled. If cuckolding Menelaus could start a war, then how should Achilles react to

Agamemnon for taking Briseis from him? In the event, Briseis eventually went back – Agamemnon swore that he had never laid a hand on Briseis.[5] Well he would, wouldn't he?

What the Briseis episode demonstrates is the symbolic importance of marriage in the time the Homeric epics were composed in the eighth century, and extending even before then. Love was an emotion which was respected – even amongst warriors – and which was worth making a stand on. Women, too, despite qualifying as spoils of war and dealt with in the cavalier way that conquering armies have traditionally dealt with captive women before and since, were paradoxically considered as intrinsically valuable, their emotions respected and their dignity upheld, to some extent.

Penelope

Penelope loves her husband. Why else would she wait twenty long years confined and condemned to working the wool and looking after the household when she could have de facto annulled her marriage and rebuilt her life with any number of suitors? Penelope was a paradigm of patience, tolerance and what the Romans called *pudicitia*, sexual propriety. She embraced family values, the proper raising of children, love and fidelity towards her husband (or at least his receding memory) all in a dignified and unobtrusive manner; she embodied everything a Greek man sought in a Greek woman. Penelope is grief-stricken by Odysseus' long absence at the Trojan War and by his subsequent long and winding journey home: she cries herself to sleep at night.[6] Penelope was the forerunner of those three Roman paragons of feminine virtue: Lucretia, Verginia and Cornelia, who lived for, and in two cases died for, their virtue. Beseiged by circling suitors, her marriage vulnerable, Penelope's love holds out and she remains resolutely faithful to her husband and to their family.

Andromache

Penelope was not the only army wife who waited patiently for her returning hero, sustained by an enduring love. Andromache was on the verge of welcoming home her hero when she learnt that he had been snatched tragically from her:

> She was at work in an inner room of the lofty palace, weaving a double-width purple tapestry, with a multi-coloured pattern of flowers. Totally unaware [of Hector's fate] she had asked her

ladies-in-waiting to set a great cauldron on the fire so that Hector would have hot water for a bath when he returned.

When the doom-laden news reached her

she ran through the halls, her heart pounding, she was out of her mind, and her ladies followed. When they came to the wall ... her eyes went black, enveloping her, and she fainted backwards, senseless.[7]

Ten years earlier the pathos in Andromache's lament as she prepared to part with her war-bound husband Hector is palpable, emphasising her love for her husband and the family values she held so dear:

Yet while my Hector still survives, I see my father, mother, kin, all in you. Alas! my parents, brothers, kindred, all, Once more will die again if my Hector falls. Your wife, your child, share in your danger; Oh prove a husband's and a father's care!

Andromache's tragedy began when Thebes, her home city, was sacked by Achilles, and her father and seven brothers died in the carnage. Her mother died of an illness and she became just one of the many spoils of war after the destruction of Troy. But along came Hector, who wooed her with opulent wedding gifts, doing the right thing when he provided his intended with material support and security, in contrast to the chancer Paris in his cavalier abduction of Helen.[8] All the more acute is the tragedy when Andromache's life is ripped apart after Achilles kills Hector – leaving her rootless and alone in the world, a displaced person relegated to the margins of society and a pathetic emblem of the fate that awaits conquered women in ancient warfare.[9] A prescient Hector had bewailed the certain fact that Andromache would be forced into slavery – weaving at another's whim and fetching the water as a slave.

Just before they part for the last time, domestic harmony prevails as Hector describes a typical scene with women weaving and men warring:

He laid his child in his dear wife's arms, and she took him to her fragrant bosom, smiling through her tears; and her husband was touched with pity at the sight of her, and he caressed her with his hand, and said: 'My dear wife, do not grieve too much ... go home and busy yourself with your own tasks, the loom and the distaff, and tell your maids to get on with their work: war is for men.'[10]

This conversation takes place on the exposed and dangerous ramparts of Troy. Even more unconventional is the implicit gender role-reversal when Andromache gives Hector military advice, a loving wife's ploy to detain Hector with a lesson in military strategy, thus keeping her husband in the relative safety of the ramparts and out of the much more hazardous open fighting taking place below on the field:

> Come on, take pity, and stay here on the wall, in case you orphan your child and make your wife a widow. Post your army by that wild fig-tree, where the wall is most vulnerable to a scaled assault, and the city is exposed. Three times already ... [the Greeks] have tried to get in there.[11]

Andromache shares with Penelope the honour of being the caring, loving mother and wife. She weaves a cloak for Hector in the domestic seclusion and safety of the interior rooms of the house and she runs that infamous homecoming bath for him. Astyanax, their infant son, is also present at the ramparts: Hector takes his son from the maid, yet returns him to his wife, a small action that provides great insight into the importance Homer placed on Andromache's responsibility as mother.[12] Andromache is never named in *Iliad* 22, referred to only as the wife of Hector (*alokhos*), in accordance with the Greek practice of maintaining the anonymity of chaste and respectable Greek women, thus underlining the importance of her status as Hector's wife and of the marriage state itself.

Nausicaa and Odysseus

The relationship between Nausicaa and Odysseus, such as it was, may be the earliest example of unrequited love we have in literature. There is no romance or physical love between the two even though Nausicaa confides in a friend that she would love her husband to be just like Odysseus, and her father Alcinous furthermore tells Odysseus he would let him marry her.[13] Interestingly, Odysseus never tells Penelope about Nausicaa, even though he does admit to affairs with Circe and Calypso.

Semonides of Amorgos

In the seventh century BC, Semonides of Amorgos in his satirical *Types of Women* describes ten distinctive types of woman based on the world of nature. Semonides, it must be said, is probably not being entirely serious, and his satirical tongue may well have been firmly in his cheek. Of the ten types, nine are less than complimentary and paint a picture of a world half full of dreadful women; only the bee woman is virtuous and has anything to commend her; being loving is one of her salient features:

> Another from a bee. Anyone getting her is lucky. She alone attracts no blame, but life flourishes with her and blossoms. She loves her husband, and he loves her. She bears him noble and famous sons. They grow old together. Conspicuous among all women is she, she is imbued with divine grace. She takes no pleasure in sitting among women when all they talk about is sex. Women like her Zeus gives to men. They are the best and most accomplished of women.

Tragic Sex

> The mother of a child is not really the parent, she's just the nurse of the newly-sown embryo. The one who mounts her is the parent, whereas she merely preserves the young offspring, as a stranger would.
>
> Aeschylus, *Eumenides* 658ff

So Aeschylus condemns womankind to a secondary, subservient role of childrearing, motherhood being erased and the dominance of the father emphasised in sexual, almost bestial language.

There are many examples of love in Greek tragedy. Euripides' Alcestis is, like Penelope and Andromache, a good wife; she is strong-minded, dutiful and religious; she loves and looks after her children and honours her gods; her marriage bed is sacred and she is prepared to die for her man.[14] To Phaedra in the *Hippolytus*, preserving her reputation is paramount, while her undying love for the eponymous hero ends in suicide: 'I cannot bear that I be found a traitor to my husband and children.'[15]

Euripides opens his *Medea* with the nurse telling us that Medea is 'out of her mind with her love for Jason'; at this point she is the perfect, compliant Greek type of wife who did everything her

husband asked, making great sacrifices for him. In return he cruelly
betrayed her love, with the most shocking of consequences for
their children. For Medea, love was for life. In the *Argonautica* she
swears 'in our lawful marriage-chamber you shall share my bed,
and nothing will separate us in our love until the appointed death
enshrouds us'. Not so for Jason. When love turns to lies, Medea has
marriage, and men, all worked out:

> What they say is that we women have a quiet time, staying at
> home, while they are off fighting in war. They couldn't be more
> wrong. I would rather stand three times in a battle line than give
> birth to one child.[16]

This concludes a speech which epitomises all that is stifling for a
woman in love with a sly and duplicitous man:

> Of all things that are living and have a brain, we women are the
> most unfortunate creatures.
>
> Firstly, we have to pay for a husband with a dowry and make
> him a master of our bodies; for not to take a husband has even
> worse consequences. And now the serious question is whether
> we take a good one or bad one; for there is no easy escape for a
> woman, nor can she say no to her marriage. She arrives as a bride
> to new ways of behaving and new manners, and needs to be a
> mind reader, unless she has learned at home, to see how best to
> manage the mood swings of he who shares the bed with her. And
> if the marriage works out well, and the husband lives with us and
> lightly bears the yoke of marriage, then my life is something to be
> envied. If not, I may as well die. A man, when he's tired of life at
> home, goes out and cures his boredom by turning to 'a friend' or
> hetaira of his own age. But we are forced to keep our eyes fixed
> on one man alone.[17]

Euripides extolled the best of women in his *The True-Hearted Wife;*
innate 'goodness' is the key to a wife's love:

> Beauty does not win love for a woman from her husband: many
> women win love by being good; for to each true-hearted wife,
> tied up in love to her husband, is Discretion's secret told. These
> are her gifts: though her husband be ugly to look at, to her
> heart and eyes shall he be handsome ... Whenever he speaks, or
> holds his peace, shall she his sense commend, Prompt with sweet

suggestion when with speech he would rather please a friend ...
For with those we love our duty bids us taste the cup of bliss not
alone, the cup of sorrow too – what is love if this is not?

A distraught, loving Evadne throws herself onto her husband's
funeral pyre; Capaneus, one of the *Seven Against Thebes,* was
blasted by a thunderbolt from Zeus.[18] In so doing, she presages the
suicide of Dido over her love for Aeneas in book two of Virgil's
Aeneid. On the other hand, a version of Helen's story in Euripides'
Helen, describes the love she felt for Menelaus when they are
reunited:

> I am so happy, the very hair on my head stands on end and my
> tears run down. I fling my arms around your neck, dear husband,
> so as to feel this delight even more.[19]

It is hardly surprising that there was to be no love lost between
Clytemnestra and Agamemnon. Clytemnestra was destroyed by the
double loss of first husband and then son – a bereft widow and mother
looking for revenge, as revealed in Euripides' *Iphigenia in Aulis:*

> I never loved you! Tantalus you slew, My first dear husband; and
> my little son. You tore him from my breast ... And a true wife
> I was, Yes, chaste and true, and cared well for your home. Such
> wives are not so common! Three girls I bore you and a son, and
> now You rob me of the first!

Homer advocated what he called *homophroneonte* in marriage –
thinking along the same lines as each other. Despite, or maybe
because of, his adulterous behaviour, Odysseus knows all about
ὁμοφροσύνη, as he makes clear in an avuncular sort of way to the
infatuated Nausicaa:

> May heaven grant you everything your heart desires – husband,
> house, and a happy, peaceful home; for there is nothing better in
> this world than that man and wife should be of one mind at home
> together. It unsettles their enemies, gladdens the hearts of their
> friends as they themselves know better than any one.[20]

Sophocles mirors this thought when he asks if there is anyone you
argue less with or turn to more than your wife to discuss serious
issues.

When a woman intruded into the traditional man's world in ancient Greece and Rome, the men in that world frequently described that woman's actions or words as being manlike, worthy of a man, or unwomanly. The socially or politically obtrusive woman (an oxymoron in itself in Greece and Rome) was defeminised, masculinised, androgenised. Epithets were applied to her which, linguistically, suggested maleness and were indicative of male behaviour: for example, *andreia* or *andros* in Greek, *vir* or *virtus* in Latin. Traditional gender definitions were turned on their heads and boundaries were breached: women were like men. In Greek tragedy, two women in particular are given this makeover of their sexuality: they are Clytemnestra and Antigone.

Both Thucydides and Sophocles, roughly contemporaneous between 497 and 396 BC, recommend that by far the best thing for war widows and for women in general is for them to hold their peace and stay silent – part of a programme ensuring general sequestration and overall social obscurity.[21] These two tragic females are anything but obscure or reticent; on the contrary, they are just two of a significant number of women who take centre stage and are vital to the plots of a number of the greatest tragedies in western literature. Crucially however, to attain their place in the spotlight they had to act like men; normal behaviour and societal norms had to be suspended and subverted. The same could also be said about comedy, where women in Aristophanes' Old Comedy take on political, religious and social roles that are characteristic of and expected exclusively of men. It is not until the emergence of New Comedy around 340 BC – brought to us by the surviving works of Menander but involving many more dramatists now lost to us – that women are always able to act like women in their portrayal of the young girl, the raped girl, the scheming wife, the old woman and the madam, reflecting, to some extent, the world as it was experienced for the ancient Greek woman.

Clytemnestra

Murderous Clytemnestra is presented variously as a slippery eel, a venomous viper,[22] and a duplicitous two-headed snake.[23] She is just like a man,[24] and fights the established male hierarchy.[25] She exhibits typical male characteristics, such as sexual independence, and she wields political power over Argos. At the same time she fails in her duties as a woman when she neglects her children, eschewing the normal role of wife and mother, with its terrible dramatic climax in the murder of her husband, the father of her children.[26] Clytemnestra is the first to admit that she acts in an unwomanly way: it is 'not like a woman to love contention'; her revenge-murder is untypical when 'the female kills the male'.[27]

The only aspect of the whole sorry affair that may be deemed consonant with normal female behaviour is Clytemnestra's ferocious maternal instinct, that which impelled her to kill the husband who slit the throat of a daughter whom she 'carried, in pain bore, loved' just to ensure the progress of a military campaign.[28] The crime is all the more chilling because the crime scene was within the household – the *oikos* – the domain of the woman of the house and the sacred symbol of family life. Clytemnestra's criminal behavoiur could not be more in contrast to the fidelity, patience and chastity exhibited by Penelope, that other army wife awaiting the return of a war hero – a paragon of feminine virtue and staunch upholder of family values. Clytemnestra as a mother sees the slaughter of Agamemnon as entirely justified and exactly what any woman would do in the circumstances; Clytemnestra as a wronged wife also wreaks vengeance for Agamemnon's overt infidelity and for parading Cassandra, his trophy concubine, before her, the 'whore of the sailors' benches'.[29] Her husband was a serial adulterer and a philanderer.[30] Adopting typically male conduct she acts in revenge by killing Agamemnon.

Antigone

Antigone too acts outside the boundaries set for women when she strives to fulfil the inviolable religious obligation all Greeks, regardless of gender, have in providing proper burial rites for their kin. If her sister, Ismene, had her own way then the burial of Polyneices would not have taken place because, in keeping with customary compliant and unobtrusive female behaviour, 'Creon has forbidden it', and that was the end of the matter. After all, had not her brother, Polyneices, betrayed 'his native city', and with a typical deprecation of their gender, too – stating they are 'only women' for whom it is natural to obey men even in 'painful matters'.[31] But this is nowhere near good enough for willful and defiant Antigone. Creon compares her behaviour to that of a man (*Ant.* 484). Indeed, before he knows any better, he assumes that the insolent (*Ant.* 480) defiance of his command can only have been perpetrated by a man. No woman would have had the chutzpah or the nerve.[32] When Creon forbids the burial of Polyneices, he is denying Antigone the chance to do one of the few valuable things society permitted women to take the lead in. Creon is repudiating her and her role in life, and that is why she vehemently opposes him, even on pain of suffering death by stoning.

But this all grist to the mill for Antigone. To her, such a death triggered by her brave defence of principles and religious *pietas* are 'a profit'; she has already advised Ismene to 'Make straight your own path to destiny', assuming a masculine role, not only in her overt social determination but also in the traditionally male role of advisor to a woman as guardian.[33]

Sophocles reinforces the tragedy when he couches Antigone's death in terms of marriage – every respectable Greek woman's goal and purpose in life. In choosing to die for her principles – something that only a man would be expected to do – she gives up her claim to marriage, motherhood, and traditional wifeliness. She will die 'unbedded' and 'unmarried' and, in so doing, renounces her womanhood and, by default, moves closer to a male role.[34] Sophocles extends his marriage metaphor when he compares Antigone's 'rocky tomb' with her 'bridal chamber'; she simulates her wedding procession when she is 'led away' from her 'father's city' into Hades.[35]

Neither Aeschylus nor Sophocles can convert these two powerful women into true heroines without masculinising them; to earn their heroic status they must be described as acting like men; they must repudiate the social norms expected of their sex, overturning typical gender behaviour. Ironically, Sophocles gives Ismene, a woman, the last word when she reflects that tragic heroines like Antigone and Clytemnestra are 'in love with the impossible' – recapitulating the norms of society.[36]

Pentheus

Pentheus, king and co-founder of Thebes, pays a heavy price for repudiating Dionysus and preventing his womenfolk from celebrating his ecstatic rites. His name, aptly enough, means 'man of sorrow' or 'man of grief', connoting in particular that caused by a loved one. Pentheus compounded his error when he imprisoned the god after Dionysus provoked Pentheus' mother, Agave, and his aunts Ino and Autonoë, along with the other women of Thebes, to mob Mount Cithaeron in a Bacchic frenzy. The story features in Euripides' *The Bacchae*. Dionysus easily escapes and inflicts Pentheus with voyeuristic tendencies by enticing him out to spy on the Bacchic rites disguised as a woman in the hope of witnessing illicit sexual activity. The daughters of Cadmus, Ino, Autonoe, Agave and Semele, spotted him in a tree and thought him to be a wild animal. They hauled Pentheus down and tore him apart, limb from limb – a ritual known as *sparagmos* – for which they were later exiled. Some say that Agave led the slaughter, tearing off his arm and then wrenching off his head. Unwittingly she stuck the head on a stick and took it back to Thebes, only to realise whose head it was after meeting Cadmus, her father and grandfather of Pentheus.

'Sparagmos' is from σπαράσσω, sparasso, 'I tear, pull to pieces', used often in a Dionysian context. In *sparagmos*, a living animal, or even a human being, is sacrificed by being torn to pieces. The action was usually followed by 'omophagia' – from ωμός, 'raw' – that is, eating the raw flesh of the dismembered. It is associated with the Maenads or Bacchantes, the female followers of Dionysus, although there is no firm evidence to link women celebrating the rites of Dionysus with dismembered animals, human sacrifice or eating raw flesh. Because Euripides depicts Agave as engaging in *sparagmos*, he presumably intended his audiences to assume she indulged in omophagia as well. Cadmus compares Agave's actions to the story of Actaeon, who was eaten by his own hunting dogs, lending further credence to suggestions that omophagia occurred. Furthermore, the *Bacchae* also describes how the Maenads went into a nearby town and carried off the children, maybe to eat them. Orpheus died when he was dismembered by ferocious Thracian women. In the flight with Jason and the stolen fleece, Medea killed and dismembered her brother, Apsyrtus, in order to delay and divert their pursuers, who would be compelled to collect the scattered body parts for proper burial.

Perhaps the most unusual example of voyeurism is a voyeuristic plant called the Gorgon. We know of it from Michael Psellus, a Byzantine Greek monk from the eleventh century AD who cites the work of Sextus Julius Africanus (*c.* AD 160–*c.* 240), a Christian traveller who compiled the *Kestoi*, an encyclopedia which contained much that was strange and miraculous in the known world. One of the entries describes the Gorgon, a plant that usually grows underground, but if a girl has sex near to it, it shoots up and watches proceedings intently. Africanus, it might be added, is noted as having the ability to restore a woman's virginity even if she has had sex many times.[37]

Oedipus

Retribution for Pentheus' *hubris* did not end there. His wife gave birth to a son, Menoeceus, who became the father of Creon and

Jocasta. And so Pentheus became the grandfather of Oedipus. Oedipus is now a byword for incest, or more specifically, for incest with one's mother. Sophocles in *Oedipus the King* plays on the hideous notion of Jocasta's womb serving both as 'begetter' and as 'begotten'. Oedipus is exposed by Laius when it is revealed that his son will one day kill him; unfortunately for all concerned, the well-meaning shepherd charged with this onerous task gives him to another shepherd, after which Oedipus is fostered by Polybus, King of Corinth, and Queen Merope as their own child. When Oedipus is later accused of being a bastard, he is compelled to search out his true origin. Oedipus murders his father, Laius, in what can only be described as an incident of road rage involving the precedence of a chariot; Oedipus is unaware that his victim was in fact his birth father.

Oedipus pressed on to Thebes but first had to deal with a Sphinx, who would detain all travelers destined for the city to pose them a riddle. If they were unable to answer correctly, the Sphinx would kill and eat them; if they got the answer right, they would be free to go. The riddle presented to Oedipus was: 'What walks on four feet in the morning, two in the afternoon and three at night?' Oedipus replied: 'Man: as an infant he crawls on all fours; as an adult, he walks on two legs and in old age, he walks with the use of a stick.' Oedipus was allowed to proceed.

By chance, Jocasta's brother Creon had decreed that any man who could rid the city of the annoying Sphinx would be crowned king of Thebes, and given the recently widowed and bereaved Queen Jocasta's hand in marriage. Oedipus, of course, qualified when he solved the riddle. He married Jocasta to fulfil the second part of the terrible prophecy, still oblivious to the fact that he had murdered his father and was marrying his mother. Oedipus tried to discover the identity of the murderer until he is warned off and told by Tiresias, a suspect himself, that he, Oedipus is in fact responsible. Jocasta, on discovering the outrage, hangs herself; Oedipus snatches two pins from her dress and pokes his own eyes out.

Oedipus, of course, lives on with us in many ways, not least as the protagonist in a series of brilliant tragedies from ancient Greece and Rome. Oedipism or auto-enucleation is a medical term for a serious self-inflicted eye injury, usually involving gouging out the eye or eyes; it is a rare form of severe self-harm. When Laius tried to avert the prophecy that his son would one day kill him, he bound the infant's feet together tightly to immobilise him; when

Oedipus eventually arrived at the palace of Polybus and Merope, they named him after the swelling to his feet and ankles, 'swollen foot'. The word 'oedema' is derived from this same Greek word for swelling, οἴδημα or oedēma. Sigmund Freud adopted the term 'the Oedipus complex' to explain the origin of certain childhood neuroses. He defined it as 'a male child's unconscious desire for the exclusive love of his mother'. It includes jealousy directed at the father and the unconscious wish for the father's death, as well as desire to have sexual intercourse with the mother. Analogous to this is the Electra complex, proposed by Carl Jung to describe a girl's psychosexual competition with her mother to possess her father in the girl's phallic stage of psychosexual development.

Comic Sex

Sex pervades ancient Greek comedy – Old, Middle and New. Aristophanes, Menander and their many contemporaries produced a wealth of comic plays in which women and aspects of their sexuality are integral to plot. The plot and script had to amuse the men in the audience – the majority if not the whole of the audience – which explains to a large extent some of the fantastic situations. For example, Aristophanes' *Ecclesiazusae, Women in the Assembly*, has women assume political control in Athens in a bid to rescue the city from the shambles orchestrated by the menfolk. The notion is absurd in contemporary Athenian society. The *Lysistrata*, in which women withdraw their sexual favours to force a ceasefire in the Peloponnesian War, is equally surreal. Aristophanes lets female empowerment and emancipation run riot in his female Utopia, especially when it extends to matters sexual: before a man or woman can have intercourse with a beautiful woman or a handsome man, they each are obliged to sleep with a less than attractive old man or woman.

> The women have decreed that if a young man desires a young girl, he can only lay her after having satisfied an old woman; and if he refuses and goes to find the maiden, the old women are authorized to grab him and drag him in.

The usual sexual clichés and stereotypes come through, to the delight, no doubt, of the male audience:

> Women kneel to bake their bread, tote their laundry on the head, just like Mother always did. They always follow the recipe, Keep

Demeter's yearly spree, just like Mother. Nag their husbands till they're dead, hide their lovers under the bed, just like Mother. Pad the grocery bill with snacks, take a drink or three to relax, prefer their pleasure on their backs, happy nymphomaniacs, just like Mother.[38]

More positively for women, the Chorus when addressing the audience in the *Thesmophoriazusae* has much to say about the good things to be found in a woman:

Let us address ourselves to the audience to sing our praises, despite the fact that each one says lots of bad things about women. If the men are to be believed, we are a plague to them: through us come all their troubles, quarrels, disputes, sedition, griefs and wars. But if we are really such a pest, why do they marry us? ... It is clear that we are better than you, and the proof of this is easy. Let us find out which is the worse of the two sexes. We say, 'It's you,' while you swear 'it's we.' [39]

Aristophanes articulates the popular male view of women, suspicious and paranoid, through a reviled Euripides who has a leading role in the same play – with some powerful female retorts:

I have been pained for a long time now to see us women insulted by this Euripides, this son of the green-stuff woman, who heaps on us every kind of indignity. Has he not hit us enough ... Does he not style us adulterous, lecherous, bibulous, treacherous, and garrulous? Does he not repeat that we are all vice, that we are the curse of our husbands? So that, as soon as they come back from the theatre, they look at us doubtfully and go searching in every corner, fearing there may be some hidden lover. We can do none of the things we used to, so many are the fantasies which Euripides has instilled into our husbands. If a woman weaves a garland for herself, it's because she is in love. Does she drop a vase while going or returning to the house? Her husband asks her in whose honour she has broken it: 'It can only be for that Corinthian stranger' ... 'A woman is the tyrant of the old man who marries her.' Again, it is because of Euripides that we are incessantly watched, that we are shut up behind bolts and bars, and that dogs frighten off the 'adulterers'. Once it was we who looked after the food, who fetched the flour from the storeroom, the oil and the wine; we can't do that any more ... this pestilent

Euripides ... we should rid ourselves of this enemy of ours by poison or by any other means, so long as he dies.[40]

Aristophanes himself pedalled the stereotype which perpetuated that women were bibulous and unreliable, neglecting their most important wifely duties as a result – a time-worn cliché, with its associated suggestion that the drink led to permissive sexual behaviour, a stereotype which persisted through the Classical era and beyond to modern ages.[41]

Oh! you hot women, you tippling women, who think of nothing but wine; you are a gold-mine to the drinking-shops and are our ruin; for the sake of drink, you neglect both your household and your shuttle!

If a woman had the temerity to ask about current affairs or political matters she was abruptly invited to shut up, with the threat of physical violence. As shocking as it is to us today, the casual presence of the notion would suggest that domestic abuse in classical Athens was quite acceptable behaviour:

Lysistrata: Before now, and for quite a long time, we kept our cool and suffered, whatever you men did, because you wouldn't let us make a sound. But you weren't exactly everything a woman could ask for. No, we knew your game and often we'd hear about a bad decision you'd made on some great matter of state. Then, hiding the pain in our hearts, we'd smirk and ask, 'How did it go in the Assembly today?' And my husband would retort: 'What's that got to do with you? Shut up!' So I'd shut up.

Old Woman: I wouldn't have shut up!

Magistrate: If you hadn't have shut up you'd have got a belting.

Lysistrata: Well, that's why I did shut up – then. But later on we began to hear about even worse decisions you'd made, and then we would ask, 'Husband, how come you're handling this so ineptly?' And he'd immediately glare at me and tell me to get back to my sewing if I didn't want my head smashed in. [42]

Signs of love and affection are comparatively rare and may reflect the business-like, pragmatic nature of most marriages, in which women were to a large degree sidelined except in their reproductive role and as providers of sexual gratification. Indeed, in *The Peace* it is 'kissing the pretty Thracian' slave girl that excites desire when the wife is out of the way in the bath. When the wife gets out of the bath, then she can make a meal:

> Come on wife, cook three measures of beans, adding a little wheat to them, and give us some figs.[43]

Aristophanes confirms how leaving the house had its difficulties for Athenian women – what with all those chores:

> It's hard for women, you know, to get away. There's so much to do; husbands to be patted and put in a good mood: servants to be wheedled out: children washed or soothed with lullabies or fed with mouthfuls of mush.

In the *Ecclesiazusae,* Blepyrus is beside himself and typically suspicious when his wife goes missing:

> What does this mean? My wife has vanished! it is nearly daybreak and she's not back! ... Ah! what a damned fool I was to take a wife at my age, and how I could beat myself up for having acted so stupidly! She's not gone out for any honest purpose, that's for sure.[44]

In New Comedy – and to some extent in Middle Comedy – the exploration of personal relationships, love lost and regained, children lost and found, was the theme of hundreds of plays in which slaves, heart-of-gold prostitutes, old women and violated virgins, mercenaries, parasites – all marginalised souls from the edge of society – were the stars. The surely recognisable characters now have real names like Chrysis, Chremes, and Demeas, and they speak more in a vernacular that is spoken in the local *agora*. Much of the Aristophanic bawdiness has gone, and the characters wear the same real clothes as the audience. The themes explored are universal – emphasising the domestic and mundane – and of interest and relevance to a much wider audience than just the inhabitants of metropolitan Athens. Menandrian comedy, a veritable showcase of wronged daughters or long lost children, for example, had family appeal because most of the men in the theatre would be themselves be the fathers of children – and half of these children would have been girls.

If Menander was to raise a laugh then he would surely have to imbue his characters and plots with traits and mannerisms that were immediately recognisable to his audiences from their own everyday experience; the plots would reflect Greek life to some degree and his characters would be recognisable as real-life Greeks. His and others' comedies are particularly important to us because they shine a rare light on aspects of non-elite Greek family life; unlike much of the rest of the literary evidence we have, they describe commonplace domestic situations and the experiences of commonplace people. The courtesan, old woman, scheming wife and love-stricken young girl are amongst the stock characters who populate Greek New Comedy.

Over 900 quotations from Menander's work are preserved in secondary sources. 'Romance' and sex are never very far a way in his domestic dramas, so women by necessity feature in these new character-driven productions. Of the fragments from eighty-two plays there are twenty-seven in which women appear in the title alone, including *Empimpramene* ('*Woman On Fire*'); *Kanephoros* ('*The Ritual-Basket Bearer*'); *Pallake* ('*The Concubine*'); *Auton Penthon* ('*Grieving For Him*'); *Chera* ('*The Widow*'); *Progamoi* ('*People About to Get Married*'); *Rhapizomene* ('*Woman Getting Her Face Slapped*'); *Synaristosai* ('*Women Who Eat Together At Noon*' or '*The Ladies Who Lunch*'); *Arrhephoros*, or *Auletris* ('*The Female Flute-Player*'); *Synepheboi* ('*Fellow Adolescents*'); *Epikleros* ('*The Heiress*'); *Hiereia* ('*The Priestess*'); *Synerosa* ('*Woman In Love*'); *Koneiazomenai* ('*Women Drinking Hemlock*'); *Theophoroumene* ('*The Girl Possessed by a God*'); and *Titthe* ('*The Wet-Nurse*').

In addition, Posidippus (316–*c*. 250 BC) wrote forty plays, and of the eighteen we know today there are the following which celebrate women in the title: *Apokleiomene* ('*The Barred Woman*'); *Ephesia* ('*The Ephesian Girl*'); *Locrides* ('*The Locrian Women*'); *Choreuousai* ('*Dancing Girls*').

We can also add the following five titles from twenty-one plays we know about from Apollodorus of Carystus who flourished in Athens between 300 and 260 BC: *Apoleipousa* ('*The Woman Who Leaves*'); *Hiereia* ('*The Priestess*'); *Proikizomene* ('*The Woman with a Dowry*') or *Himatiopolis* ('*The Female Clothes-Seller*'); *Lakaina* ('*The Laconian Woman*') and the melodramatically and onomatopoeically titled *Sphattomene* ('*The Woman Being Slaughtered*'). From Diphilus we have, for example, *Diamartanousa* ('*The Woman Who Is Failing Utterly*') and *Aleiptria* ('*Masseuse*') – just two out of eleven with women in the titles from the fifty-four we have titles for; Philemon adds *Ananeoumene* ('*The Born Again Woman*') and *Ptoche* ('*The Poor Woman*').

All of life is here, with woman scripted and performing in a vast range of everyday scenarios. We can sum up these new types of *dramatis personae* and the new kinds of plots with:

> Long-lost children end up living next-door to their grieving parents, young men compromise women who seem to be prostitutes but fortuitously turn out to be marriageable maidens in love with their attacker, and gentle courtesans welcome home nubile virgin sisters to the lusty arms of well-meaning and well-endowed Athenian bachelors.[45]

In Menander's *Perikeiromene* ('*The Cropped Girl*') the independence and assertiveness of Glykera, the poor girl who has been shorn, is significant. The perpetrator is a Corinthian soldier, Polemon, who had always treated the girl as his wife but violently and angrily assaulted her when he discovered she had kissed another man. The domestic violence and the forced haircut is typical, it seems, of the uncivilised behaviour of mercenaries. The man who had been caught kissing Glykera was in fact her twin brother – all's well that ends well – and a reconciliation with and marriage to the soldier ensued. This is a typical scenario, full of coincidence and improbability in which the girl plays a central part: it reflects not only the fact that life is just as strange as fiction but also that a woman's place in the family, personal relationships and society at large was now being acknowledged to some extent. In this rich dramatic world, women had a role to play in the course of human relationships. It emerges too in the avaricious prostitute who turns out to be a canny but caring madam, concealing her generosity behind a mask of greed and grasping; or in the bombastic soldier who not only boasts of the countless enemies he has slain but also how well he treats the woman he loves.

Significantly, we know of no play of Menander's which does not deal with *eros*, love, in some form or another. Love can often take the shape of a formal marriage, another recurring theme in the New Comedy: marriage, as we know, was always arranged between the father and his intended son-in-law with the bride's assumed consent sidelined until the wedding night. What Menander, and presumably his playwriting colleagues, show us is that it was possible by now for a woman to have some say in the marriage arrangements – not least the choice of husband – and to influence the courtship through her own desires and actions. Menander and his audience were pioneering the view that this was the right thing to do and that the wishes of the daughter and future wife could and should be taken into account.

Love is clearly a factor in Menander's *Men at Arbitration* in which two men squabble over who owns some trinkets. This domestic crisis had driven asunder a newly married couple, still very much in love. Despite some challenging obstacles, love prevails. Given that the plot of the play may have reflected aspects of real life, despite some highly unlikely dramatic elements, Menander shows that love was obviously an ingredient in some marriages in or around his time (*c.* 342–*c.* 290 BC).

Love again shines through in a Menandrian fragment which describes a distraught, faithful husband of five months bewailing the fact that his wife is not faithful and that he loved her and (thought that) she loved him. The passage is doubly significant in that it is the only example in ancient Greek where the three distinct words for human love – *erao, phileo* and *agapeo* – occur in close textual proximity.

But Menander was no early feminist; his largely male audience would have relished these misogynist aphorisms as they tripped off the acid tongues of his splenetic actors:

> Don't trust a woman, even when she's dead
> A woman is the wildest of all wild animals
> A woman knows nothing apart from what she wants to know
> A bad woman is a treasure trove of bad things
> Don't trust your life with a woman
> It isn't easy to find a good woman
> Sea, fire – and woman as the third evil
> It's better to bury a woman than marry her
> A woman is silver-coated muck
> Even women can behave reasonably
> When there's no woman around, nothing bad ever happens
>   to a man
> A woman who flatters you is after something

Satyr Plays

Satyr plays were a type of tragicomedy, similar to burlesque and, as the name suggests, starred choruses of satyrs acting out their obscene, sexually charged antics replete with fithy jokes and erect phalluses. The form was developed by Pratinas of Phlius in around 500 BC to provide some light, intermittent relief from the doom and gloom of the tragedies on the bill. In the dramatic contest that was the Athenian Dionysia, each competing playwright entered four plays in the competition, three tragedies and one satyr play. These satyr plays were short and half the length of a tragedy. One such example has survived complete: Euripides' *Cyclops*, featuring Odysseus' encounter with the cyclops, Polyphemus, in Book 9 of the *Odyssey*. The largest fragment of Aeschylean satyr is his *Dictyulci* ('The Net Fishers') in which the baby Perseus is washed up with his mother Danaë and is found by Silenus and the satyrs. Large fragments of a satyr play of Sophocles called *Ichneutae* ('The Trackers') survive, in which the satyrs are enlisted by Apollo to track down his stolen cattle, and discover the baby Hermes. The genre was still popular and performed as late as the second century AD.

Mime

Sex and male–female relationships have a big part to play, too, in the scurrilous mimes of Herodas, who was active in the third century BC. Typically, mimes were coarse, vernacular, and replete with sexual references – in this Herodas was typical. In *Mime 1* the old nurse, now the local bawd, calls on Metriche, whose husband is away in Egypt, and tries to interest her in an eligible young man who has fallen in love with her at first sight. Metriche declines with dignity, but consoles the old woman with a generous cup of wine – Mrs Sarah Gamp in Dickens' *The Life and Adventures of Martin Chuzzlewit* springs to mind. In *Mime 2* we meet the pimp who describes Myrtale, a woman who has been assaulted:

> She is in rags, from head to heels, where that miserable rascal tore her to pieces, dragging her away and violating her … I am a whoremonger; I do not deny it. Battaros is my name.

In *Mime 5* the jealous Bittina quizzes Gastron, in a wonderful turn of phrase:

> Just tell me, Gastron; have you grown so satiated that you are no longer satisfied to shake your thighs with me but must be having sex with Menon's Amphythæa?

Mimes 6 and 7 are covered in the section on *olisboi*, dildos.

Declamation

Declamation was an advanced element in Greek rhetorical education, prized not just because it trained students to compose and deliver extemporised arguments but also because it inculcated what were deemed appropriate morals in its students and practitioners.

Domestic disputes involving women make frequent appearances in these declamations and, as in comedy, are confined to a few narrow stereotypes: suffering maidens, adulterous wives, bothersome mothers, prostitutes and evil stepmothers. These stereotypes originate from Menander and other New Comedy playwrights in which women, as noted, are frequently characterised as unfaithful, expensive, extravagant, jealous, angry, vociferous and evil. Teachers of declamation adapted these themes to foster certain attitudes about women, converting the generally constructive and sympathetic perspective in New Comedy to a pejorative and vituperative one. Such indoctrination was long term, and was achieved by laying the foundations for these negative stereotypes in students' – largely boys' – minds from as early an age as possible and reinforcing them throughout their school careers.

4

Marriage, Love, the Wedding, Adultery and Rape

Marriage

In elite families, marriage was, on the surface, little more and nothing less than a pragmatic business transaction. Love was an incidental by-product and, where it did arise, would probably be due to the kindling of mutual respect and companionship over years of rubbing along together. This conduct was the sort of thing which, as we saw, Homer recommended. You can almost hear Hesiod sigh when he articulates the conundrum, speaking for countless subsequent generations of Greek men, that 'men could not live with [women] and could not live without them'. In saying this he interjects prejudice, discrimination, misogyny, fear and distrust into one half of the human population against the other. In opening her ill-fated box, Pandora had lifted the lid off the bad things in life; she had ended the Golden Age and ushered in a world which from now on was going to consist of the vicissitudes of a limited and suffering mortal life. And who's fault was it? It was the fault of women. Before women arrived on the scene, everything was fine, but the 'grim cares of mankind' were now out of the box and unleashed upon the world; all men could do now was hope for hope.

And so, benighted with this womanly manifestation of a poisoned chalice, man has to make the most of things; here is Hesiod's acid prescription for a good wife:

Marry a virgin, so that you can teach her careful ways, in particular, marry one who lives near you, but have a good look around and ensure that your marriage will not be the laughing stock of the neighbourhood. For a man wins nothing better than a good wife, and nothing worse than a bad one, a greedy soul who roasts her man without fire, as strong as he might be, brings him an early old age.[1]

There was no escape. In the *Theogony,* Hesiod dismisses bachelorhood as a way out. A wretched old age awaits the single man as there will be no one around to provide home care:

> Zeus ... made women to be an evil to mortal men, with a nature to do evil ... whoever avoids marriage and the sorrows that women cause, and will not wed, reaches deadly old age without anyone to tend his years.[2]

According to Plutarch, a man gets the wife he deserves. If he is narcissistic his wife will be vain and immodest, if he is a libertine himself she will be a slut, but if he is self controlled and loves the finer things in life, then his wife will be chaste and compliant.[3]

It was the father's responsibility to have his daughters successfully married off. There may have been some concern to provide his girl with a good man, but the compelling factor would be the social, financial and political opportunities a son-in-law might bring to the *oikos* through his own family and commercial or military aspirations. Therefore, the selection of a son-in-law was to a large extent an investment decision; the long term goal, apart from getting a male heir to prolong the *oikos,* was to recoup the dowry and capitalise on it. A girl's feelings and trepidation over first meeting her husband close to or even on the wedding day would have cut little ice in many families. Whether this was always the case in less wealthy families we have no way of knowing, but it is reasonable to assume that the opportunities for and desire to achieve financial and social aggrandisement through a daughter's marriage were progressively lessened the poorer the family.

However, the father was all powerful in the triangle he formed with his daughter and her – or should it be his? – intended. To complicate things, the father could always change his mind, presumably if he got a better offer for his daughter. This is what supposedly happened to Neobule and the seventh-century-BC poet Archilochus. Archilochus was previously engaged to the girl before her father Lycambes reneged and married her off to someone else. Archilochus retaliated in verse so bitterly that Neobule, her father and her sisters all hanged themselves in despair. In telling the calamitous tale Archilocus incidentally gave a foretaste of what was to come in the form of twenty-first-century electronic hate mail and 'trolling'.

Archilocus piles on the agony in an elegy in which the victims tragically speak from the grave:

> We here, the daughters of Lycambes who earned a hateful reputation, swear by the reverence in which this tomb of the dead is held that we did not shame our virginity or our parents or Paros, pre-eminent among holy islands, but Archilochus spewed out a frightful reproach and a hateful report against our family.[4]

Love

Love, then, was often a nebulous, elusive and incidental thing. Athenaeus tells of people who have dreamt that they have fallen in love with someone they know, such must have been the yearning for real love. The first-century-AD Stoic Musonius Rufus was pro-marriage but took an ascetic view, teaching that, because it was not necessary to be married in order to procreate, the only benefits, echoing Homer's *homophroneonte,* was companionship or *symbiosis*. To Rufus it was vital for a married couple to look out for one another 'in sickness and in health and in every circumstance'. To him, having sex for the pleasure of it was unjustified and illegal.[5] We recall that Nausicca in the *Odyssey* had seen Odysseus as *homophron*, 'of like mind'.

However, love was certainly not always absent: we can see it on emotional and loving inscriptions etched on gravestones and in epitaphs. Indeed, tombstone inscriptions provide us with unique insight into how women were remembered in death by loving husbands and sons, and occasionally how they themselves wished to be remembered. Loving fathers were able to demonstrate paternal and maternal love for deceased sons and wives in this very public, enduring way. Fourth-century-BC Telemachus is typical, 'laid to rest at the right hand side of his mother and not deprived of her love'. Indeed, one of the tombs of Ceramicus depicts:

> Damasistrate and her husband clasp hands at parting. A child and a kinsman stand beside the chair, but husband and wife have no eyes save for each other, and the calm intensity of their parting gaze answers all questionings as to the position of the wife and mother in Attic society.

Archedice from fifth-century Athens receives fulsome praise:

> The dust hides Archedice, daughter of Hippias, the most important man in Greece in his day. But though her father, husband, brothers and children were tyrants, her mind was never overwhelmed by arrogance.

As does Aspasia:

> Of a worthy wife this is the tomb – here by the road that is busy with people – of Aspasia, who has passed away; in recognition of her noble disposition Euopides set up this monument for her; she was his consort.

Dionysia of fourth-century Athens belies the stereotype that all women were wastrels and extravagant:

> It was not clothes, it was not gold that this woman admired during her lifetime; it was her husband and the good sense that she showed in her behaviour ... your tomb is adorned by your husband, Antiphilus.[6]

A bereaved husband acknowleges Melite, his wife, as good and loving, a love that she returns in equal measure:

> You were the best, and so he [Onesimus] laments your death, for you were a good woman.

The picture shows her holding out her hand to him as she says:

> And to you farewell, dearest of men; love my children.

Parental love is also represented in the moving epitaphs for sons and daughters, indicating real emotion and devotion for lost loved ones. Phrasicleia died in Athens around 540 BC before she was married; we can sense the feeling of failure felt in not attaining the status of 'wife':

> I shall be called a maiden always. This is the name the gods gave me inplace of 'wife'.

Bitte poignantly announces to the world that:

I lie here, a marble statue instead of a woman, a memorial to Bitte, and of her mother's sad grief.

Xenoclea, mother of two girls, died of grief after the death of her eight-year-old son, Phoenix, who drowned out at sea.[7]

In Plutarch's *Consolation to His Wife* we have a long, moving consolationary letter which expresses not only his love for her but also their common grief on the death of their two-year-old daughter, Timoxen:

> Just as she was herself the most delightful thing in the world to embrace, to see, to hear, so too must the thought of her live with us and be our companion, bringing with it joy in greater measure, no, in many times greater measure, than it brings sorrow ... and we must not sit idle and shut ourselves in, paying for those pleasures with sorrows many times as great.[8]

Whatever the facts about Sappho and her sexual preferences we know that she was probably married and had a daughter, Cleis; one story going back to Menander (Fr. 258 K) says that Sappho committed suicide by jumping off the Leucadian cliffs for love of Phaon, a ferryman. Was this an attempt to heterosexualise her?[9]

Hipparchia of Maroneia (*fl.* 325 BC) was a Cynic philosopher who met Crates, the famous Cynic. She fell in love with him and his eccentric ways, and, despite her parents' opposition, married him. In the fourth century BC, the lawyer Isaeus has a speech in which his client's father is shown to love his intended bride so much that he would be prepared to pay the earth in order not to lose her.[10]

Aristippus had an interesting take on love for his mistress. When his slave criticised his obsession with her, he answered:

> 'I give Lais a great deal, that I myself may enjoy her, and not that no one else may.' And when Diogenes [the Cynic] said, 'Since you, O Aristippus, cohabit with a common prostitute, either, therefore, become a Cynic yourself, as I am, or else abandon her.' Aristippus answered him, 'Does it appear to you, Diogenes, an absurd thing to live in a house where other men have lived before you?' 'Not at all,' said he. 'Well, then, does it appear to you absurd to sail in a ship in which other men have sailed before you?' 'By no means,' said he. 'Well, then,' replied Aristippus, 'it is no more absurd to be in love with a woman with whom many men have been in love already.'[11]

This brings to mind Julia, the wayward daughter of Augustus, who used the same metaphor when wittily describing her debauched behaviour. When asked how her children all looked like her husband Agrippa despite her permissive behaviour, she is alleged to have quipped that being pregnant allowed her to pursue her extramaritial affairs without fear of getting pregnant: 'I never take on a passenger unless the ship is full'. Unfortunately for Julia, a somewhat less accommodating ship was later to take her into insular exile on Pandateria.[12]

The pursuit of love often led to recourse to the dark arts. There are examples of love *defixiones*, binding spells, where a lover will invoke underworld deities in a heartfelt bid to win the love of his life. A man called Successus dedicates his wife in a bid to see his love for her requited: 'May Successa burn, let her feel herself aflame with love or desire for Successus.' Let us hope that Successus was successful in winning Successa over. There is plenty of fire here but none of the brimstone we often meet in these spells.

Solon introduced the stricture that would not allow marriages to be contracted on a commercial basis or for land, but rather only for pure love, affection, and the birth of children. Draconian as these laws were, they do provide further evidence that love and affection was becoming the foundation of Athenian marriages – otherwise why would he have cited it as a legal precondition?

Solon is cited in the case of Ismenodora, a mature, attractive, wealthy widow who falls in love with the much younger Bacchon. Bacchon's mother opposes the match based on the gulf in the backgrounds between the couple, but his friends point out that he can only benefit from her status and wealth. Others, though, prefer to champion chaste pederastic relations in the belief that these, and not heterosexual unions, are the way to genuine *eros*.[13]

Antisthenes, the pupil of Socrates, tells us that Pericles loved Aspasia so much that he used to kiss her twice every day, once when he entered her house, and once when he left it. Kissing in public, though, was discouraged. Plutarch said in his advice to young married couples, 'It is shameful to embrace and kiss and caress each other in the presence of others.' Before him, Cato the Elder (23–149 BC) had a pragmatic approach to kissing when he asserted the right that male relatives had of kissing their women (*ius osculi*) when they met, not to show affection or courtesy, but to ascertain whether they had been drinking – an early form of breathalisation which first saw the light in Euripides and Aristophanes. Cato was probably not altogether typical when he famously expelled Manilius from the Senate for kissing his wife in front of their daughter and, even more eccentrically, admitted that *he* only ever kissed his wife during thunderstorms.[14] By far the most erotic description of ancient kissing comes from Achilles Tatius in his second-century novel *Leucippe and Clitophon*:

> A woman's body is moist in the clinch, and her lips are soft in response to kisses. On account of this she holds the man's body in her arms, with it completely joined to her flesh, and he is surrounded with pleasure when he has intercourse with her. She stamps her kisses on his lips like seals on wax ... and when she has experience, she can make her kisses sweeter by not only wishing to use her lips, but also her teeth, grazing round her lover's mouth and biting his kisses ... At the height of orgasm she goes mad with pleasure and opens her mouth in passion. At this time tongues keep company with each other, and so far as possible they also make love to one another; you can make your pleasure greater by opening your mouth to her kisses.[15]

We hear about Periander who fell hopelessly in love with Melissa, the daughter of Procles of Epidaurus, when he saw her dressed like a Peloponnesian woman – 'she had on no cloak, but a single tunic only, and was acting as cupbearer to the young men' – and he married her.[16]

A rare expression of shared love comes in the story of Plangōn the Milesian, a celebrated *hetaera* or prostitute. Athenaeus rakes up the story:

> And [Plangon], as she was exquisitely beautiful, was loved by a young man of Colophon, who already had Bacchis of Samos as his mistress. So, when this young man began to pay attention to Plangōn, she, having heard of the beauty of Bacchis, wished to make the young man abandon his love for her. When she was unable to do that, she required as the price of her favours Bacchis' celebrated necklace. He, because he was very much in love, begged Bacchis not to destroy him with despair; and Bacchis, seeing the state the young man was in, gave him the necklace. Plangōn, when she saw how Bacchis was quite without jealousy returned the necklace, but kept the young man: and ever after Plangōn and Bacchis were friends, loving the young man in common; and the Ionians were amazed and ... gave Plangōn the name of Pasiphila ['Dear to all'].[17]

Athenaeus describes the great love Harpalus the Macedonian must have felt for Pythionice when he

> spent so much money on her; and she was a courtesan. And when she died he erected a monument to her which cost him many talents. And as he was carrying her out to burial ... he had the body escorted by a band of the most eminent artists of all kinds, and with all sorts of musical instruments and songs ... any one who goes to Athens ... will see a tomb built by the wayside, of such a size that there is none other near which can be compared with it. And at first, as would be natural, he would say it to be the tomb, beyond all question, of Miltiades, or Cimon, or Pericles, or of some other of the great men of Athens. And above all, he would feel sure that it had been erected by the city at the public expense, or at all events by some public decree; and then, again, when he heard it was the tomb of Pythionice the courtesan, what must he feel?[18]

Athenaeus reminds us that Aristotle of Stageira had a son named Nicomachus by a courtesan called Herpyllis and lived with her till his death; and that Plato loved Archaeanassa, a courtesan of Colophon, so much that he even composed this song in her honour:

> My mistress is the fair Archaeanassa From Colophon ... wretched are those, whom in the flower of youth, when first she came across the sea, she met; they must have been entirely consumed.[19]

We have seen how Medea was driven mad by love for Jason, and how Clytemnaestra was driven insane by her love for her children. Love and sexual passion were analogous to insanity and illness; they were physically debilitating – being hopelessly in love was akin to being lashed by a storm. Just ask Ibycus, a love poet of the sixth century BC:

> Eros is never quiet. No, like a Thracian north wind ablaze with lightning, rushing from Aphrodite accompanied by parching madnesses, black ... powerfully, from the souls of my feet [it] shakes my whole being.[20]

Or it was like being melted down like wax, according to Ascelepiades the third-century-BC epigrammist:

> Didyme by the branch she waved at me has swept me off my feet, alas! and gazing on her beauty, I melt like wax before the fire.

And if she is black, so what? So is coal, but when we light coal, it shines as bright as roses.[21]

And:

Drink, Asclepiades. Why these tears ? What ails you? It is not just you that cruel Cypris has taken captive; not for you alone has bitter Love sharpened his arrows. Why while still alive do you lie in the dust? Let us drink the strong drink of Bacchus.[22]

Ascelepiades battered with a hammer; Anacreon wounded with a flaming arrow – Eros and Aphrodite were fickle and could be cruel and punitive. To Posidippus of the early third century BC, Aphrodite 'always brings new pain and desire'.[23] Sappho's description of *eros* conjures up images of involuntary tremor and uncontrollable fever:

I'm speechless and fine fire licks beneath my skin, I'm blind and buzzing fills my ears.
Sweat runs down, I'm shaken deep by a shiver; I feel as green and close to death.[24]

Eros is a soul shaker, a wind on mountain oaks and a limb-loosener:

Once again Eros, the loosener of limbs disturbs me, Bittersweet, uncontrollable creature.[25]

Phaedra's malady is caused by her love for her stepson; the chorus observes that her body is 'ravaged'. Her colour all wrong, she is weak at the knees, demonstrably a victim of Eros and Aphrodite:

Eros, god of love, distilling liquid desire into lovers' eyes, bringing sweet pleasure to the souls of those against whom you battle, never hurt me but come in due measure and harmony. For neither arrows of fire nor starlight burn more than the arrows of Aphrodite, which Eros, Zeus's son, hurls forth.[26]

Plutarch too gives us a revealing description of the effects of love. Around 300 BC, Antiochus I Soter fell violently in love with Stratonice, his mother-in-law, though she already had a son by his father, Seleucus I, king of Syria. Despite efforts to curb his ardour, Antiochus lost the will to live and proceeded to starve himself to death. His doctor, Erasistratus, diagnosed that his patient was dying for love but did not know the object of his desire. So, he spent days observing in his chamber and whenever any beautiful person of either sex entered it, watched to see how Antiochus reacted. When Stratonice came in, as she often did, either alone or with Seleucus, he demonstrated all the symptoms described by Sappho: the faltering voice, the burning blush, the languid eye, the sudden sweat, the pounding pulse and in the end, the passion overcoming his spirits, fainting and a deathly pallor. Seleucus generously allowed Antiochus to marry Stratonice in 294 BC; she gave him five children.[27]

Solon's long litigious arm reached into the bridal chamber. In a law recorded by Plutarch in the *Life of Solon* he decreed

> that the bride and bridegroom shall be shut in a bedroom, and share a quince together; and that the husband of an heiress shall have sex with her three times a month; for though there may be no children, it is honour and affection which a husband ought to pay to a virtuous, chaste wife; it removes all those petty differences, and will not allow their little quarrels to end in divorce.

Respect, affection, and regular sexual intercourse is, then, the Solonic recipe for a happy marriage. Plutarch then goes on to expatiate on the benefits of mothers breastfeeding their children. It inculcates tenderness and care, providing a unique bonding experience to the lasting benefit of both mother and baby. The problem with nurses, dry and wet, is that they are motivated by pay rather than affection. What is more, Plutarch adds, women have two breasts so that in the event of bearing twins a woman has a dual source of nutrition.

The Wedding

Homer gives us an early description of a wedding as depicted on the shield of Achilles:

> On it he [Hephaestus] wrought in all their beauty two cities of mortal men. And there were marriages in one, and festivals. They were leading the brides along the city from their maiden chambers under the flaring of torches and the loud bride song was arising.[28]

The tradition was that, come nightfall, the father of the bride gave his daughter's hand to his new son-in-law, thus in full view of the guests formalising the transfer of guardianship. After the earlier betrothal (*engue*), the handing over of the bride was the second step to legitimatise the marriage (*gamos*). Witnesses guaranteed the legality of the original verbal contract in case any litigation arose after the wedding. This is probably when the solemn unveiling (*anakalypteria*) took place and the bride revealed herself to the groom for the first time. The unveiling and the groom's acceptance of the bride was established on a fragment from Pherecydes of Syros, a sixth-century philosopher, by Zeus in his marriage to Chthonie (Gaia):

> [Zeus] made a large, beautiful robe and on it he wove Ge and Ogenus [Oceanus] and the house of Ogenus ... 'wishing to marry you I honour you with this. Hail to you and be my wife.'

She replies – presumably to accept (but the fragment breaks off) – and it became the custom amongst gods and men.

Many vase paintings depict the role of both mothers in the ceremony. The bride's mother carried torches lit from her hearth, which protected her daughter during the procession, while her mother-in-law held torches lit from her hearth and received the bride into her new husband's home.

Once ensconsed in her new home, the first ritual, the *katachysmata*, took place at the new hearth. This is mentioned in a fragment from the fifth-century-BC comedian Theopompos: 'Bring the katachysmata; quickly pour them over the groom and the bride!' The *katachysmata* was also poured over the heads of newly bought slaves. It contained dates, coins, dried fruits, figs and nuts, and signified good seasons and good auspices for the new member of the household. The groom led his new wife to the hearth of her new *oikos*, where Hestia waited, sceptre in hand, to receive her into the household. The link provided by the *katachysmata* between slave and bride clearly illustrates the similarities in social standing beteen the two groups within the *oikos* and the community.

The bride's ritual bath was an elaborate ceremony. The *loutrophoros*, 'one who carries the bathwater', used a vessel specially designed for transporting the water for prenuptial baths and was synonymous with ancient Greek marriage. The women of the family joined the bride to parade to the bath house; then the bride would bathe in preparation for her marriage.

The object of getting married was, of course, to have children; there was no other reason. 'Trying for a baby' would have commenced straightaway and would continue until successful. The birth of a child was understood to temporarily pollute the *oikos*;

pregnant women were sometimes the cause of and also subject to *miasma* – bad air or odour. During the first forty days of her pregnancy, a pregnant woman was not permitted to enter any holy shrine. After forty days, however, the pregnant woman was expected to visit the sanctuaries of those deities connected with childbirth. Anyone who came into the house where there was a pregnant woman was considered polluted, if non-infectiously, for three days, after which the impure person was considered cleansed of the birth pollution. A baby's naming ceremony, its *amphidromia*, took place on either the fifth or the tenth day after birth.

Adultery

Adultery is the most frequently mentioned sexual transgression in Greek literature. The conventions surrounding mythical adultery exemplify the double standards relating to gender and sexual conduct in Greek society. The most famous case in Greek mythology is Helen and Paris, the *casus belli* of the Trojan War. The philandering of Paris is compared starkly with his brother Hector's moral rectitude and his love and affection for Andromache, his wife, and for Astyanax, their infant son:

> Hector saw him, and berated him with shaming words: 'Pernicious Paris, good looking but woman mad you trickster; I wish you'd never been born or died unmarried.'[29]

On Olympus, a heartbroken Hephaestus seeks redress when he learns that Ares is sleeping with Aphrodite, Hephaestus' wife. The sad, pathetic story is revealed in the 'Song of Demodocus':

> The minstrel struck the chords to prelude his sweet song and sang of the love of Ares and fair-crowned Aphrodite, how first they lay together secretly in the house of Hephaestus; how Ares gave her many gifts, and brought shame on the bed of the lord Hephaestus. But Helius, who had seen them as they lay together in love, came straight to him with news. When Hephaestus heard the painful tale, he went to his workshop, contemplating evil deep in his heart, and set on the anvil block the great anvil and forged unbreakable bonds which would not be undone.[30]

Odysseus is not just synonymous with Mediterranean travel, he is also inextricably linked with serial adultery. While Penelope waited patiently at home for twenty years, swatting off so many salacious

suitors and working her wifely wool, wily Odysseus enjoyed
ten years of adventure tourism and long-term horizontal
collaboration with some of the region's more voluptuous and
excitingly dangerous women – notably Circe and Calypso. The
male sexual freedom exercised here obviously reflected the norm
in Homer's day, and probably was common practice in the heroic
age he was writing about centuries before. As such, the message
from the epic poems would have resonated down the ages as each
generation handed its values down through the years; it would
become accepted routine for men to philander and mandatory
for women not to. Indeed, Calypso is very reluctant to give up
Odysseus and indignantly complains about the Olympian sexual
double standards in which a god can pursue a mortal woman or
man *ad libitum* while her own case demonstrates that a goddess
has no hope of capturing a mortal man. She cites the precedent set
by Iasion in his dalliance with Demeter in that 'thrice-ploughed
field' when he paid the ultimate price courtesy of a thunderbolt
from Zeus.

A woman's suspicions of her husband's adultery could have
fatal consequences, as Cyanippus' wife was to discover in this
cautionary tale:

> Cyanippus, a Thessalian by birth, was always going out to
> hunt, but his wife, whom he had recently married, suspected
> him of having an affair with another woman, because he would
> frequently spend the night in the forest; so she followed him and
> hid in a thicket to wait for events to unfold. Her movements,
> however, rustled some leaves and the dogs, thinking that she was
> a wild animal, rushed upon her and tore to pieces the loving wife
> as if she were a brute beast. Cyanippus saw this astounding event
> and killed himself.[31]

As stated, the double standards were to prevail down on earth.
In Greek law a man could stray and commit adultery with virtual
impunity – married women and young boys were off limits, but
prostitutes and other women of questionable repute as well as
older males were fair game. The seduction of married women was
considered a serious offence and dealt with severely: the cuckold
had the legal right to kill an adulterer or a rapist *in flagrante
delicto*. Female adulterers were ruined for life; they were classed as
prostitutes and forbidden to marry or take part in public ceremonies.
Stobaeus enshrines this for us in a passage he claims was written by
Perictyone, Plato's mother, but it was almost certainly written by

a man.[32] In it 'she' asserts that, concerning her husband, a woman must behave lawfully and honestly, never thinking of herself, but guarding and protecting her marriage bed, upon which everything depends. A woman must put up with everything from her husband, drunkenness, infidelity, ignorance, meanness, but that she should not give in to such behaviour herself, as mistakes which are forgiven in men are not in women, and that vengeance is wreaked on women who behave badly towards their husbands.

Only the Pythagoreans and the Stoics in the writings of Musonius Rufus advocated sexual fidelity in marriage for both partners.

If a woman complained about her husband's infidelity then she was unlikely to make much progress – not legally, domestically or socially. The perpetrator would be neither prosecuted nor ostracised. Nor would he feel shame or guilt. One woman who tried to protest was Hipparete, the daughter of Hipponicus III, but she may have wished she had not bothered. She was a wealthy Athenian lady who married the Athenian statesman and general Alcibiades in about 424 BC. Hipparete loved Alcibiades but she was uncomfortable with his whoring and sued him for divorce. Plutarch tells us that, when the case came to court:

> Alcibiades came up and grabbed her and carried her off home with him through the market place, no man daring to oppose him or take her from him.[33]

Being hauled off ignominiously over her husband's shoulder through the busy city obviously had no effect either on his behaviour, and it would have done nothing for her pride. Presumably, the case was dropped; she lived with him until her death and gave birth to a daughter and a son, whom they called Alcibiades.

Perhaps Hipparete should have known better? She had been but a pawn in the power play between her father and her husband. Alcibiades in earlier days had made an unprovoked physical attack on Hipponicus; in a kind of perverted pennance Alcibiades went to Hipponicus' house, took off his clothes and 'desired him to scourge and chastise him as he pleased'. Hipponicus, taken aback no doubt, not only forgave Alcibiades but also offered him Hipparete's hand in marriage.

Cases of adultery initiated by the woman were deemed so serious that it was known to have sparked off wars, at least in legend. Helen and Paris and the Trojan War is the famous example, but Parthenius of Nicaea writes that Neaera, the wife of a Milesian man, Hypsicreon, fell in love with Promedon of Naxos when he visited her husband at their house.[34] Nothing happened while Hypsicreon was around, but Promedon came back to Miletus again while Hypsicreon was away. Neaera saw her chance and went into Promedon's room intending to have sex with him, but Promedon refused to indulge, fearing the anger of Zeus Xenios – the god responsible for hospitality to guests. Neaera then locked the doors from the inside and persisted until Promedon gave in. The next day, Promedon left Miletus, racked with remorse having betrayed his friend's hospitality. To escape punishment by her husband, Neaera followed Promedon to Naxos and took up a suppliant's position at the sacred hearth in Prytaneum, from which the Naxians refused to hand her over. Hypsicreon and the Milesians declared war on Naxos.

This cautionary tale is interesting because it depicts the woman as a troublesome and evil adulteress to be avoided at all costs. Significantly, when Promedon left consumed by guilt that morning, he was not agonising over any guilt for his adultery, but rather because he had betrayed his friend's hospitality.

Citizenship was central to ancient Greek political and social life. For example, in Athens it was vital that both parents have Athenian citizenship before any offspring could be awarded full citizenship. Women were key players in the allocation of this citizenship; their trump card consisted in that, to qualify as an Athenian, you had to be born of an Athenian father *and* of an Athenian mother. Female adultery was a disqualification for citizenship so wives had to be denied any opportunities for adultery, and girls had to be kept pure until marriage when they could help produce more legitimate citizens. Wanton premarital sex and bastards were anathema to family-preserving brothers, fathers and prospective husbands. So, generations of paranoid and insecure husbands and fathers apparently resolved the issue by keeping their wives and daughters sequestered and excluded. Social intercourse and opportunites for illicit sexual intercourse were kept to a minimum.

Crucially, if paternity could not be established, then the child could not be a citizen. A husband had to know that he was the father of his child; a father had to know where his unmarried daughter was and what she was up to and with whom. Furthermore, adultery was thought not just to blemish a woman's chastity, but to corrupt her mind as well.

The court case described by Lysias, *On the Murder of Eratosthenes*, illustrates the ramifications of adultery in the domestic setting. Euphiletos stands trial accused of the murder of Eratosthenes, his wife's lover. As stated, according to Athenian law, if a husband caught his wife's lover in the act of adultery, he could either kill him or demand financial compensation. Euphiletos came upon Eratosthenes having sex with his wife and killed him in front of witnesses. Lysias does not record the verdict.

Aristophanes includes any number of references to adulterous relationships. In the *Thesmophoriazusae* we have seen how men typically call women

> adulterous, lecherous, bibulous, treacherous, and garrulous ...
> Does he not repeat that we are all vice, that we are the curse of
> our husbands?

In the *Ecclesiazusa*, 'they receive their lovers in their houses just as they always did'; then there is

> the woman who spreads open a large cloak before her husband's
> eyes to make him admire it in full daylight in order to conceal
> her lover by so doing, and afford him the means of making his
> escape.[35]

So the men kept the women in their place while they could philander more or less with impunity. In wider society women were also kept under control by *gunaikonomoi* – women regulators – from the fourth century BC. These officials monitored the dress and behaviour of women at weddings and funerals and during religious festivals.[36]

If adultery was only considered shameful in certain social contexts, then the seduction of virgin girls had no such qualification. The lyric poet Archilochus (*c.* 680–*c.* 645 BC) describes one such scenario in which he aims to deflower a young girl 'among the flowers, trembling as she is like a fawn', fondles her breast, feels her whole body and ejaculates, sending 'his white force aside'. Beforehand, the virgin girl had tried to dissuade him with the prospect of having sex with Neobule instead – a girl to whom we have noted the poet was engaged until her father called off the engagement with tragic consequences for her and her family. Whatever, our seducer rudely rejects Neobule out of hand, despite an appealing description of a sexy, young and eager woman – someone else can have her, he says; she's 'overripe', she's not a virgin, she can't get enough, she's bitter and twisted, she takes on too many lovers, she can go to hell. Character assassination complete, he romantically confesses that he prefers to take the virgin, promising her that he will withdraw, phrased in an interesting metaphor: 'I'll come ashore at your garden grass', meaning that he will ejaculate over her pubic hair.[37]

Rape

Rape was from a legal standpoint just as complicated as adultery. The gods, as noted, were serial rapists; Zeus uses it not just for sexual gratification but to demonstrate and exert his virility and omnipotence. If you were to ask him why he raped, he may well have replied, 'Because I can.' But 'rape' was not always what we today understand to be rape, based around the issue of consent. As we shall see in our discussion of the Greek sexual vocabulary, the verb *harpazein* meant 'to carry off', as *raptare* did in Latin; to convey the connotative meaning of non-consensual sexual violation, the Greeks added *bia* – 'with force'. Forced sex in Latin was usually expressed as *stuprum,* 'fornication', with the addition of *cum vi* or *per vim*, with violent force. *Raptus ad stuprum* was abduction with a view to committing a sex crime. The legendary rape of the Sabine women was literally the abduction of the Sabine women, a shameless act of nation-building; no doubt the actual raping, as we understand it, took place when the Romans got the Sabine women and girls home.

When a Greek girl was abducted or kidnapped, the issue was not one of lacking consent by the victim, but rather the absence of legal consent from the father, husband or guardian; the precedent was set in the *Homeric Hymn to Demeter* when Zeus and Hades were complicit in the snatching of Persephone and her incarceration in the Underworld. This was not 'actual rape': it was a well-conceived arrangement to install a queen by an arranged marriage to Hades. The procedure, of course, was the norm in the real world above. Persephone and her mother Demeter would have seen it very differently.

Raping a slave was only considered a criminal offence when the slave's owner had not given consent – more a case of damaged goods than atrocious sexual violence against a human being. In wars fought by the Greeks and conflicts prior to that, particularly in the often horrendous aftermaths of sieges, the systematic rape of women, men and children on the losing side was par for the course, a duty even, and has been, to a greater or lesser extent, ever since. That said, some more enlightened generals did try to curb the practice.

5

Sex and Sexuality: Animal Lovers, Necrophilia, Dildos and Masturbation

This chapter covers aspects of sexuality and attitudes to it; it takes in hermaphroditism, sexual pleasure, deviant behaviour and sexual variations, erotica, 'pornography', prostitution, and erotic dreams.

When discussing sex and sexuality in the ancient Greek world it is important to try and view things as an ancient Greek might have. What I wrote about Roman sex and sexuality in my earlier books largely holds good for the Greek way of seeing sex.[1] To re-emphasise briefly, it is important but undoubtedly difficult to try and see sexuality as the Greek man and woman might have seen it, that is from a vantage outside of our own modern, twenty-first-century perspective, with all the baggage that it has accumulated in the intervening time. The ubiquity of the erotic in poetry and plays, of phalluses on ceramics, would clearly suggest that Greeks were accustomed to and even liked looking at sex; the shame, embarrassment and oppression which accompanies erotica or 'pornography' (itself an English nineteenth-century term) in many societies today would probably have been quite alien to them. To the Greek it was all probably quite normal. By and large, sex and sexuality seem to have been relatively unremarkable facets of everyday life. Importantly, erotic images would have been observed by as many women as men, suggesting that women were probably just as relaxed about it and unphased by it as their male counterparts.

As stated, the function of women and the purpose of marriage was to produce babies, ideally male babies. The Greek was not left on his or own here. Hippocratic help and advice was at hand to achieve the preferred sort of offspring: to produce a male child, copulation of the rapid thrusting variety – at the end of the woman's period was best.[2] To produce a girl, what the Greeks gained in technique they definitely lost in spontaneity: the recommendation was to tie up the right testicle during sexual intercourse, which should take place in the middle of the woman's period.

Hermaphroditism

We have a mythological explanation for hermaphroditism when Salmacis wrapped herself around Hermaphoditus so tightly that they became one. Hermaphrodites (*androgyni*) used to be thought of as prodigies in Greece and Rome until the time of Pompey in the first century BC, who made them figures of fun, putting them on the stage in his theatre. They were joined in the limelight by such unusual celebrities as Eutyche, a woman who was later led to her funeral pyre by twenty children to celebrate the thirty individual babies she had delivered to the world; by Alcippe, who had given birth to an elephant; and by the slave girl who delivered a snake. Sightings of centaurs were not uncommon, it seems: Pliny saw one immersed in honey. A baby was born in Saguntum, soon after the city was devastated by Hannibal: it took one look around, evidently did not like what it saw, and immediately unbirthed itself and returned to its mother's womb. Pliny adds as a footnote that the Greeks call such people *ektrapeloi*, 'freaks'.

Diodorus Siculus, in an alternative mythical origin story in the late first century BC, described hermaphrodites as 'marvellous creatures', *terata*, who are able to see into the future, for good and bad:

> Hermaphroditus, as he has been called, who was born of Hermes and Aphrodite and received a name which is a combination of those of both his parents. Some say that this Hermaphroditus is a god and appears at certain times among men, and that he is born with a physical body which is a combination of that of a man and that of a woman, in that he has a body which is beautiful and delicate like that of a woman, but has the masculine quality and vigour of man. But there are some who declare that such creatures of two sexes are monstrosities, and coming rarely into the world as they do they have the quality of presaging the future, sometimes for evil and sometimes for good.

Much later, around AD 500, Isidore of Seville described hermaphrodites as having the right breast of a man and the left of a woman, who can both sire and bear children. After Pompey made celebrities out of them they had, by Pliny's time, become objects of delight and fascination, *deliciae*, much in demand in the slave markets.

Diodorus Siculus leaves us an intriguing story about a man from Macedonia called Diophantus living in Abae in Arabia; he married an Arabian woman and had a son who died young, and a daughter called Heraïs whom he married off to a man named Samiades. After a year, Samiades left on a long journey, leaving Heraïs who fell ill 'of a strange and altogether incredible infirmity'. An aggressive tumour presented at the base of her abdomen which became more and more swollen, accompanied by fevers; her physicians diagnosed an ulcer at the mouth of the uterus. On the seventh day without cure the tumour burst to reveal a penis projecting from her groin with testicles. When this happened, only her mother and two slaves were present; they looked after Heraïs to the best of their ability and said nothing of what had happened. Heraïs recovered and tried to get on with her life, still wearing women's clothes, looking after her house and remaining true to her absent husband. It was assumed by the few people in the know that she was an hermaphrodite, and that since conventional sexual intercourse was not an option, she would have sex with her husband anally. Samiades returned but Heraïs, out of shame, could not bear to be near him. He was angry and quarrelled with his father-in-law and took legal action; the jurors debated whether the husband should have jurisdiction over his wife or the father over his daughter. When the court found in favour of Samiades, Heraïs undid her dress and exposed her penis – much to the astonishment of all present. Heraïs swapped her women's clothes for a man's. The doctors concluded that her penis had been concealed in an egg-shaped part of her vagina, encased by a membrane; an opening had formed through which urine was discharged. Heraïs underwent surgery, changed her name to Diophantus, joined the cavalry, and fought in the king's army.[3]

Modern urologists have identified this as a clear case of hypospadias, where the hole through which urine passes (*meatus*) is not at the tip of the penis; instead the hole may be anywhere along the underside of the penis or even within the scrotum and the foreskin is all at the back of the penis leaving none at the front. The penis may be bent when erect – 15 to 50 per cent of cases are in such a condition, called 'chordee'. Corrective surgery aims to straighten the penis, relocate the *meatus* to the tip of the penis and to carry out a circumcision by removing the excess foreskin. Hypospadias is a common birth defect found in up to 1 in every 200 boys.

Diodorus described a similar case in Epidaurus some thirty years later involving a patient called Callo, an orphan and priestess of Demeter. Callo was only able to urinate through a kind of penis (*pecten*). Nevertheless, she married but was unable to have natural sexual intercourse and 'was obliged to submit to unnatural embraces' – sodomy. She eventually developed a painful tumour on her genitals; none of the doctors she attended would treat her, other than an apothecary who cut into her groin only to reveal testicles and an imperforate penis. 'Cutting into the glans he made a passage into the urethra, and inserting a silver catheter drew off the urine. Then, by scarifying the perforated area, he brought the parts together.' The apothecary demanded double fees, justifyng this because he had received a female patient and made her into a healthy young man. Callo, meanwhile, 'laid aside her loom-shuttles and all other instruments of woman's work, and taking in their stead the garb and status of a man changed her name ... to Callon'. Unfortunately for him, because she had been a priestess and had witnessed things to which men should not be privy, she was duly tried for impiety.[4]

Diodorus is at pains not to seem prurient in detailing these cases but is anxious to dispel man's 'consternation and mystification' and the superstition it brings. He goes on to tell us about an Italian who had married an hermaphrodite, but the senate, mired in superstition, ordered the 'creature' to be burned alive. A similar case at Athens led to the person being burned alive out of ignorance.[5]

Similar paranoid superstition is evident when Pliny the Elder describes instantaneous gender transgression or gender reassignment – 'no dream', *non est speculum,* he attests. Although the examples are from the wider Mediterranean world, there is no reason to doubt that they were typical of the region as a whole and would have occurred in ancient Greece and in the wider Greek world. In 171 BC a girl from Casinum instantaneously changed into a boy before her parents' eyes; the augurs banished her to a remote island. Licinius Mucianus records the case of Arescon, a 'man' from Argos who married a man as Arescusa; 'she' then grew a beard and developed other male features and married a woman; there was a similar sighting in Smyrna. Pliny himself saw a bride turn into a man on his/her wedding day. The mother of a boxer,

Nicaeus of Byzantium, was born from her mother's adulterous affair with an Ethiopian: the mother was born white but Nicaeus, her son one generation later, was born black. Pliny goes on to say that certain Indian tribes have children from the age of seven and are old by the time they reach forty, while others conceive aged five and die three years later; the children of others go grey immediately after birth. Women who want a black-eyed baby must eat a shrew during their pregnancy.[6]

Equally miraculous were the observations of Phlegon of Tralles, a freedman of Hadrian's. Phlegon's publications included *On Long Lived Persons*, a diverting list of Italian and Roman centenarians culled from the censuses; but it his paradoxographical *Marvels* which interests us here – a semi-humorous compilation of ghost stories, congenital abnormalites, strange hybrid creatures, hermaphrodites, giant skeletons and prophesying heads. Again, although the stories are culled from Roman life, it is reasonable to assume that the Greeks experienced similar cases. He records, for example, an hermaphrodite from 125 BC who caused such a stir that the *Sibylline Oracles* were consulted; a highly thought of slave woman who in AD 49 gave birth to an ape; a four-headed child which was presented to Nero; and a child born with its head protruding from its shoulder.[7]

Hipponax

Hipponax (*fl.* 540 BC) gives us both incest and fellatio in his iambic fragments, adumbrating the seamier depths of Ionian life. He calls Bupalus 'the mother-fucker (μητροκοίτης) with Arete' (the name means 'virtue'); elsewhere Hipponax tells us that Arete performs fellatio on him. The vitriol apparently stemmed from the fact that Hipponax had hopes of marrying Bupalus' daughter but was rejected because he was so ugly. Hipponax's response was so devastating that Bupalus hanged himself.[8] Hipponax was no lover of women generally, if the famous line, 'there are two days when a woman is a joy: the day someone marries her and the day when someone carries out her dead body' is indeed by Hipponax.

Fetishistic food sex – eating, drinking, defecating and fornicating, often at roughly the same time – is a frequent theme, as in fragment 92, in which Hipponax describes a sexual encounter in a stinking toilet. A Lydian-speaking woman performs some mysterious and obscene rites on the poet, which include whacking his genitals with a fig branch and inserting a foreign body up his anus, provoking incontinence and an attack by dung beetles – a repugnant and bizarre scene which inspired the 'Oenothea' episode in Petronius's *Satyricon*.

Wonderful pithy one-liners include 'drank like a lizard in a bog', 'croaking like a raven in a privy', 'sister of cow manure', 'filthy arse … self-exposer' (βορβορόπιν … ἀνασυρτόπολιν), 'Mimnes, you whose arse gapes open all the way up to your shoulders (εὐρύπρωκτος, euryproktos)', and 'interprandial shitter' (μεσσηγυδορποχέστης).

Hipponax, however, was also capable of some elegant poetry, if fragment 119 is anything to go by: 'If only I might have a maiden who is both beautiful and tender …'

Buttocks partialism
Female buttocks have been an erogenous zone and a symbol of fertility and beauty since the dawn of history. Statues created as early as 24,000 BC, such as the Venus or Woman of Willendorf found in Austria, have exhibited exaggerated buttocks, hips and thighs. Pygophilia is sexual arousal caused by the buttocks.

Athenaeus tells the engaging story of the well-read *hetaera* Mania, mistress of Philip II, quoting Sophocles:

> Mania once was asked, by King Demetrius, for a perfect sight of her fair buttocks; and she, in return, demanded that he should grant her a favour. When he agreed, she turned her back, and said, 'O son of Agamemnon, now the Gods grant you to see what you so long have wished for.'[9]

There is more buttock-revealing, or at least a request for it, as well as an exquisite put-down, with Gnathaena:

> They say that one fine day a youth from Pontus was sleeping with Gnathaena, and in the morning he asked her to show her buttocks to him. But she replied, 'You have no time for that now, it's time for you to feed the pigs.'

Demophoon, a friend of Sophocles', was also partial to his *hetaera's* buttocks:

> And it is said this woman had fair buttocks, And when Demophoon tried to hold them, 'A pretty thing,' said she, 'that what you get From me, you may present to Sophocles.'

In the endless pursuit of the acme of physical beauty the buttocks were very important, as indeed they were in social intercourse. The ideal was portrayed on a Greek bronze, now lost, but a fine first-century-BC Roman copy in marble called the 'Kallipygean Venus' can be seen in the Naples Archaeological Museum. Athenaeus tells the story of a Syracusan farmer who had two daughters that could not agree on which had the best buttocks, so they enlisted the opinion of a young male passer-by. He preferred the buttocks of the older sister and fell in love with her. His inquisitive younger brother fell likewise for the younger sister; the two married their callipygian girls, who commissioned a temple to the 'Kallipygean Aphrodite' and erected a cult statue. The Christian Clement of Alexandria was later to describe the masterpiece as 'shamefully erotic examples of pagan religious art'.

Women on top

Gnathaena's granddaughter, Gnathaeniŏn, had a similarly sharp repartee. One day when her boyfriend, the actor Andronicus, was out of town she was persuaded to name her price, despite being retired from the trade, by a smith:

> But being but a rude and ill-bred clown, he, one day sitting with some friends ... boasted that he never consorted with her in any other way, except that she rode on top of him, five times over.

When Andronicus returned and heard about this he was none too pleased and complained:

> That she had never granted him such liberties ... Gnathaeniŏn replied that she was her own mistress, and the smith was so begrimed with soot and dirt that she did not wish to embrace him; but after receiving a large sum of gold, she gave in to his request, and cleverly contrived to touch the part of him, which, though small, stuck out the furthest.

The equally witty Mania prefers to be on top too, particularly when entertaining a wastrel:

> They say a man who was a complete profligate entertained Mania at supper; and when he asked her, 'Do you like being on top or down the best?' She laughed, and said, 'I'd rather be on top, my friend, For I'm afraid that if I lie down, you'd bite the plaited hair off my head.'[10]

Petronius and Apuleius, two Roman novelists of the early empire, describe the lubricious movements of the dominant woman. Horace compares the whore, *meretricula*, with a horse rider. The *mulier equitans* appears to have been popular, with the woman 'riding' on top; it was also called the 'Hector horse' as mythological Hector and Andromache allegedly liked sex that way. There are numerous visual representations of the sexually dominant woman, many from the ceramics found in the Rhone Valley dating from AD 70 to 250. Some show the woman to be the soldier in a reversal of the *miles amoris* scenario – *orte scutus est* – 'look out, that's a shield you've got there!'; the man is flaccid. A medallion shows the woman on top with the text *vides quam bene chalas*, 'see how well you open me up.' The famous *Navigium Veneris*, 'navigation of Venus', or more loosely 'cock steering', medallion is still attached to its original jug and shows a very dextrous man steering his penis into his partner's ample rear, in much the same way as he would manipulate a boat's rudder. Although these examples all date from years after ancient Greece had succumbed to the Romans, ceramic evidence shows that Greek man and woman were up to the same antics.

Sexual positioning

Premium *hetaerae* could set their prices according to what sexual positions they were proficient in. One who had mastered twelve positions charged the most for one position called *keles* – 'racehorse' – in which the woman was on top.

For the low-rent *khamaitypés* (χαμαιτυπής), the options were much less comfortable and dignified; they had to perform 'in the dirt' as they had no beds or rooms. They are depicted on vases as either performing rear entry 'dog-style' or on all fours on the ground, also taking it from the rear. The Epicurean Lucretius in the first century BC was to describe this as *more ferarum*, 'the way that animals do it'.

One vase shows a prostitute standing in improvised dog-style holding on to a tree trunk to steady herself. Her legs are spread apart, the man enters her from behind, his hands on the sides of her buttocks; she is helping in the thrusting. The artist has painted a smile on the prostitute's face, suggesting that she was enjoying it, or pretending to. Another vase demonstrates the *cyon*, or the 'dog', from which the term 'dog-style' presumably comes, and which has the woman on all fours and the man entering from the rear. In a famous vase in the British Museum, we can see a *hetaera* sitting on her client's lap facing him, assisted by two slave girls in rising and falling on her man's penis. The 'leapfrog' – or an act of sodomy where the woman is 'folded in two' with her hands flat on the ground – appears on yet another vase.

Agalmatophilia

Agalmatophilia, from the Greek *agalma*, 'statue', and *–philia*, love, is a paraphilia involving sexual attraction to a statue, doll or mannequin. This attraction may encompass a desire for sexual contact with the object, viewing such encounters or sexual pleasures as manifestations of a desire of being transformed or transforming another into the preferred object. Athenaeus describes such an instance, albeit an unfulfilling one:

> Cleisophus of Selymbria ... fell in love with a statue of Parian marble that then was at Samos, and shut himself up in the temple to gratify his affection; but when he found that he could make no impression on the coldness and unimpressibility of the stone, then he discarded his passion.

Another man got away lightly, perhaps, for his 'transgression':

> At Delphi, in the museum of the pictures, there are two boys wrought in marble; with one of which, the Delphians say, a visitor fell in love so strongly, that he made love to it, and shut himself up with it, and presented it with a crown; but when he was discovered, the god ordered the Delphians, who consulted his oracle about it, to let him off.

Agalmatophilia first became a subject of clinical study with the publication of Richard von Krafft-Ebing's *Psychopathia Sexualis*, in which he recorded the case of a gardener in 1877 falling in love with a statue of the Venus de Milo and being discovered attempting to have sex with it.

Bestiality

When we think of bestiality, or zoophilia (which is presumably not very often for most people), we tend to assume that it is the man or the woman who is the instigator rather than the animal. Not so Athenaeus: he can offer a catalogue of instances where the animal has been the driving force in zoophilic relationships, although we have no way of knowing if there was an actual sexual element involved:

> And even brute beasts have fallen in love with men: for there was a cock who took a fancy to a man of the name of Secundus ... and the cock was nicknamed the Centaur ... And, at Aegium, a goose took a fancy to a boy; as Clearchus relates in the first book of his Amatory Anecdotes ... And Hermeias says that a goose also took a fancy to Lacydes the philosopher. And in Leucadia a peacock fell so in love with a maiden there, that when she died, the bird died too ... at Iasus, a boy whose name was Dionysius who, when leaving the palaestra with the rest of the boys, went down to the sea to bathe to be met by a dolphin which came forward out of the deep water to meet him, and taking him on his back, swam away with him a considerable distance into the open sea, and then brought him back again to land ... Coeranus was saved by a dolphin. And when, at last, he died of old age in his native country, as it so happened that his funeral procession passed along the sea-shore close to Miletus, a great shoal of dolphins appeared on that day in the harbour, close to those who were attending the funeral, as if they also were joining in the procession and sharing in the grief.

We learn too of an affectionate, maternal elephant called Nicaea crossing the species boundary. The wife of the king of India on her deathbed entrusted her one-month-old child to the elephant, which demonstrated extraordinary affection for the infant. It could not bear the child to be out of its sight and whenever it did not see him, it became dejected:

> And so, whenever the nurse fed the infant with milk, she placed it in its cradle between the feet of the beast; and if she did not do so, the elephant would not eat ... while the child was sleeping, it would beat away the flies ... And whenever the child cried, it would rock the cradle with its trunk, and lull it to sleep. And very often the male elephant did the same.

Bestial practices it seems are as old as mankind. One of the earliest depictions is a cave painting from Val Comonica in Brescia, Italy, circa 8000 BC, which clearly shows a man pleasuring a donkey. A common Egyptian curse went, 'May a donkey fuck your wife and children!' We will hear about a woman having sex with a goat in Herodotus' descriptions of some bizarre Egyptian habits; in the meantime, there is also the example of the highly sacred Egyptian

Apis bull with its strong association with fertility. When a new bull was born to replace the deceased one, only women were allowed to look after it for the first forty days of its life. To encourage fertility throughout its life, women would lift up their cloaks and display their vulvas. Theocritus describes shepherds and goats in 'hideous coupling' at Thyout, while a petroglyph found at Naquane, north Italy, shows a man happily sodomising a quadruped while gaily waving at the viewer. In the various books on dream interpretation from ancient Greece we hear of women fantasising about sex with mice, horses, donkeys, rams, wolves, lions, crocodiles, snakes, baboons, ibis and falcons.

Necrophilia

Hittite law from the sixteenth century BC to the thirteenth century BC explicitly permitted sexual relations with the dead. According to Herodotus, necrophilia was a problem in Egypt:

> The wives of [Egyptian] men of rank when they die are not handed over immediately to be embalmed, nor such women as are very beautiful or of greater regard than others; it is only on the third or fourth day after their death (and not before) that they are delivered to the embalmers. They do this in order that the embalmers may not abuse the women, for they say that one of them was caught doing so to the corpse of a woman lately dead, and his colleagues blew the whistle on him.

Herodotus alludes to Periander 'baking his bread' in Melissa's 'cold oven' in that superb euphemism:

> [Periander] stripped all the women of Corinth naked, because of his own wife Melissa [whom he had killed]. He had sent messengers to the Oracle of the Dead on the river Acheron in Thesprotia to enquire about a deposit that a friend had left, but Melissa, appearing as a ghost, said that she would tell him nothing, nor reveal the location of the deposit. Why? Because she was cold and naked. The clothes, she said, which Periander had buried her in had not been cremated, and were of no use to her. Then, to prove to her husband that she was telling the truth, she added that Periander had put his loaves into a cold oven. When this message was brought back to Periander he knew that it was true because he had actually had intercourse with Melissa's corpse. Immediately, he proclaimed that all the Corinthian women should come out into the temple of Hera, which they did

as if attending a festival, wearing their finest clothes; Periander set
his guards there and stripped every one of them, ladies and slaves
alike, and heaped all their clothes in a pit, in which, as he prayed
to Melissa, he set fire to them. When he had done this and sent a
second message, the ghost of Melissa told him where the friend's
deposit was.[11]

The Babylonian Talmud relates that King Herod of Judea (73–4
BC) was besotted by a virgin girl who killed herself to avoid
marrying him; he preserved her body in honey for seven years in
order, some say, to have regular sex with her corpse. Xenophon of
Ephesus leaves us with the odd and unedifying story of the poor
Spartan Aigialeus and his common-law wife Thelxinoe who died;
Aigialeus kept her body at home embalmed Egyptian-style.[12] 'I
speak to her as though she is still alive,' he says, and 'I lie down
next to her and have my meals with her.' This is reminiscent of
Euripides' *Alcestis* (348–53), where Admetus promises to keep
a likeness of his dying wife in his bedroom. Diodorus Siculus
reminds us that poorer Egyptians would keep mummies at home
rather than placing them in tombs because they believed that
the dead could enjoy earthly pleasures such as food and drink.[13]
Aigialeus says of Thelxinoe's corpse, 'I'm forever kissing her
and passing the time with her,' with the strong suggestion of
necrophilia.[14]

Dildos

Miletus was the manufacturing and exporting centre of the
olisbos, from ὀλισθεῖν (*olistheîn:* to slip, glide) and known to
us as the dildo. The world's oldest known dildo is a twenty-
centimeter phallus from the Upper Palaeolithic period, some
30,000 years ago, found in Hohle Fels Cave near Ulm in Germany.
What can only be described as dildo-like breadsticks, known
as *olisbokollikes* (singular *olisbokollix*), were known in ancient
Greece before the fifth century BC. More often, dildos were made
either of wood or pressed leather and were liberally smeared with
olive oil before use.

A third-century-BC mime by Herodas, *A Quiet Chat [Mime 6],*
features a conversation between two young women, Metro and
Coritto. Metro wants to borrow Coritto's dildo but Coritto says
that Nossis has it, who got it from Euboula:

That woman wore me down; she begged me so much that I
weakened and gave it to her, Metro, before I had even used

it myself. After seizing it like a godsend, she gives it away [to Nossis]! ... If I had a thousand I would not have given her one, even if it were all worn out.

Coritto then explains that she bought it from Kerdon, the maker of the dildo, who covers up his black-market trade by pretending to be a cobbler who 'works at his house and sells secretly'. Metro then vividly describes Kerdon's expertise:

But the things he makes, all of them, are worthy of Athena; you would believe you could see her hand, instead of Kerdo's. He came here with two, Metro! When I saw them, my eyes nearly popped out with desire. The men certainly have no rams like those! – we are alone – that's for sure! And that's not all: their smoothness – a dream; and the stitches – of down, not of thread! Hunt as you might, you could not find another cobbler so kindly disposed toward women.

She then leaves to seek him out. In *Mime* 7, Metro takes some friends to Kerdon's shoe shop and the sexual innuendo continues with footware a metaphor for sex toys.

The *olisbos* is also mentoned in Aristophanes' *Lysistrata* (107ff) when Calonice, bewailing the absence of the men at war, remarks:

And so, girls, when fucking time comes ... not the faintest whiff of it anywhere, right? From the time those Milesians betrayed us, we can't even find our eight-fingered leather dildos. At least they'd serve as a sort of flesh-replacement for our poor cunts ... So, then! Would you like me to find some mechanism by which we could end this war?

(loose translation of Aristophanes' *Lysistrata*,
translated by George Theodoridis)

Masturbation
Man and woman have been masturbating since the dawn of time. A clay figurine of the fourth millennium BC from Malta shows a woman masturbating. In ancient Sumer, masturbation was thought to enhance potency, either solitary or with a partner. In ancient Egypt, male masturbation when performed by a god was considered a creative or magical act: Atum created the universe by masturbating, and the ebb and flow of the Nile was attributed to the frequency of his ejaculations. Egyptian Pharaohs were required to masturbate ceremonially into the Nile.

To the ancient Greeks, masturbation was a normal and healthy substitute for other sexual pleasures – a handy safety valve against destructive sexual frustration. This may explain why there are so few references to it in the literature: it was common practice and did not merit much attention. Nevertheless, it may well have been deemed, publicly at least, to be the preserve of slaves, lunatics and other such so-called undesirables. Elite opinion would have regarded it as a waste of time and semen, since it was one of the prime cultural responsibilities of the Greek male to further the family line and extend the *oikos*.

One term for it was *anaphlao*, a verb which Aristophanes disparagingly uses to describe the Spartans masturbating in the *Lysistrata* (1099). *Anaphlasmos* is used for masturbation in Eupolis' *Autolycus* (21) (*c.* 446–411 BC). The decidedly odd Diogenes the Cynic routinely masturbated in public, defending his actions by saying 'If only it were as easy to banish hunger by rubbing my belly.'[15] Interestingly, Diogenes attracted censure not just for for masturbating in public but also for eating in the agora – indicating perhaps that masturbating in a public place was regarded as no more serious a crime than eating in a public place. Satyrs were inveterate masturbators; sixth-century-BC *kraters* survive showing them in the act with their pronounced erections.

Diogenes Laertius believed that Hermes discovered masturbation and, taking pity on his son, Pan, who was pining for Echo at the time, he taught him how to masturbate to relieve his pangs. Pan, in turn, taught the habit to young shepherds:

> Fish showed themselves more sensible than men almost; for whenever they needed to eject their sperm, they went out of doors and rubbed themselves against something rough. He was amazed that while men were unwilling to pay out money to have a leg or arm or any other part of their body rubbed ... yet on that one member they spent many talents time and again and some had even risked their lives in the bargain. In a joking way he would say that this sort of intercourse was a discovery made by Pan.[16]

Erotic dreams

The standard text on dream interpretation in antiquity is the *Oneirocritica*, researched and compiled by Artemidorus of Ephesus in the second century AD and based on his own work and that of sixteen predecessors, now all lost. The eighty-two sections in book one interpret the appearance in dreams of subjects as diverse as head size, eating and sexuality.

Interpretations of dreams about the penis vary from the obvious and logical to the arcane. According to Artemidorus, penis dreams are related to one's parents because of the association with reproduction; they also are indicative of children because the penis makes children. Penis dreams can also signify a wife or a mistress because the penis is the vehicle for sexual intercourse with wives and mistresses. It indicates brothers and all close relatives since the *oikos* relies on the penis. It is a symbol of both strength and vigour which explains why some call the penis 'one's manhood'. Less obviously, it corresponds to speech and education because the penis, like speech, is very fertile. The penis is also a sign of wealth and possessions because it too expands and contracts and is productive.[17]

Legal, consensual intercourse with a wife bodes well, while coercive sex has the opposite implication. On the other hand, dreaming about intercourse with prostitutes working in brothels signifies a bit of a scandal in the offing and a small financial outlay in the future. Going into a brothel and getting out is good; Artemidorus describes an acquaintance who dreamt that he went into a brothel and could not get out; he died in real life a few days later, apparently the logical outcome of his dream, because a brothel, like a cemetery, is a place 'common to all and the destruction of many human seeds takes place there'. Prostitutes sitting in their stalls, selling their services, receiving their fee or visibly copulating are a good sign, but streetwalkers in a dream are even better.[18]

Familiarity is everything: if a man dreams he is having intercourse with a woman he does not know, if she is attractive and elegant, is decked out in fine and expensive clothes and gold necklaces, and gives herself willingly, this augurs very well for the dreamer and indicates forthcoming success. However, 'if she is an ugly, shapeless, shabbily dressed old hag dragging out a life of pain, and she does not consent to sex, it signifies the opposite.'

Going back to sex with the woman the dreamer knows and is consensual, the man will benefit from such a woman because a woman who gives her body freely would very likely also give him

her investments. Often a dream of this kind has helped the dreamer when coping with the mystery of woman, since the woman in such a dream also allows him to touch her secret parts.

It is a bad thing to dream of having sex with a legally married woman because that dream delivers the same punishments as the law subjects a man to when caught committing adultery in real life – death.

Dreams relating to female homoeroticism were all about secrets. All will be revealed to the partner when a woman dreams she is pleasuring another woman. The same happens when a woman dreams she is the object of pleasure, with the disadvantage, though, that she will either be separated from her husband or she will be widowed.[19]

To Artemidorus, oral sex was one of those aspects of sexuality he considered to be outside the law. Anyone dreaming that he has had fellatio performed on him by a friend, relative or a child will grow to hate the perpetrator; if the child is an infant then that infant will die because he can no longer kiss him or her. If fellatio is performed by someone he does not know then he will pay a penalty for 'the useless emission of semen'. If, on the other hand, the man performs fellatio on someone, man or woman, he knows then he will come to hate that person, again because they can no longer kiss each other. If he does not know the person on whom he performs fellatio then harm will come to all except those who make a living by using their mouths, such as flute players, trumpeters, orators and philosophers.

When it comes to the interpretation of incestuous dreams about having sex with one's mother then things are, unsurprisingly, not so very straightforward:

> The case of one's mother is both complex and manifold and admits of many different interpretations ... the manner of the embraces and the various positions of the bodies indicate different outcomes.

With face-to-face intercourse between a dreamer and his mother who is still alive and whose father is in good health, it means that he and his father will become enemies because of the jealousy that naturally arises between rivals. But if his father is sick, he will soon die, since the dreamer will look after his mother both as a son and as a husband. But it is lucky for every artisan and labourer. If the dreamer is estranged from his mother, they will become friends again because of the sexual intercourse. It also signifies that a son will return from a foreign country to his own land, if his mother still lives there. If she does not, then he will travel back to wherever she lives. If the dreamer is poor but his mother is rich, he will receive from her whatever he wishes or she will die soon after and leave her estate to him.

If, though, his mother is dead in the dream, the dreamer will himself die very soon afterwards. Land is a preponderant issue: for a man who is involved in a lawsuit over land rights or related matters, it is good to have intercourse with one's dead mother. 'Some people say that it indicates bad luck only for farmers. For they will cast their seeds down into, as it were, dead land. That is, it will bear no fruit.' If a man has the dream in his native land, he will soon leave it since it is impossible to remain so close to home after such a crime. If he feels grief or remorse because of the incest, he will be banished from his native land. If not, he will go abroad of his own volition.

It is not good to have sex with a mother who is looking away; it is also unlucky to dream of having intercourse with one's mother while she is standing up:

> For men use this position only when they have neither bed nor mattress. Therefore it signifies coercion and oppression. It is also bad to have intercourse with one's mother while she is kneeling and worse while she is prostrate. For it signifies great poverty because of the mother's immobility.

Woe betide anyone who has a dream in which he takes his mother 'from underneath while she is in the "rider position"; this means death to the dreamer.'

In conclusion, Artemidorus helpfully teaches:

> It is not auspicious to use many different positions on one's mother. For it is not right to insult one's mother ... the worst dream by far is one in which the dreamer practices fellatio with his mother. For this signifies to the dreamer the death of children, the loss of property, and serious illness. I know of a man who, after this dream, lost his penis. For it was understandable that he was punished in the part of the body with which he had sinned.[20]

6

In Bed with the Boys and Girls

Aristotle tells us where he believed pederasty all started:

> The fashion of making favourites of boys was first introduced among the Greeks from Crete, as Timaeus informs us. But others say that Laius was the originator of this custom, when he was received in hospitality by Pelops; and that he took a great fancy to Pelops' son, Chrysippus, whom he put into his chariot and carried off, and fled with to Thebes. But Praxilla the Sicyonian says that Chrysippus was carried off by Zeus. And the Celts, too, although they have the most beautiful women of all the barbarians, still make great favourites of boys; so that some of them often go to rest with two lovers on their beds of hide. And the Persians, according to the statement of Herodotus, learnt from the Greeks to adopt this fashion.[1]

In Plato's *Symposium* we learn how hermaphrodites and homosexuals came about. Aristophanes, a character at the drinking party, formulates a kind of spoof creation myth when he muses that human beings were once divided into three sexes: male, female and androgynous. These hermaphrodites once had four arms, four legs, and two sets of genitalia, either two male sets, or two female, or one of each:

> The sexes were not two as they are now, but originally three in number; there was man, woman, and the union of the two, of which the name [androgyne] survives but nothing else ... and then as a term of reproach ... primeval man was round, his back and sides forming a circle; and he had four hands and the same

number of feet, one head with two faces, looking opposite ways, set on a round neck and precisely alike; also four ears, two sets of genitals.

But Zeus spoilt all that when the hermaphrodites, in their considerable might, tried to assault Olympus and attack the gods (190b–c). Zeus, with one greedy eye on the offerings the hermaphrodites brought him, decided against a genocidal thunderbolt blast and opted to cripple them instead by chopping each in half, in effect separating the two bodies. From now on they would have to amble around on just two legs desperately seeking their other half to recover their primal nature, with what would become their heterosexual orientation determined by the genitals of that missing person. They do say that for all us of there is someone out there …

I believe I have a plan which will enfeeble their strength and so extinguish their turbulence; men shall continue to exist, but I will cut them in two and then they will be diminished in strength and increased in numbers; this will have the advantage of making them more profitable to us … He spoke and cut men in two, like a sorb-apple which is halved for pickling, or as you might divide an egg with a hair; and as he cut them one after another, he told Apollo to give the face and the half of the neck a turn in order that man might look on this part of himself: he would thus learn a lesson of humility. Apollo was also ordered to heal their wounds and compose their forms. So he gave a turn to the face and pulled the skin from the sides all over that which we call call the belly, like the purses which draw tight, and he made one mouth at the centre, which he fastened in a knot (the navel has the same name); he also moulded the breast and took out most of the wrinkles, much as a shoemaker might smooth leather upon a last; he left a few, however, in the region of the belly and navel, as a reminder of their punishment … and they sowed the seed no longer as hitherto like grasshoppers in the ground, but in one another [by moving the genitals to the front of the body]; and through sexual intercourse they might breed, and the race might continue.

Those women separated from women run after women, thus creating 'lesbians'. The men split from other men become homosexuals (191e). Those that come from original androgynous beings with both organs are destined to be heterosexuals.

Aristophanes thinks that homosexuals are the bravest as only they grow up to be politicians (192a), while many heterosexuals are adulterous (191e). Aristophanes in the *Symposium* concludes with a caution: men should fear the gods and always worship them lest they get the axe out again leaving man hopping about on one leg, hopelessly split apart (193a). Only if man loves god will he escape this fate and find completeness.

To the ancient Greeks sexual orientation carried little of the stigma it has had and can still have in modern societies. There is no vocabulary in Greek or Latin for homosexual or heterosexual which may suggest that the difference did not exercise the Greeks and Romans in anything like the way it has troubled later societies in the last 2,000 years. Indeed, such words as 'pornography', 'homosexual' and 'lesbian' (in its sexual sense) are nineteenth century in origin. Greek society was not obsessed with gender-based sexual desire or behaviour, but was rather more concerned with the role that the participants played in the homoerotic sex act – essentially, whether they were an active penetrator or being passively penetrated.

This active-passive model corresponded with dominant and submissive roles in wider society. What was important was not that one practiced sodomy; it was *how* one did it. To sodomise was fine up to a point; there was, however, no excuse for being sodomised. So reviled was buggery that one of the punishments for adultery with a married woman was to have a raddish shoved up your rectum: 'raddish reaming' or 'radish rape', a symbol of the erect male penis delighting in revenge (the verb is ῥαφανιδόω, *rhaphanidoo*). Another humiliating penalty was singeing off the adulterer's pubic hair to make the adulterer look effeminate. If a husband caught his wife and an adulterer in the act, he was at liberty to do whatever he liked to him. As already noted Lysias' *On the Murder of Erotosthenes* is a defence speech given by a man who killed an adulterer and was accused of various indelicacies at the same time – impiety and entrapment, public humiliation and a court appearance were the usual consequences. Allowing one's body to be gratified by others in oral or anal sex was a sign of weakness, an absence of masculinity. It was accepted, however, for a man to bed males lower down the social hierarchy, such as slaves or male prostitutes, so long as he assumed the penetrative role and was in no way passive or submissive. Penetration was manly and powerful; passivity was weak and effeminate, something that women, foreigners and slaves did that was wholly stigmatic and invited opprobrium.

'Greek love' is sometimes used to refer to anal intercourse, and even today, 'doing it the Greek way' still describes anal intercourse. To the ancient Greeks romantic and sexual relationships between males and between women was indicative of a balanced sex life, having both men and women as lovers was considered quite normal so long as one partner was an adult and the other was aged between twelve and fifteen.

Eva Cantarella describes the situation:

> Homosexuality was not an exclusive choice. Loving another man was not an option out of the norm, different, somehow deviant. It was just a part of life experience; it was the show of an either sentimental or sexual drive that, over a lifetime, alternated and was associated (sometimes at the very same time) with love for a woman.[2]

Homosexuality was a rich source of comic material. Aristophanes' acerbic wit is evident at the beginning of the *Thesmoriazusae,* where his rival, Agathon, is ridiculed for his reputation as 'an old queen' and male whoremonger. The old man in the play, Euripides, does not know Agathon even though he has had sex with him – to which Aristophanes quips (l. 35) that he would not know him because he would have only have seen him from behind. Aristophanes makes much of Cleisthenes' alleged gay tendencies and his effeminate mannerisms – what Eva Keuls magnificently calls 'his hospitable rear end'.[3]

Famous adult male couples include Pausanias (*fl.* 420 BC)and the thirty-year-old tragic poet Agathon; as well as the example of Alexander the Great and his boyhood friend Hephaestion. Agathon hosts a dinner party, as described in Plato's *Symposium,* at which the discussion of love is on the agenda. Pausanias distinguishes between a higher and lower kind of love: all the vulgar lover desires is sexual gratification, and his objects are women and boys. The noble lover aims exclusively for young men, with whom he establishes lifelong relationships based on mutual respect for each other's intelligence. Diogenes Laertius wrote that Alcibiades, the fifth-century Athenian general and politician, 'in his adolescence drew away the husbands from their wives, and as a young man the wives from their husbands'. Of the general Hephaestion (*c.* 356–324 BC), Curtius tells us that he was 'by far the dearest of all the king's friends; he had been brought up with Alexander and shared all his secrets', although this could simply mean that they were just very good friends and committed comrades in arms.

Attitudes towards same-sex love varied from region to region. For example, in parts of Ionia there was general disapproval, while in Elis and Boiotia it was accepted and even celebrated.

Pederasty

Relationships between elite older men and teenage boys was not uncommon. This is the ancient Greek tradition of pederasty – *paiderastia*. A boy was a boy until he could sport a full beard, at which time he became a man. Pederasty could prevail from about age twelve to about seventeen. The older man was the *erastes*, and his role was to educate, protect, cherish, give moral guidance and be a role model for his *eromenos*, his boy. The object was to pass down through the generations the values of the elite through a programme of education and social training. This would prepare the younger partner for a well rounded career, be it in military or civilian life; it was an important milestone on the road to manhood.

Pederasty was also a sexual relationship, with the critical proviso that penetrative sex was banned because it was considered antisocial and demeaning for the passive partner. Penetration, such as it was, was therefore intercrural, between the boy's thighs, rather than anal or oral.

The practice also served to adumbrate the distinction between physical love, *eros,* and non-sexual love, *philia.* The man could demonstrate *eros,* but not the boy. If he welcomed penetration he was acting as a pathic, a *kinaedos,* or a catamite, a weak and womanlike man; in sexual relations it was women who were routinely penetrated and they were, of course, socially, sexually and politically inferior. Sensibly, at the start of the relationship there was a cooling-off period when the young object of desire rebuffed all advances until he could be sure of the good intentions of the *erastes* and that he was not being courted out of lust, or, as we say today, being groomed. Plutarch's quotation from Philip II may confirm the prevalence of and dignity implicit in pederasty:

It is not only the most warlike peoples, the Boeotians, Spartans, and Cretans, who are the most susceptible to this kind of love but also the greatest heroes of old: Meleager, Achilles, Aristomenes, Cimon, and Epaminondas.

Theocritus, Achilles Tatius, and Solon all celebrate pederasty and homosexuality generally. Solon writes in his *Boys and Sport*:

> Lucky is the man who loves and after early play whereby his limbs are made supple and strong retiring to his house with wine and song, plays with a fair boy on his breast all day long!

In Aristophanes's *Birds* we have a typical pederastic scenario when one elderly man says to another in disgust:

> Well, this is a sorry state of affairs ... You meet my son just as he comes out of the gymnasium ... and you don't kiss him, you ignore him, you don't hug him, you don't feel his balls! And you're supposed to be a friend of ours!

Education and good manners were inextricably associated with pederastic male love. A youth who is fired by his love for an older male will naturally attempt to emulate him; the older male, inspired by his desire for the beauty of the youth, will do everything he can to improve that beauty. This from Aristophanes' *Clouds* exemplifies the kind of advice that was on offer:

> How to be modest, sitting so as not to expose his crotch, smoothing out the sand when he arose so that the impress of his buttocks would not be visible, and how to be strong.

Two of Plato's works, *Phaedrus* and *Symposium*, project contemporary attitudes toward pederasty. At the beginning of *Phaedrus*, Phaedrus and Socrates are discussing a speech that Lysias, an orator, has written. The speech was 'designed to win over a handsome boy'. Socrates asserts that man 'cannot have a less desirable protector or companion than the man who is in love with him'. The *Symposium* goes into even greater detail where several guests all expatiate on why a love of boys is a good thing.

Scholars are divided over whether pederasty in classical Greece arose when it partly replaced heterosexuality, due to a lack of available women other than *hetaerai* and perhaps the flute-girls performing in the symposia. But the obligatory late age of marriage for men alone must have fuelled the pursuit of boys by twenty-something bachelors, particularly amongst the wealthier, more educated classes.

The Sacred Band of Thebes

The Sacred Band of Thebes, Ιερὸς Λόχος, *Hieròs Lókhos,* what we might call 'special Special Forces', was a military unit recruited exclusively from men and their male lovers. It is an example of how the ancient Greeks enlisted love and camaraderie between troops to boost morale. The detachment comprised 150 pairs of homosexual soldiers; the organisational model was along the lines of the practice of *pederestaia,* consisting of an older *erastes* and a younger *eromenos.* They are first mentioned in 324 BC in the oration *Against Demosthenes* by the Athenian logographer Dinarchus.

The Sacred Band ranked second only to the Spartans in terms of combat ferocity and endurance. The strategy was to pair them in battle with their lovers because they would fight like tigers for them with total disregard for their own safety. Achilles and Patroclus – whether they had a homosexual relationship or not – must have been exemplary role models for the Sacred Band. Their regular training included wrestling and dance; they retired at thirty years of age having been recruited when around twenty years old. As shock troops, their battlefield tactic was to disable the enemy by targeting and killing their best men and leaders. Apparently, they were only once defeated in battle: their incredible run of success began in the Battle of Leuctra in 371 BC against the Spartans and only ended when the force was annihilated by Philip II of Macedon in the Battle of Chaeronea in 338 BC. Philip was moved by their valour. According to Plutarch:

> When after the battle, Philip was surveying the dead, and stopped at the place where the 300 were lying and learned that here was a band of lovers and loved, he burst into tears and said, 'Die miserably anyone who thinks that these men died or suffered anything to be ashamed of.'

Plato, indeed, had said, 'if there were only some way of contriving that a state or an army should be made of lovers they would overcome the world.'

Athenaeus reveals how Alexander the Great had homosexual leanings. He was so much besotted with Bagoas the eunuch that he once kissed him in front of the whole theatre; when the whole theatre shouted in approval of the action, he kissed him again. We also hear that:

> Charon of Chalcis had a boy of great beauty, a great favourite of his: but when Alexander, on one occasion, at a great entertainment

given by Craterus, praised this boy, Charon made the boy go and salute Alexander: but Alexander said, 'No, for he will not please me as much as he will vex you.' For though the king was of a very amorous disposition, still he was at all times sufficiently master of himself to have due regard to decorum, and keeping up appearances.[4]

Athenaeus adds that 'Sophocles, too, had a great fancy for having boy-favourites, equal to the addiction of Euripides for women'. Hieronymus of Rhodes, in his *Historical Commentaries*, adds that Sophocles once led a handsome boy outside the walls in order to have sex with him. The boy laid his own cloak on the grass, and they used Sophocles' cloak to cover them. When they had finished, the boy went off with Sophocles' cloak, and Sophocles was left with the boy's cloak. Naturally, this affair became the subject of gossip, and when Euripides was told about it he mocked Sophocles, saying that he too had had this boy but he did not have to pay any extra, whereas Sophocles had been treated with contempt because of his licentiousness. When Sophocles heard this, he composed the following retaliatory epigram alluding to Euripides' adultery:

It was the sun, not the boy, who stripped me of my cloak, Euripides; but the north wind went with you, when you made love to another man's wife. You are not wise, when sowing another's field, to bring Eros to court for being a snatch-thief.[5]

A reputation, real or fabricated, for promiscuity was frequently used to dishonour and denigrate women who were, for one reason or another, deemed to be 'difficult'. Men too were tarred with this brush in attempts to destroy them politically. The distasteful spat between Aeschines and Timarchus is a good example of such calumny as described in Aeschines' *Against Timarchus*.

In 347 BC, Aeschines addressed the assembly of Ten Thousand in Megalopolis, Arcadia, urging them to unite and defend their independence against Philip of Macedon. He was, however, criticised by Timarchus for dilitoriness with his embassy to Philip, culminating in a charge of high treason. Aeschines responded aggressively by claiming that Timarchus had forfeited his right to public debate because of his debauched conduct as a young boy, when he was no better than a whore prostituting himself to many a man in the Piraeus. Timarchus was sentenced to *atimia*, disenfranchisement, and was thus politically destroyed. Pseudo-Plutarch in his *Lives of the Ten Orators* says that Timarchos hanged himself. Aeschines was cleared of the charge of treason.

Effeminacy and cross-dressing

Effeminacy in men was beyond the pale – *para phusin* or 'outside nature'. It implied passivity and receptiveness, *epithumein paschein*, both weaknesses contrary to the proper sexual conduct of the Greek male, who ought to be virile, dominant, penetrating and thrusting. The physiological explanation offered by Aristotle explains that a natural effeminacy in men arises from a congenital malformation or impotence, accounted for by a blockage in the tubes which take semen to the penis and testicles. This then backs up towards the anus (*hedra*), creating a store of fluid which is sensitive to stimulation.[6] In social circles, the effeminate male, the Roman *cinaedus*, was mocked and reviled.

Cross-dressing had some surprising advocates. In delineating the Greek origins of the Roman festival of the Lupercalia, the heroic, alpha male Hercules, according to Ovid, indulged in a bout of cross-dressing with Omphale. Hercules puts on Omphale's clothes, and Omphale dresses up in typically Herculean lion skin and wields his club, symbolic of manhood and power.[7] Explaining why the Luperci run naked, Ovid reveals that it is because of the unsuccessful rape attempt on Omphale by Pan, the randy half-goat and symbol of fertility. Omphale's clothes were the problem – Pan was unable to get through them and penetrate her; to prevent such a calamity ever recurring, Pan insisted that the Luperci always be naked. The luperci were the 'brothers of the wolf' (*lupus*), a corporation of priests of Faunus dressed in goatskin at the Lupercalia.

Surprisingly perhaps, 'lion-hearted' (θῡμο-λέοντα, *thūmo-léonta*) Achilles too was not averse to a spot of dressing up if it saved him from the call-up for the Trojan war. To help her son dodge the draft, Thetis concealed him at the court of Lycomedes, king of Skyros. Disguised as a girl he lived amongst Lycomedes' daughters, under the pseudonym Pyrrha, the red-haired girl. Ungratefully, he raped one of the daughters, Deidamia, and fathered a son, Neoptolemus (also called Pyrrhus, after his father's alias).[8] Odysseus is told by the prophet Calchas that the Greeks would not capture Troy without Achilles' support, so he went to Skyros masquerading as a peddler selling women's clothes and jewellery with a shield and spear secreted in his wares; Achilles instantly takes up the spear, Odysseus sees through his disguise and persuades him to join the Greek forces.[9]

That other famous alpha male, Julius Caesar, was also involved in cross-dressing. Apparently, aged twenty, he lived the life of a girl in the court of King Nicomedes IV, and was later referred to behind his back as the 'Queen of Bithynia' – 'every woman's man and every man's woman'. Suetonius describes his long-fringed sleeves and loose belt as a bit odd, prompting Sulla to warn everyone to 'beware of the boy with the loose belt'.[10]

There is, of course, cross-dressing and there is cross-dressing. Some women were compelled to dress as a man if they wanted to excel in a man's world which precluded the advancement or involvement of women in certain activities and professions. We shall learn Agnodice's story later – a young midwife in 500 BC who dressed as a man so as to be able to practice and who was instrumental in changing the law relating to female midwifery. Two of Plato's students, Axiothea of Phlius and Lasthenea of Mantinea, wore men's clothes in order to access his lectures; Thecla, an intrepid disciple of Paul of Tarsus, dressed as a man to ensure her safety in her wanderings. In 380 BC Callipateira, or Pherenike, the daughter of Diagoras of Rhodes, the famous Olympic prize-winning boxer, became the only laywoman to gain access to the Olympic Games. Callipateira's son, Peisírrhodos, her three brothers and her nephew, Euklēs, as well as her father had all been Olympic victors. Their next performances were too good to miss, so Callipateira conspired to sneak in, disguised as a man. Pausanias, in his guide to Olympia, tells how:

> They say that no woman has been caught, except Callipateira ... She, being a widow, dressed up just like a gymnastic trainer, and brought her son Peisirodus to compete at Olympia. Peisirodus ... was victorious, and Callipateira, as she was jumping over the trainers' enclosure, 'bared her person' and her sex was discovered.[11]

She was hauled before the *Hellanodíkai* (the judges of the games) on a capital charge of sacrilege. In her defence Callipateira shrewdly argued that, if there ever was a woman who could be allowed to defy the ban, then it was she – with a father, three brothers, a son and a nephew who had achieved victory eight times at previous Games. The judges could only concur and she was acquitted. They had, nevertheless, learnt their lesson; a law was passed stipulating that, in future, trainers should strip before entering the arena.

Female homoeroticism

The evidence regarding female homoeroticism is decidedly thin. However, Sappho's erotic poems eloquently demonstrate that female homoerotic relations were an integral part of a girls education in *thiasoi*, girls' schools, in Mytilene, possibly as a precursor to marriage. Sappho (*c.* 630–570 BC) ran such a *thiasos,* a community in which Greek girls could receive a basic education and, at the same time, were exposed to homosexual love, sometimes for and from their teachers. Sappho herself writes of her love for various students – and sometimes their love for each other. As the *polis* evolved, however, marriage as we know it became established as a social institution, bringing an end to the *thiasoi* and with it much of early Athenian female independence and homosexuality, neither of which had any place within the constraints of this emergent social organisation.

Despite, critical acclaim from no less an authority than Plato, it was not too long before Sappho was subjected to male abuse and ridicule. Comedies and satirical biographies predictably portrayed her as a stereotypically short, fat and ugly woman who turned to women because she could not attract a man. Others slandered her as a prostitute because homoerotic acts were seen as indistinguishable from whorish acts. Aristotle is truly surprised that the 'people of Mytilene honour Sappho'. Why surprised? Because 'she is a woman'.[12] When Plato's Aristophanes describes women who desire other women words fail him because there is (quite literally) no such word; he uses the term *hetairistria* with its obvious connotations.

Nevertheless, Sappho had her followers, not least the poetess Nossis (*fl.* 300 BC), an epigrammist who claimed to rival Sappho and sings of a love for other women in seven of her surviving poems.

Interestingly, that master of the bawdy joke, Aristophanes, never alludes to female homoeroticism, suggesting perhaps that the subject was too sensitive or potentially offensive to put before the paying Athenian public. On the other hand, he uses the verb *lesbiazein* to refer to fellatio because the inhabitants of the island of Lesbos had a predilection for orofacial sex.[13] By the second century AD Lesbos had developed a connotation with female homoeroticism, probably due to the Sapphic factor. Before the end of the nineteenth century, the word 'lesbian' could refer to anything related to the island of Lesbos, including a type of wine; 'lesbianism' to denote erotic relationships between women is recorded from 1870. In 1890, the adjective 'lesbian' had an entry in a medical dictionary to describe tribadism as 'lesbian love'; by 1925, the word became a noun in English for the female equivalent of a sodomite. From a medical point of view, the feeling was that love between women was 'not quite right', if the Greek physician Asclepiades *(c.* 124–40 BC) is representative of medical opinion.

Over the centuries the issues surrounding Sappho have spawned endless (largely speculative) debate and passionate arguments as to Sappho's character, public life and sexual orientation. Even though there is no direct reference to either homosexual or heterosexual sex in her work, hypocritical religious leaders down the ages ordered her books to be burned, including Pope Gregory VIII, who called her a lewd nymphomaniac in 1073. He was probably influenced by the early Christian writer Tatian (120–*c.* 180 AD) who described Sappho as a 'sex mad little whore'. Tatian, in turn, was influenced by the homophobic apostle Paul:

> This Sappho is a sex mad little whore, and sings of her own promiscuity; but all our [Christian] women are chaste, and the young girls at their distaffs sing of divine things more nobly than that woman of yours. So be ashamed.[14]

It is worth pointing out that this Tatian is the same Christian man who described the 'invention' of marriage as being the work of the devil.

Sappho's compatriot, the choral lyric poet from the seventh century, Alcman, shines light on the aristocratic girls who received training in dance and singing for their future roles in religious festivals. One of his poems describes the attraction his female singers felt towards the chorus leaders Hagesichora, Agido and Astymeloisa. This maiden song, *partheneion,* opens with a choral song in which Agido and then Hagesichora's beauty are praised. They sing that 'the hair of my cousin Hagesichora blossoms like unalloyed gold, and as for her face, it shines like silver'. Even her ankles are beautiful. Their desire for the girls in the other semichoir is surpassed by their love for Hagesichora; moreover, Aenesimbrota was probably a purveyor of love potions, for the girls can go back to her place and procure their heart's desire:

> Nor will you go to Aenesimbrota's and say, 'may Astaphis be mine, and may Philylla look upon me with desire, or Damareta, or sexy Ianthemis – no, it is Hagesichora who keeps watch over me.'[15]

'Long-legged' Astymeloisa inspires longing that is limb loosening; her glance is 'more melting than sleep or death ... she flies through the sky like a shining star, a golden sapling or a downy feather ... if she came closer and took my tender hand I'd soon be begging at her feet'.[16]

Anacreon hints at a female same-sex relationship enjoyed by a girl who scorns him and 'gazes eagerly at another's pubic hair – a girl's'.[17]

Much later, Plutarch tells us that Spartan noblewomen took young girls as lovers. He says that same-sex erotic relationships between older and younger women were prevalent amongst Spartans: 'This love was so acceptable to them, that even the beautiful and good women took girls as lovers.'[18] Plutarch in one line explodes the male stereotype that 'lesbians' were all ugly and of ill repute. Aristotle believed the relative high-standing of women in Spartan society was a major flaw in their political system. In the *Politics*, he states that Spartan women, despite the fact that they wrestle and do other sports in the gymnasium, were still not trained sufficiently to cope with their freedom, and so turned promiscuous and dissolute, 'lesbian', as a result.

7

In Bed with a Whore: Pornai, Hetaerae and Other Prostitutes

Prostitution of various kinds was no less important than the institutions of marriage and slavery, and was big business in Athens and in other towns, cities and ports. When the average age of marriage for men was thirty, if a young Greek wanted sex, he had little option but to turn to young men, slaves or prostitutes. This was considered acceptable practice. This late age of marriage in men, a relative shortage of available women, and service overseas in the various wars fought by the *poleis* and Leagues combined to ensure a thriving trade in prostitution. Customers were cautioned not to fritter away their inheritances in the brothels around the Greek world.

If a fragment from *The Brothers* by the comic playwright Philemon is to believed, Solon established state-run brothels in the city in order to democratise the pleasures of sex and satisfy 'certain needs of an urgent kind'.

Philemon describes how Solon regulated an institutionalised sex trade in Athens:

[Solon], seeing Athens full of young men, with both an instinctive compulsion, and a tendency to stray in an inappropriate direction, bought women and established them in various places, equipped and common to all. The women stand naked so that you get what you see. Have a good look ... The door is open. One obol. Pop in. There is no shyness, no idle chat, nor does she recoil. Get stuck in, as you wish, in whatever way you wish. You come out. Tell her to go to hell. You've never seen her before.[1]

In 1997 archaeologists unearthed an ancient brothel in Thessaloniki in northern Greece full of phallic items and other erotic paraphernalia dating back to the second century BC. Writing in *Archaeology* magazine at the time of the brothel's discovery, Yannis N. Stavrakakis said:

> Polyxeni Veleni of the Museum of Thessaloniki has identified a circular bathhouse measuring nearly 25 feet in diameter, at the center of which was a sauna. The chamber held as many as 25 separate baths. Adjacent to this room were two pools for hot and cold water and a rectangular hall. Several artifacts found in the hall – a red vessel with a phallic spout, a clay dildo with pulsating shaft, and an embossed glass vessel depicting Aphrodite – indicate it was probably a brothel. A door connected the bath and brothel so patrons could enjoy both. Dining was offered in a taverna on a level below. Veleni believes the complex was part of a larger building, probably a gymnasium.

What then was on offer? A ready supply of prostitutes would have been available, fed by the abject poverty in which many Greeks lived, particularly those migrating into the metropolitan and colonial centres. These would have been bolstered by girls and women captured in war, where the victors often excercised their right to sell the vanquished into slavery or to the sex trade.

Alexis of Thurii tells us how apprentice prostitutes were provided with platform shoes and false buttocks to entice customers – one of the earliest references to grooming, the odious practice we assume to be a development of the twenty-first century:

> They get hold of inexperienced young girls and utterly transform them, not just their faces and figures, but their minds too. If one of them is too short they sew thick cork soles into her sandals. Too small in the hips they pad her out until everybody exclaims, 'what a charming arse'; too fat in the tummy then they rig her up with corsets; and if she happens to have ginger eyebrows then they blacken them with soot. But any special beauty she has she must expose to the public.[2]

Pornai

The *pornai* (πόρναι) were at the foot of the social ladder, owned by pimps or a *pornoboskós* (πορνοβοσκός) working in brothels in 'red-light' districts such as Piraeus or Kerameikos, north west of the Acropolis:

> Building Z in the Kerameikos was built and rebuilt several times and in its third phase (late Fourth Century BCE) probably served as a tavern and brothel, as attested by the hundreds of drinking and eating vessels and the many loom-weights discovered inside. Spun wool was one of the items very high up on every urban dweller's shopping list. Given the technology of the day the spinning of wool was as mindless an enterprise as it was essential, and therefore it was ideal for slave labour, and because it could be easily put down and picked up again it was a perfect task for those with frequent periods of freedom from some other job. Brothel workers regularly spun between clients.[3]

Streetwalkers were a few rungs higher. Sandals with inscribed soles have been excavated which left an imprint ΑΚΟΛΟΥΘΕΙ AKOLOUTHEI, 'Follow me!', on the ground. Eubulus, a comic writer, describes them:

> [They are] plastered over with layers of white lead ... their jowls smeared with mulberry juice. And if you go out on a summer's day, two rills of inky water flow from your eyes, and the sweat rolling from your cheeks to your throat makes a vermilion furrow, while the hairs blown about on your face look grey, they are so full of white lead.

Young virgin prostitutes could charge more, as could the pretty prostitute; but not her older, jaded colleagues. Exclusivity, difficult to gauge and ensure, cost more, as did Greek group sex. Musicians and dancing girls working the *symposia* and banquets were next up the ladder.

What do we know about the sex life of a Greek prostitute? The Greek language, like Latin, is fertile in words for a prostitute. As we have seen, one is *khamaitypḗs* (χαμαιτυπής), which literally means 'one who hits the ground', suggesting their sex took place precisely there. Much of the vilification they attracted derives from their venality, a popular theme in Greek comedy, and the fact that prostitutes were, as well as stallholders and shopkeepers, the only women in Greek society who handled money. But a grasping approach to life is only to be expected: a prostitute's career was necessarily short-lived; youth and physical attraction were everything, so income diminished over time. To compensate and to provide for old age prostitutes had to acquire as much money as possible from a very limited window of opportunity.

Avoiding pregnancy was obviously paramount in the profession. Hippocrates leaves us one of the few descriptions of contraception, in his *On the Seed*. Here he details the case of a dancer 'who had the habit of going with the men'; to avoid pregnancy he recommends that she 'jump up and down, touching her buttocks with her heels at each leap' to evacuate the semen. *Pornai* may have had recourse to abortion or infanticide.

Greek pottery also tells us something of the daily struggle endured by prostitutes, replete as the ceramics are with banquet scenes, sexual activities, toilet scenarios and images showing abuse. In the toilet scenes the prostitute usually has sagging breasts and flabby rolls of flesh; one *kylix* shows a prostitute urinating into a pot. To denote commercial sex, the presence of a prostitute is often indicated by a purse; as we have already discussed, the sexual position most frequently depicted is the leapfrog – an act of sodomy where the woman is 'folded in two' with her hands flat on the ground. A number of vases show abuse, where the prostitute is threatened with a stick or sandal and forced to perform acts considered degrading by the Greeks: fellatio, sodomy, or sex with two or more partners. There were also many male prostitutes, some of whom had a female clientele. Most, however, serviced male customers.

Hetaerae

At the top end of the prostitute's hierarchy were the *hetaerae*, who were often intelligent, sophisticated and attractive high-class whores. The word translates as '*female companion*' and corresponds with what we term a mistress, hostess, escort or call girl.

High-class prostitutes were often educated and witty – clever repartee went with the job. The best description of this is by Athenaeus:

> And there were other courtesans who had a great opinion of themselves, paying attention to education, and spending a part of their time on literature; so that they were very ready with their rejoinders and replies.

Nicarete (*fl.* 300 BC) was a philosopher of the Megarian school said by Athenaeus to have been a *hetaera* of good family and education:

> She was very well calculated to excite affection by reason of her accomplishments, and she was a pupil of Stilpon the philosopher.[4]

Many *hetaerae* were exceedingly well connected: we can name Theodota, companion of Alcibiades; Naeara, the subject of a discourse of pseudo-Demosthene; Phryne, the model for Praxiteles' Aphrodite of Knidos, who was his mistress but also friend to the orator Hypereides, who defended her against a charge of impiety; and Leontium, companion of Epicurus and herself a philosopher. Pythionice was the mistress of Harpalus, Alexander the Great's treasurer; and Thaïs was Alexander's mistress and then Ptolemy I's after him.

Some were celebrated in verse: Lyde of Antimachus, and her namesake Lyde, who was also a courtesan and the mistress of Lamynthius the Milesian. He and a poet called Myrtilus wrote poems, the one in elegiac, and the other in lyric verse; they both titled their poems *Lyde*:

> Antimachus, too, smitten with love for the Lydian girl Lyde, trod the ground where the Pactolus river flows; and when she died, in his helplessness he placed her in the hard earth, weeping the while, and in his woe he left her there and returned to lofty Colophon; then he filled his holy scrolls with grieving, and rested after all his pain.

Then there was the female flute-player Nanno, the mistress of Mimnermus, and Leontiŏn, the mistress of Hermesianax of Colophon. He dedicated three books of elegiac poetry to her, in the third of which he gives a catalogue of love affairs.

If any one woman bucked the conventional role played by women in Athenian society, one who flouted and embarrassed the social norms, it was Aspasia of Miletus. She was mistress, alleged *hetaera* and partner of Pericles and mother of their son, Pericles the Younger. She ran a salon which became *the* place to go for Athenian intellectuals and was frequented by Socrates, amongst other celebrities of the day. Some scholars believe that she taught rhetoric and public speaking with Pericles and Socrates amongst her students. Contemporaries Plato, Aristophanes and Xenophon all mention her. Such is the importance of Aspasia to our understanding of women in ancient Greece that one author was forced to write, 'To ask questions about Aspasia's life is to ask questions about half of humanity' – such is the dearth of our knowledge about ancient Greek women in general.[5] As was typical in the Greek and Roman worlds, obtrusive and intelligent women like Aspasia attracted more than her fair share of sexual abuse and vilification, and she gained a reputation as a brothel-keeper and a prostitute. Indeed, she may well have been an *hetaera* in between looking after the two Pericles in her life.

What is more, at the beginning of the Peloponnesian War, Aspasia was not immune from the criticisms fired at Pericles and at those close to him. Aspasia 'was accused of corrupting the women of Athens in order to satisfy Pericles' perversions and was tried for impiety'. This upset Pericles terribly, even though she was acquitted; Athenaeus says that Pericles pleaded her case weeping 'more tears than when his life and property were endangered'. The playwright Duris made her responsible for the Athenian attack on Samos in 440, and in 425 Aristophanes parodied the prologue of Herodotus's *Histories*, suggesting that the Archidamian War was caused by Pericles declaring war on the Megarians, who had abducted two girls from Aspasia's brothel in 430:

> But now some young drunkards go to Megara and carry off the courtesan Simaetha; the Megarians, hurt to the quick, run off in turn with two harlots from the house of Aspasia; and so, for three whores, Greece is set ablaze. Then Pericles, incandescent on his Olympian height, let loose the lightning, caused the thunder to roll, upset Greece and passed an edict, which ran like the song, that the Megarians be banished both from our land and from our markets and from the sea and from the continent.[6]

It was not all bad press for Aspasia, however, as attested by this eulogy from the satirist Lucian writing in the second century AD:

> We could choose no better model of wisdom than Milesian Aspasia, the admired of the admirable 'Olympian'; her political knowledge and insight, her shrewdness and penetration, shall all be transferred to our canvas in their perfect measure.[7]

Phryne (*c.* 371 BC) was a model both for the sculptor Praxiteles and for the painter Apelles on account of her divine figure. Her real name was Mnēsarétē, which means, somewhat ironically, 'commemorating virtue', but because of her jaundiced complexion she was also called, less flatteringly, Phrýnē, 'toad' – a nickname often adopted by prostitutes.[8] Athenaeus celebrates her beauty, telling us:

> But Phryne was a really beautiful woman, even those parts of her which were not generally seen – because it was not easy to see her

naked as she used to wear a tunic which covered her whole body, and she never used the public baths. But on the solemn assembly of the Eleusinian festival, and on the feast of the Poseidonia, she took off her clothes in full view of all the assembled Greeks, and having undone her hair, she went to bathe in the sea. It was from her that Apelles obtained his picture of Aphrodite Anadyomene; and Praxiteles the sculptor, who was her lover, modelled the Aphrodite of Cnidus from her body. On the pedestal of his statue of Eros, which is placed below the stage in the theatre, he wrote the following inscription: 'Praxiteles has devoted extreme care to representing all the love he felt, drawing his model from his inmost heart: I gave myself to Phryne for her wages, and now I no more charms employ, nor arrows, Save those of earnest glances at my love.'[9]

The statue of Eros was consecrated in the temple of Thespiae, as well as a statue of Phryne herself which was made of solid gold and consecrated in the temple of Delphi. It stood proudly between the statues of Archidamus III and Philip II. When Crates the Cynic of Thebes saw the statue he called it 'a votive offering of the profligacy of Greece'. Pausanias reports that two statues of Apollo stood next to her statue and that it was made of gilded bronze.[10]

Athenaeus says that Phryne was so rich that she offered to pay for the rebuilding of the walls of Thebes, which had been destroyed by Alexander the Great in 336 BC, the only condition being that the following inscription must be inscribed: 'Destroyed by Alexander, restored by Phryne the courtesan.' Diogenes Laërtius gossips about a failed attempt Phryne made on the virtue of the philosopher Xenocrates.

The salient event in Phryne's life was her trial. Athenaeus tells us that she was prosecuted for an undisclosed capital charge and defended by the orator Hypereides, who happened to be one of her lovers.[11] The high point of the trial was when Hypereides removed Phryne's robe and exposed her breasts before the judges to arouse their sympathy when it seemed as if the verdict was not going their way. Whatever this action actually did arouse goes unreported but her beauty filled the judges with such a superstitious fear that they could not bring themselves to 'condemn a prophetess and priestess of Aphrodite' to death. Phryne was acquitted.

Athenaeus offers a less erotically charged account of the trial as given in the *Ephesia* of Posidippus of Cassandreia. He says that Phryne just clasped the hand of each juror, tearfully pleading for

116

her life, but keeping all her clothes on. It is likely that the baring of breasts was a later invention from some time after 290 BC although it should be noted that women were eminently capable of evoking the sympathy of the judges, mothers and children could be brought in to courts for that purpose. The baring of breasts was neither obligatory nor restricted to prostitutes to arouse compassion.

Athenaeus reports that Apollodorus, in his book on courtesans, says that there were two other women named Phryne, one of whom had the nickname Clausigelos, *Weep-laughter*, and the other Saperdiŏn, *Goldfish*. Herodicus, in his *Essay on People Mentioned by the Comic Poets*, Book 6, says that one of them was called Sestos, because she 'sifted' (ἀποσήθειν) and stripped all her lovers bare.

Lamia, a very meretricious Greek courtesan, famously charged a lusting king Demetetrius of Macedonia 250 talents (about £4,300) for her services; to pay this off the the king instated a tax on soap. Demosthenes desired the Sicilian-born Greek courtesan so badly that he offered '1,000 drachmas for a single night'. She took one look at him and upped the figure to 10,000 drachmas (£30,000), a figure he was still happy to pay.

Another famous *hetaera* was Thargelia. Plutarch tells us that she was born in Ionia and 'made her onslaughts on the most influential of men'. Like Aspasia, Thargelia was well known for her beauty, grace and wit. As already noted, according to the Greek sophist Hippias in his book *A Collection*, Thargelia married fourteen times.[12] Thargelia was also said to be involved in intelligence work: amongst her handlers was Cyrus the Great, for whom she did some spying. Plutarch noted that

> Thargelia, a great beauty, extremely charming and at the same time sagacious, had numerous suitors among the Greeks. She brought all who had to do with her over to the Persian interest, and by their means, being men of the greatest power and station, she sowed the seeds of the Median faction up and down in several cities.

Citizens of some Greek city-states saw Thargelia's name as being synonymous with 'traitor'.

Some *hetaerae* became very wealthy – be they alive or dead. One, Gnathaenion, reputedly travelled like royalty when she went to a religious festival in the Piraeus to meet a client, a foreign merchant. She rode in a litter with three donkeys, three maidservants and one young nurse in her entourage. In the Hellenistic era Harpalus, a Macedonian, became quite besotted with an Athenian courtesan named Pythionice and squandered a lot of money on her. When she died he built a very expensive monument in her honour, and then hired a large choir of famous artists to accompany her body in a funeral procession through the streets. To provide for their retirement, many prostitutes bought slave girls or took in abandoned female infants to raise and train as prostitutes to carry on the family business. Occasionally, a slave prostitute would be bought by a client and set up as his concubine.

Athenaeus also reveals that Epicurus had Leontiŏn; nothing changed when she joined The Garden and took up philosophy:

> But she did not stop being a prostitute when she began to learn philosophy, but still whored herself to the whole sect of Epicureans in the gardens, and to Epicurus himself, in the most open manner.[13]

Lais and Theodote were extraordinarily beautiful:

> Apelles the painter, having seen Lais while she was still a virgin, drawing water at the fountain Peirene, and marvelling at her beauty, took her with him on one occasion to a banquet with his friends. And when his companions laughed at him because he had brought a virgin with him to the party, instead of a *hetaira*, he said, 'Do not wonder, for I will show you that she is quite beautiful enough for future enjoyment within three years.' And a prediction of this sort was made by Socrates also, about Theodote the Athenian, as Xenophon tells us in his Memorabilia [3.11], for he used to say, 'That she was very beautiful, and had breasts finely shaped beyond all description. And let us,' said he, 'go and see the woman; because you cannot judge beauty by hearsay.' But Lais was so beautiful that painters used to come to her to paint her bosom and her breasts. Lais became a rival of Phryne, and had a huge number of lovers, never caring whether they were rich or poor, and never treating them with any insolence.[14]

Lais, however, died because of her beauty. Athenaeus records that Polemon says that she was murdered by some women in Thessaly because she was having an affair with a Thessalian called Pausanias

> and that she was beaten to death, out of envy and jealousy, by wooden footstools in the temple of Aphrodite; and that is why that temple is called the temple of the impious Aphrodite.

For prostitutes Thessaly was not a good place to be. Pharsalia, a dancing-woman from Thessaly, came to a bad end when Philomelus gave her a golden crown of laurel leaves. She was afterwards torn to pieces at Metapontum by the soothsayers in the marketplace when claims were made that a voice could be heard coming out of the laurel.

Prostitutes and concubines were an important element of army baggage trains. Athenaeus describes one of Darius' trains. Parmenion found:

> Three hundred and twenty-nine concubines of the king, all skilled in music; and forty-six men who were skilful in making garlands, and two hundred and seventy-seven confectioners, and twenty-nine boilers of pots, and thirteen cooks skilful in preparing milk, and seventeen artists who mixed drinks, and seventy slaves who strain wine, and forty preparers of perfumes.

The partying was obviously not going to stop for this army on the move.

Neaera is probably ancient Greece's most famous prostitute; her story comes down to us in a collection of speeches recorded in Athens by Demosthenes. The prosecutor, Apollodorus, sued his political rival, Stephanus, for pretending that his daughter was a citizen, even though her mother was clearly an immigrant prostitute. In Athenian law, if Neaera's immigrant status was proved then the daughter did not qualify as a citizen of Athens.

Neaera was one of seven child-slave girls bought by the madam of a high-class brothel in Corinth. Neaera had a number of famous and wealthy clients, two of whom became resentful of making regular payments to the madam and arranged to buy her outright for 30 *minas*, roughly what a labourer could earn in eight years. When it was time for the men to marry, they offered Neaera the chance to buy her freedom for 20 *minas*. The men saw this as a discounted price but it was probably no more than they were going to get on the open market, since she was now somewhat older. A condition of the deal was Neaera's promise to leave Corinth.[15]

An Athenian called Phrynion bought Neaera. She went to Athens with him in expectation of marriage or, at least, concubinage, but was disappointed to find herself working as a low-rent prostitute. Taking two servants and other goods, she fled to Megara where she set up in business for two years and eventually met Stephanus, who offered to take her back to Athens. Here he negotiated a deal with Phrynion in which an arbitrator decided on fair compensation for Phrynion's loss.

All went well until Apollodorus launched his suit; Neaera was then in her seventies. She had never been an Athenian citizen, but the crux of the case revolved around the parentage of the children of Stephanus and Neaera. If Stephanus was proved to have fathered the children by another wife – an Athenian citizen – the citizenship of the children was assured, but if convicted, Stephanus would lose not only his political rights and citizenship but any land he owned as well, since non-citizens could not own property in Athens.

The Symposium

The symposium was an important Greek social institution (from the Greek συμπόσιον, from συμπίνειν, to drink together). It was essentially a drinking party, one that provided the setting for two important Socratic dialogues, Plato's *Symposium* and Xenophon's *Symposium*, as well as featuring in the elegies of Theognis of Megara. It was often much more than just 'a lads' night out'; rather it was, in its finest form, a forum for intellectual and philosophical discussion. Sometimes the symposium was a vehicle for men of respected families to celebrate the easing of young men into aristocratic society, and to make the most of other special occasions, such as victories in athletics or drama or poetry contests. Plato describes how the flute-girl who showed up at one of his symposia was shown the door, so as not to distract the guests from the philosophising.[16]

Symposia would typically be held in the *andrōn* (ἀνδρών), the men's quarters; the participants, symposiasts, between fourteen and twenty-seven drinkers, would recline on seven, eight or nine pillowed couches set against three walls of the room. In Macedonian symposia the emphasis was not just on drinking but hunting, too, and young men were allowed to recline and imbibe only after they had blooded their first wild boar.

Catering included food and, obviously, lots of wine. Entertainment was laid on, which might include games, songs, flute-girls (*auletride*) or boys, and slaves performing various acts, carnal and otherwise. Sex in one form or another would often be on the agenda. *Hetaerae* and entertainers were hired to perform and converse intelligently with the guests. Amongst the instruments in the women's repertoire was the *aulos*, a kind of oboe, and the stringed barbiton or lyre; some girls might pluck a harp, others were dancers or gymnasts. Athenaeus describes them well:

And there were other courtesans who had a great opinion of themselves, paying attention to education, and spending a part of their time on literature; so that they were very ready with their rejoinders and replies.[17]

Xenophon describes a good night out at a symposium:

> When the tables had been moved out of the way and the guests had poured a libation and sung a hymn, a man from Syracuse came in with the evening's entertainment. He had with him a fine flute-girl, a dancing-girl – one of those skilled in acrobatic tricks – and a very handsome boy, who was expert at playing the cither and at dancing; the Syracusan made his money by presenting their acts as a show ... it was agreed that performers both gave top rate entertainment ... the other girl began to accompany the dancer on the flute, and a boy at her elbow handed her twelve hoops one at a time. She took these and as she danced threw them whirling into the air, throwing them at the right height so as to catch them in a regular rhythm.[18]

Socrates too was obviously impressed by the night's entertainment of erotic hoop-spinning and acrobatics. He concluded with a somewhat contradictory statement that women were almost the equal of men ... only not intellectually or physically:

> This girl's feat, gentlemen, is only one of many proofs that woman's nature is in no way inferior to man's, except in its lack of judgment and physical strength. So if any one of you has a wife, let him confidently teach her with confidence whatever he would like to have her know.

Oeneus, in the play of the same name written by the tragic poet Chaeremon, gives a good example of how beauty and sexuality were fully admired and appreciated:

> And one did lie with garment well thrown back, Showing her snow-white bosom to the moon: Another, as she lightly danced, displayed the fair proportions of her left-hand side, Naked – a lovely picture for the air to wanton with; and her complexion white strove with the darkening shades. Another bared her lovely arms and shoulders all: another, with her robe high round her neck, concealed her bosom, but a slit below showed all of her shapely thighs. I was led on, not without hope, by desire for her smiling beauty.

In fourth-century Athens a top price of two drachmas was payable to these girls for an evening's entertainment. Sex was extra according to the service required. Athenaeus tells us that it was usual for these girls to be auctioned off to the highest bidder at the end of the evening.

The most famous symposium is described in Plato's dialogue of the same name and was hosted by the poet Agathon to mark his first victory at the drama contest of the 416 BC Dionysia. Amusingly, Plato tells us that the celebration was upstaged by the surprise entrance of the young buck Alcibiades, dropping in drunk and half-naked, the flotsam of an earlier symposium that day.

The most important man at any symposium was the symposiarch. It was he who would decide the strength of the wine and its dilution, a critical decision depending on whether serious discussions were on the agenda or just indulgence. Wine was only drunk after the dinner, and women were barred.

In a fragment from his *c.* 375 BC play *Semele*, Eubulus has the god of wine, Dionysos, describe for us the right and wrong way to drink:

For sensible men I prepare only three kraters: one for health (which they drink first), the second for love and pleasure, and the third for sleep. After the third krater is drained, wise men head for home. The fourth krater is not mine any more – it belongs to bad behaviour; the fifth is for shouting; the sixth is for rudeness and insults; the seventh is for fights; the eighth is for smashing up the furniture; the ninth is for depression; the tenth is for madness and unconsciousness.

It was the role of the symposiarch to stop things from getting out of hand, but Greek literature and art tell us that the third-*krater* limit was not always observed. *Plus ça change.*

8

Spartan Sex and Power Sex in Macedon

Sexual mores and, in particular, the relative social freedom women enjoyed in Sparta and Macedon, are quite remarkable. In both places sex and women were, as in Minoan Crete, much less constricted and oppressed than in other parts of Greece.

Sparta

Controversy continues to rage over whether the Spartans practiced pederasty like many of the other *poleis*. Xenophon says quite categorically that: '[Lycurgus] ... laid down that in Sparta lovers should refrain from molesting boys, just as much as parents avoid having intercourse with their children or brothers with their sisters', thus putting it on a par with the act of incest. Xenophon, though, adroitly notes the reason why this statement is seldom believed when he adds: 'It does not surprise me, however, that some people do not believe this, since in many cities the laws do not ban lusting after boys.' All of our written sources on Sparta come from these other cities, where pederasty was de riguer amongst the elite – and it was the hostile elite that wrote the histories of Sparta.

Aristotle blamed all of Sparta's problems on the fact that the women were very much in control of things there, because homosexuality was largely absent in Spartan society. Tabloid historian Herodotus loved a good story, and it is significant that he nowhere mentions homosexuality in Sparta, something he would surely have been at pains to expose were the evidence there.

Spartan anxiety over the continuation of the royal line emerges in Herodotus book five when King Anaxandrides' wife is found to be infertile. The Ephors insist that the line of Eurysthenes be continued and suggest Anaxandrides divorce his wife and marry someone else more productive. Anaxandrides refuses, saying

> his wife was guilty of nothing and the magistrates' advice that he should send her away and marry another woman instead was most improper – he would do nothing of the sort.[1]

There is evidently in Anaxandrides a respect for the sanctity of marriage and a feeling that divorce should not be undertaken lightly, something not commonly found in Athenian marriage. Furthermore, in claiming his wife had done nothing wrong, Anaxandrides may be implying that the infertility may not be his wife's fault and that the failure to produce children does not automatically lie at the woman's door. Nevertheless the Ephors castigate him if he refuses to comply. Anaxandrides complies, but this is 'an unheard of thing' in Sparta.[2]

The dynastical requirement for an heir assumed precedence above the Spartan monogamous culture. Anaxandrides' actions, however, would suggest that women had a wider role and a deeper appreciation in society that extended beyond motherhood and their function of bearing and raising sons. We have observed how Aristotle believed that the Spartan political system was flawed and weakened because the relatively free women in Spartan society were insufficiently trained to deal with those freedoms and so turned to promiscuity as 'lesbians'. Plutarch, also noted already, tells us that Spartan noblewomen took young girls as lovers.

Plutarch uses a Spartan girl's behaviour as an exemplar of how a young wife should behave when it comes to sex with her husband. A young Spartan girl, when asked by a friend of hers whether she had initiated sex with her husband, answered that she had not, but that he had with her. Plutarch was of the opinion that this was the right way to behave:

> Never shun or scorn the caresses and dalliances of his amorous inclinations, when he himself starts things off; but never herself initiating sex. For the one smacks of impudent harlotry, the other displays a female pride and arrogance devoid of conjugal affection'.[3]

Elsewhere, Plutarch describes what can only be called a singularly nonchalant, pragmatic approach to marriage and its consummation, behaviour which chimed with and was derived from a strict military lifestyle:

> To get married the women were carried off by force (ἐγάμουν δὲ δι' ἁρπαγῆς), not when they were young and pre-pubescent, but when they were in full bloom and mature. After the woman was abducted the 'bridesmaid' took over: she cropped the bride's hair, gave her a man's cloak and sandals to wear, and laid her down on a straw mat on the floor, alone, and in the dark. Then the groom, neither drunk nor worn out by sex, but composed and sober, after dining in his mess as usual, sneaked out to the room where the bride lay, undid her virgin's belt, and took her in his arms to the marriage bed.[4]

Afterwards the man would back to the barracks to sleep with the other soldiers. This relationship continued in its clandestine way:

> [The husband] visiting his bride by stealth taking every precaution, full of dread and fear lest any of her household should notice his visits, his bride also contriving and conspiring with him that they might have stolen moments together whenever the occasion allowed.

Plutarch adds that some of these Spartans became fathers before they ever saw their wives in daylight. He sees it as a fine example of restraint and self-moderation, a good thing because it kept mutual affection and the sexual appetite fresh and keen, not 'sated and dulled by too much sex ... and there was always left behind in their hearts some residual spark of mutual longing and delight.'

The poems of Spartan Alcman (*fl.* 700 BC) celebrate and champion women. His sixty or so hymns are actually the lyrics of songs performed at public festivals by choruses of girls, known as *partheneia* ('maiden-songs', παρθένος). Some see in some of the poems evidence of female homoerotic love:

> If only Astaphis were mine, if only Philylla were to look my way and Damareta and lovely Ianthemis; no, Hagesichora wears me out with love.

> (fr. 1, vv. 64–7)

And:

> I were to see whether she might love me. If only she came nearer and took my soft hand, I would be her suppliant immediately.

> (fr. 3, vv. 79–81)

For Alcman, women are part of the beauty that forms the rich tapestry of nature. He describes a woman's hair and the golden chain she wears around her neck in the same breath, as it were, as the purple petals of a Kalchas flower and the purple depths of the sea; the 'bright shining' colour of the windflower and the multicoloured feathers of a bird as it nibbles green buds on the vine.

Sparta had no brothels and Spartans were, apparently, free from prostitution and adultery, preferring instead to honour the sanctity of marriage and fidelity. Helen of Troy, however, was, of course, a famous Spartan and did her compatriots no favours when it came to sexual mores. She was one of the world's greatest adulteresses and responsible for the outbreak of a major regional conflict.

The relative freedom and respect enjoyed by Spartan women generally, their social obtrusiveness, and their education and sexual liberation triggered salvos of misogynistic and abusive slurs aimed at the alleged national permissiveness. This is all typified by Euripides in *Andromache*:

> Spartan girls could not be chaste even if they wanted to be. They leave home, and with naked thighs and their dresses loose, they share the running tracks and gymnasiums with young men.

This extreme conservative attitude was of course coloured by the fact that Sparta and Athens were arch-enemies. Attacking an enemy's morals through their womenfolk was a popular strategy in the ancient world. As it happened, Sparta was not alone in the practice of naked exercise. Athenaeus writes that Ionian Chios shared the custom of exercising in the nude with Sparta.[5]

It comes as no surprise that the conversation in the Deipnosophists eventually turns to 'love and amatory matters', or, more specifically, to Spartan women and sex:

> At Lacedaemon all the young women used to be shut up in a dark room, while a number of unmarried young men were shut up with them; and whichever girl each of the young men caught hold of he led away as his wife, without a dowry. That's why they punished Lysander, because he left his former wife, and wished to marry another who was much more beautiful. But Clearchus of Soli, in his treatise *On Proverbs*, says, 'In Lacedaemon the women, on a certain festival, drag the unmarried men to an altar,

and then thrash them; in order that ... they may become more affectionate, and in time may start thinking about marriage.'

By Athenaeus' time that first anecdote had become ancient history and only survived as a ritual in Spartan weddings, in which the bride's hair would be cut short and, wearing a man's cloak and sandals, would be left alone in a dark room where she would be 'captured' by her new husband.

Under Lycurgus Spartan children were state-owned. It was because of this that wife-swapping and husband-swapping, as well as the common ownership of children regardless of their fatherhood, was sanctioned. This was an attempt to free men from the characteristic 'empty and womanish passion' of jealous possessiveness exhibited by women.[6] Some may call this a natural manifestation of maternalism, but to the Spartan 'to share with other worthy men in the begetting of children' was a means of 'keeping the marriage free from all wanton irregularities'. Lycurgus mocked other cultures which would rather murder or make war rather than sanction free love and free marriages.

The Spartans were famous for their belief that homoerotic relationships were valuable contributors to military camaraderie, good morale and fighting prowess. The Sacred Band of Thebes was, of course, the epitome of this, a special unit made up of homosexual partners and discussed above. Prominent amongst these was Epaminondas (d. 362 BC), Cicero's 'first man of Greece'. Plutarch tells us that Epaminondas had two male lovers: Asopichus and Caphisodorus; the latter died with him at the battle of Mantineia.[7] The two warriors were buried together, something which usually only happened with a husband and wife.

Macedon

In Macedon women close to or in the royal family enjoyed an elevated status totally unheard of in the rest of Greece, even in Sparta. Queens, princesses and mistresses enjoyed power, status and wealth in the labyrinthine machinations of the empire started by Philip II. Women were used as pawns in the various powerplays orchestrated over decades to cement alliances, act as regents, reinforce and extend dynasties and eliminate enemies. Some of these women excelled in the military, notably Cynane, the daughter of Philip II, and her daughter Eurydice II. Very often these women were casually eliminated as so much dispensable collateral.

How did this phenomenal run of powerful, influential political and militaristic women happen? Eurydice I (b. 407 BC) was a Greek queen from Macedon, wife of king Amyntas III of Macedon. She was the daughter of Sirras of Lyncestis and had four children, Alexander II, Perdiccas III, Philip II, all of whom would be kings; she was the paternal grandmother of Alexander the Great. Eurydice played a revolutionary public role in Macedonian life and was assertive and influential in a political world hitherto dominated by men. Her political activities changed the course of Macedonian history: Eurydice I was the first known royal Greek woman to be active in the political arena and to successfully exert political influence. The elite Macedonians were polygamists – a facet of their social world which served to complicate an already Byzantine period of history. Philip II himself had seven wives – Athenaeus conveniently gives us a list of the various kings' complicated conquests:

> But Ptolemaeus the son of Agesarchus, in his *History of Philopator*, giving a list of the mistresses of the different kings, says, 'Philippus the Macedonian promoted Philinna, the dancing woman, by whom he had Arrhidaeus, who was king of Macedonia after Alexander. And Demetrius Poliorcetes ... had a mistress named Mania; and Antigonus had one named Demo, by whom he had a son named Alcyoneus; and Seleucus the younger had two, whose names were Mysta and Nysa.' But Heracleides Lembus, in the thirty-sixth book of his *History*, says that Demo was the mistress of Demetrius; and that his father Antigonus was also in love with her: and that he put to death Oxythemis as having shared in many of the crimes of Demetrius; and he also put to the torture and executed the maid-servants of Demo.[8]

Pre-eminent amongst Philip II's seven or so wives was Olympias – mother of Alexander – never far away from the centre of powerful things and a key player in many of the significant events of the period. Olympias (*c*. 370–316 BC) was totally dedicated to the best interests and political future of her son. In many ways she foreshadowed the scheming, uncompromising and obsessive wives, mistresses and mothers of the early Roman emperors who were hell-bent on ensuring the elevation of their sons to the highest office. Livia, the Agrippinas and Messalina would have learnt much from Olympias, who may well have been implicated in the assassination of her husband, Philip II, and certainly had a hand in the murder of one of his wives and their daughter.

Alexander the Great

The alleged homosexual leanings of Alexander the Great – Hephaestion, Bogoas and Charon – are covered in the chapter on homoeroticism. Let us now look at the women in the life of Alexander and see how they were used, treated and how they conducted themselves. These elite Macedonian women were more cosmopolitan, better travelled, more politically astute and considerably more exotic, dangerous and volatile than their sisters elsewhere in ancient Greece.

Plutarch leaves us with a description of a rather shy, sexually naïve Alexander the Great:

> But as for the other captive women, seeing that they were surpassingly stately and beautiful, he just said in jest that Persian women hurt his eyes. And displaying in rivalry with their fair looks the beauty of his own sobriety and self-control, he passed them by as though they were lifeless images for display.[9]

Diodorus Siculus adds to Alexander's reputation for sexual self-restraint, with a hint of effeminacy:

> Then he put on the Persian diadem and dressed himself in the white robe and the Persian sash and everything else except the trousers and the long-sleeved upper garment. He distributed to his companions cloaks with purple borders and dressed the horses in Persian harness. In addition to all this, he added concubines to his retinue in the manner of Darius, in number not less than the days of the year and outstanding in beauty as selected from all the women of Asia. Each night these paraded about the couch of the king so that he might select the one with whom he would lie that night. Alexander, as a matter of fact, employed these customs rather sparingly and kept for the most part to his accustomed routine, not wishing to offend the Macedonians.[10]

Curtius may have summed it up best when he describes the concern shared by Alexander's parents over his apparent indifference to matters sexual; this had potentially serious consequences for the dynasty:

> He scorned sensual pleasures to such an extent that his mother was anxious lest he be unable to beget offspring.

1. *Right*: The snake goddess from Knossos or perhaps a court lady, dated around 1600 BC. The skirt is full length and has seven flounces. She wears a polonaise, or double apron, over the skirt. The bodice has elbow-length sleeves and leaves the breasts and neck exposed, maximising the sex appeal of the girl. Note the prominence of the breasts and the small waist. Coloured faience. (Courtesy of Herakleion Archaeological Museum)

2. *Below*: Ajax raping Cassandra. Tondo of an Attic red-figure cup, *c.* 440–430 BC. (Courtesy of Louvre Museum, Department of Greek, Etruscan and Roman Antiquities, room 43, case 16)

3. *Above*: Achilles tending Patroclus wounded by an arrow. Tondo of an Attic red-figure kylix, *c.* 500 BC, from Vulci. (Altes Museum, Berlin)

4. *Below*: Amazonomachy. Lower tier of an Attic red-figure lekythos, *c.* 420 BC. (Metropolitan Museum of Art Department of Greek and Roman Art. Accession number 31.11.13)

5. *Right*: 'Circe Offering the Cup to Odysseus' (1891) by John William Waterhouse (1849–1917); note the pig on the right. (Courtesy of Oldham Gallery)

6. *Below*: Ganymede being snatched by an eagle, which will take him to Mount Olympus to be cupbearer to the gods.

7. Cnidus Aphrodite. Marble, Roman copy after a Greek original of the fourth century. (National Museum of Rome. Accession number Inv. 8619)

8. Aphrodite as an hermaphrodite. (Courtesy of Lady Lever Gallery, Port Sunlight)

9. *Right*: Priapus, ever erect, on a House of the Vetii wall painting in Pompey. He is actually weighing his phallus; the fruit symbolises fertility.

10. *Below*: Calypso mourning over Odysseus on the Isle of Ogygia. (Courtesy of Minneapolis Institute of Art)

11. Pentheus being ripped apart, from the House of the Vetii, Pompeii. The daughters of Cadmus – Ino, Autonoe, Agave and Semele – spotted him in a tree spying on women engaged in a Bacchic rite and thought him to be a wild animal. They hauled Pentheus down and tore him apart, limb from limb. The ritual became known as *sparagmos*.

12. Leda and the swan in a wall painting from Herculaneum. An early example of divine bestiality.

13. The classic marble group depicting Pan having sex with a goat. He did not leave it there, being credited with having taught young shepherds how to masturbate. From Herculaneum.

14. Clytemnestra hesitates before killing the sleeping Agamemnon (1817). Aegisthus urges her on. Pierre-Narcisse, Baron Guérin (1774–1833). (Courtesy of the Louvre)

15. A depiction of Eros and Psyche from the 'Casa di Terenzio Neo', Pompeii. (Courtesy of Naples Museum)

16. *Right*: A beautifully simple erotic scene on a vase. (Courtesy of Pergamon Museum, Berlin)

17. *Below*: An erotic scene of a very different kind on the rim of an Attic red-figure *kylix*, *c*. 510 BC. The painting shows penetration orally and anally – both of which were deplored. It was imperative that a man always did the penetrating, be it with man or woman. (Courtesy of the Louvre)

18. A couple in bed in a 480 BC painting now in the museum at Paestum.

19. Sex depicted on a *skyphos*. What Lucretius called '*more ferarum*': 'like animals do it'. (Courtesy of the Louvre)

20. Satyr copulating with a buck; as depicted on a black figure cup, around 520 BC. (Courtesy of the British Museum)

21. Detail from a fourth-century BC red figure vase showing a symposium in full swing, with flute player and *hetaira*. (Courtesy of Naples National Museum)

22. A woman about to be raped by two men. (Courtesy of the Louvre)

23. An erotic scene from the rim of an Attic red-figure *kylix*, *c.* 510 BC by the Pedieus Painter. There is a suggestion of violence here, too. (Courtesy of the Louvre, Department of Greek, Etruscan and Roman Antiquities; room 43, case 4. Accession number G 13)

24. Banquet scene: man reclining on a bench while a naked youth plays the *aulos*. Tondo of an Attic red-figure cup, dated between 460 and 450 BC.

25. Masturbating satyr on a sixth-century BC black figure vase. (Courtesy of Staatliche Museen zu Berlin. F1671)

26. Bronze statuette of the Roman fertility god Priapus, made in two parts and shown here in assembled and disassembled forms. Dated from the late first century BC. It was found in Rivery, in Picardy, France in 1771 and remains the oldest Gallo-Roman object in the collection of the Museum of Picardy. This figurine represents the deity clothed in a *cuculus*, a Gallic coat with hood. The upper section is detachable and conceals a phallus.

27. *Right*: Man consorting with
boy – an example of *pederestaia*.
Late sixth-century black-figure vase.
(Courtesy of Boston Museum of
Fine Arts 08.292)

28. *Below*: A homoerotic scene; note
the erect penises. Black figure, dated
around 540 BC. (Courtesy of the
British Museum)

29. *Left*: A fertility festival scene showing a joyful woman sprinkling phalluses growing in the ground. Red-figure vase from 430 BC. (Courtesy of the British Museum, E8. 10)

30. *Below*: Drunk satyr cavorting and balancing a *kantharos* on his penis. Detail from an Attic red-figured *psykter*. From Cerveteri; dated between 500 and 490 BC. (Courtesy of British Museum, Accession number GR 1868.6-6.7)

To encourage a relationship with a woman, Philip and Olympias were said to have hired a top-end, high-priced Thessalian *hetaera* named Callixena for Alexander's delectation.

Whatever, diffident and shy or not, Alexander soon made up for lost time. Mistresses and *hetaerae* notwithstanding, Alexander had three wives: Roxana of Bactria, Stateira, and Parysatis, daughter of Ochus. He was the father of at least one child, Alexander IV of Macedon, by Roxana, born soon after his death in 323 BC. Stateira may also have been pregnant when he died; another child, Heracles, is said to be his born around 327 BC. The mother was the concubine Barsine, the elite and noble daughter of satrap Artabazus of Phrygia, and wife of Memnon.

Parysatis was the youngest daughter of Artaxerxes III of Persia who was murdered in 338 BC and eventually succeeded by her second cousin, Darius III, in 336 BC. Parysatis and her sisters continued to live the good life at the Persian court, accompanying the Persian army during Darius's campaign against Alexander. After the Battle of Issus in 333 BC, Parysatis and many of her family were captured in Damascus by Alexander's general Parmenion. According to Arrian, in 324 Parysatis married Alexander at Susa, just one of the renowned Susa Weddings. That same day, Alexander married Darius's eldest daughter, Stateira, thus strengthening his ties to both branches of the royal family of the Achaemenid Empire. The marriage celebrations went on for five days, during which time ninety other Persian noblewomen were married to Macedonian and other Greek military men who were loyal to Alexander.

Alexander's ill-conceived aim at the spectacular event was to unite the Persian and Macedonian cultures, with the intermarriages producing offspring of mixed descent from both empires. It was a truly clumsy attempt at racial engineering; after Alexander's death most of the Macedonians repudiated these wives.

According to Arrian of Nicomedia:

He gave Drypetis to Hephaestion, she too a daughter of Darius and a sister of his own wife; his intention was that the children of Hephaestion should be cousins to his own children. To Craterus he gave Amastris daughter of Oxyathres, brother of Darius, and to Perdiccas the daughter of Atropates, satrap of Media. To Ptolemy the bodyguard and to Eumenes the royal secretary he gave the daughters of Artabazus, Artacama to one and Artonis to the other. To Nearchus he gave the daughter of Barsine and Mentor, and to Seleucus the daughter of Spitamenes of Bactria.

Similarly he gave to the other companions the noblest daughters of the Persians and Medes, some eighty in all.

The marriages were celebrated according to Persian custom. Chairs were placed for the bridegrooms in order, and after the drinks the brides came in and sat down, each by the side of her groom. They took them by the hand and kissed them; the king began the ceremony, since all the weddings took place together. More than any action of Alexander this seemed to show a popular and comradely spirit. The bridegrooms after receiving their brides led them away, each to his own home, and to all Alexander gave a dowry. And as for all the Macedonians who had already married Asian women, Alexander ordered a list of their names to be drawn up; they numbered over 10,000, and Alexander offered them all gifts at their wedding.[11]

Drypetis was the younger daughter of Darius III. She was taken prisoner by Alexander at Issus in 333 BC, along with her sister Stateira, her mother (another Stateira), and her grandmother Sisygambis. The Persian women then became part of Alexander's baggage train for the next two years.[12] Unlike many other women in the train, they were treated by Alexander with 'as much respect as if they were his own sisters'; he also promised that the two princesses were to be given husbands of appropriate rank.[13] If Darius thought that he still had a say in his daughters' futures he was very wrong: there was never any question but that the princesses were now Alexander's property. Letters between Darius and Alexander before Gaugamela show how Darius offered Alexander one of his daughters in marriage (probably Stateira); Alexander responded curtly that what Darius offered was already his.[14]

Alexander was forced to make a highly embarrassing retraction at one point in his dealings with the Persian royal women – a victim of his own cultural norms and of his ignorance of how other cultures treated their women. In 331 BC when the army left Susa, the royal family stayed behind at the palace. Alexander sent some fabric to Sisygambis, with the suggestion that she might like to make some clothes with it and teach her granddaughters Stateira and Drypetis the art of dressmaking. Although this was standard practice for Greek women it was a deep insult to their more socially liberated Persian counterparts.

In Hephaestion Drypetis could not have wished for a more powerful or affluent husband: he was Alexander's second in command. However, the marriage was to be short-lived. In 324 BC

Hephaestion died after a brief illness; a few months later Alexander also died. Roxana, Alexander's other wife, had Drypetis and Stateira killed to clear the decks. Roxana was pregnant and would stop at nothing to ensure that, if she gave birth to a son, then he should be the unrivalled heir to Alexander's empire.

Roxana's (c. 343–c. 310 BC) reputation preceded her. She was the most beautiful woman in all of Asia and deserving of her Persian name, Rauxsnaka, meaning 'little star'. She was the daughter of Oxyartes, a Bactrian nobleman who served Bessus, the satrap of Bactria and Sogdia. The marriage ceremony with Alexander exuded romance: the wedding feast was held high up on the Sogdian rocks; the couple shared a loaf of bread (still a custom today in Turkestan) which Alexander dramatically sliced with his sword.

Alexander's army had captured the Sogdian Rock fortress in 327 BC along with a number of civilians hiding there; among them was the family of Oxyartes, including Roxana. Alexander had first seen her at a banquet, where she and other Sogdian girls were performing a native dance to entertain the king and his entourage. It was then that he became transfixed by Roxana and married her, despite counsel to the contrary.[15]

The opulent honeymoon captured the public imagination. An impression of it was painted by the sculptor and artist Aetion. The picture was very popular with the crowds at the next Olympic Games, and went on a travelling exhibition to Italy where, in the second century AD, Lucian saw it and described the erotic scene as it unfolded:

> The scene is a very lovely chamber, and in it there is a bridal couch with Roxana, a very beautiful maiden, lounging upon it, her eyes cast down in modesty, for Alexander is nearby. There are smiling Erotes: one is standing behind her removing the veil from her head and showing Roxana to her groom; another like a good servant is taking the sandal off her foot, already preparing her for bed; a third Eros holds Alexander's cloak and is pulling him with all his energy towards Roxana. The king himself is holding out a crown to her.

Roxana then disappears from the scene; apart from a reference to a miscarriage in India there is no further mention of her until Alexander's death. A version of the *Alexander Romance* also

includes descriptions of the couple, the king's 'letters' to his mother
Olympias about Roxana, and how 'Roxiane' grieved for her dying
husband:

> And Roxiane cried aloud and tore at her clothes and wished to
> fall at her husband's feet. Alexander moaned and groaned and
> placed his hand upon her, and gave her by glance into the care of
> his comrade Perdiccas.

Love at first sight it may have been between Alexander and Roxana
but there was an obvious political exigency to the match – Sogdiana
had proved somewhat intractable and the political alliance forged
by the marriage can only have helped. In 328 Alexander was able
to demonstrate his sensitive side when Spitamenes, one of the
Sogdian commanders, had been betrayed and decapitated by his
wife no less, the mother of Apama I. When the woman presented
the head to Alexander he expelled her from the camp, lest she upset
his 'mild-mannered' troops with her savage ways.

In the meantime, Alexander had affairs with other women, one
being with Cleophis, the captured queen of a small kingdom in
India, by whom Alexander fathered a son.

When Alexander died in 323 BC, Roxana was pregnant. The sex
of the baby was absolutely pivotal to the history of the region. She
gave birth to a son six months later and wasted no time in trying
to ensure his succession; she named him Alexander. After some
hostilities he was declared joint king with a mentally challenged
son of Philip II, Philip III Arrhidaios.[16] Perdiccas was made
administrator.

As noted, Plutarch tells that, with Perdiccas's support, Roxana
promptly murdered Alexander's other wives, Stateira and her sister,
Drypetis, in order to remove any obstacles to young Alexander IV.
As a daughter of Darius', if Stateira should also fall pregnant and
have a boy, then he might have a strong claim on Alexander's
throne. Roxana lured Stateira into a trap with a forged letter;
Perdiccas had Alexander's signet ring and he alone was able to
set the royal seal upon any forgery. Stateira and Drypetis were
poisoned, and their bodies dumped down a well.

When Perdiccas was assassinated in 320 BC and Antipater died,
Roxana and Alexander IV passed into the ineffective and weak
protection of Polyperchon, who was soon up against Cassander,
Antipater's son. In 317 Alexander IV was stripped of his royal
title, and Roxana fled with him to her mother-in-law, Olympias,

who was given the responsibility of raising Alexander as a true pedigree Macedonian. Roxana was still regarded by many as a barbarian. The army went over to Olympias; she captured Philip III and his wife, and had them tortured and killed. Cassander invaded Macedonia, facing an army antagonised, their morale weakened by Olympias's cruelty. She took refuge in fortified Pydna with Roxana and the young Alexander. Polyperchon was abandoned by his army, and Pydna was soon starved into surrender. Olympias gave herself up on promises of safety, but she was stoned to death on Cassander's orders, a fate which she faced with dignity and stoicism. Cassander compounded the atrocity by denying her funeral rites – a fate worse than death. Roxana and her son were imprisoned at Amphipolis and finally killed in 310 after Cassander had duplicitously promised to return the kingship to Alexander when he came of age.[17] Diodorus describes the last days of Roxana:

> Cassander now saw that Roxana's son Alexander was growing up and there were some who were spreading the word in Macedonia that Cassander ought to release the boy from custody and hand over to him his father's kingdom. Afraid for his own safety, Cassander ordered Glaucias, who was in charge of the boy's custody, to assassinate Roxana and her son, and to hide their bodies.

This effectively ended the direct involvement of Alexander the Great and the royal house of Macedon in the tortured politics of the region.

Alexander's affair with the courtesan Barsine started after her husband Memnon's death. Plutarch records:

> Alexander, so it seems, thought it more worthy of a king to subdue his own passions than to conquer his enemies, and so he never came near these women [concubines], nor did he associate with any other before his marriage, with the exception only of Barsine. This woman, the widow of Memnon, the Greek mercenary commander, was captured at Damascus. She had received a Greek education, was of a gentle disposition, and could claim royal descent, since her father was Artabazus who had married one of the Persian king's daughters. These qualities made Alexander the more willing ... to form an attachment to a woman of such beauty and noble lineage.[18]

Noticing a change in Alexander's attitude to life, Justin adds:

> As he afterwards contemplated the wealth and display of Darius, he was seized with admiration for such opulence. Hence it was that he first began to indulge in luxurious and splendid banquets, and fell in love with his captive Barsine for her beauty, by whom he had afterwards a son that he called Heracles.[19]

Heracles, if Justin is right, was brought up at Pergamum by his mother; both mother and son were murdered by Polyperchon in 309 BC on the orders of Cassander.

Campaspe, also known as Pancaste, was another of Alexander's mistresses, and, if Aelian is to be believed, the woman to whom he lost his virginity. This beautiful Campaspe was painted by Apelles, the greatest artist of the day; Pliny the Elder records how Alexander detected that Apelles had a greater appreciation of Campaspe than he, so he kept the nude portrait but gave Campaspe to Apelles.[20] The story may be apocryphal but, either way, Campaspe became a synonym for a man's mistress. Apelles also used Campaspe as his model for his famous painting of *Aphrodite Rising out of the Sea*, the *Venus Anadyomene*.

We have heard much of Olympias slipping menacingly in and out of what can only be called, even if anachronistically, these Machiavellian games of power. She was the daughter of Neoptolemus I, king of the Molossians, a tribe in Epirus, and sister of Alexander I. Plutarch in his *Moralia* asserts that she was originally called Polyxena, changing her name to Myrtale before her marriage to Philip II of Macedon, apparently as part of her initiation into a mystery cult. Philip and Olympias fell for each other when both were initiated into the mysteries of Cabeiri on Samothrace.[21] She adopted the name Olympias in 356 BC, when Philip's horse came home in the Olympic Games. The omens were good: the night before the wedding, Plutarch tells us, Olympias dreamed that a thunderbolt struck her womb and started a fire. Soon after, Philip dreamed that he put a lion seal on Olympias' womb, interpreted by Aristander that Olympias would give birth to a son who bore the characteristics of a lion. That son was Alexander the Great.

Olympias was by nature a jealous and unpredictable woman; her husband's marriage in 337 BC to Cleopatra (called Eurydice by Philip) only damaged the relationship further when she took off with Alexander to voluntary exile in Epirus at the court of

Alexander I. Things deteriorated further when Philip offered their daughter, another Cleopatra, to young Alexander in marriage. The wedding did not go well. Philip was murdered by Pausanias, one of his *somatophylakes*, his personal bodyguard; Olympias was suspected of being involved. She then had Eurydice and her child executed to reinforce Alexander's claim as king of Macedonia, confirming that Philip was not his father but Zeus was.

Other women connected with Alexander include Athenais, a prophetess from Erythrae in Ionia. According to Strabo, she was significant as the woman who gave Alexander the all-important confirmation of his allegedly divine descent.

Lanike (also known as Hellanike or Alacrinis), daughter of Dropides, was the sister of Cleitus the Black and Alexander's nurse. Cleitus was an officer in the excellent Companion cavalry, a unit of eight squadrons of 225 horsemen in the Macedonian army. He saved Alexander's life at the Battle of the Granicus and was repaid by him when Alexander ran him through with a lance during a drunken brawl some years later. Cleitus had somewhat tactlessly expressed his disapproval of 'barbarians' and of their increasing influence over Alexander. Cleitus called the Sogdians 'wild beasts', and was reluctant to remain amongst them as Alexander's satrap; Roxana, Alexander's wife, was of course a Sogdian 'barbarian'. When he killed Cleitus the king saw it that he was simply granting his wish to be free from bestial barbarians. Cleitus was 'the Black' to distinguish him from Cleitus the White.

Polyaenus gives us the story of a brave woman called Timoclea.[22] While the armies of Alexander were plundering Thebes, a Thracian, Hipparchus, broke into Timoclea's house. In spite of the circumstances, things seem to have begun well because it was only after dinner that Hipparchus raped Timoclea and forced her to reveal the whereabouts of her fortune. Timoclea confessed that she had hidden her vases and cups down a well, along with other ornaments and furniture. She took the Thracian to this well; he climbed down only to be met with an avalanche of stones which Timoclea and her servants rained down on him, eventually burying him. The Macedonians arrested Timoclea, who was hauled before Alexander. She was unrepentant and proud that she had avenged the brutality shown to her by Hipparchus: Alexander was impressed and applauded her chutzpah, allowing her and her relatives to go free.

Ada of Caria (*fl.* 377–326 BC) was a member of the House of Hecatomnus and ruler of Caria, first as Persian satrap and later as queen under the control of Alexander. She married her brother

Idrieus, who died in 344 BC, but as satrap was expelled by her other brother Pixodarus in 340 BC and fled to Alinda, where she carried on her rule in exile. When Alexander invaded Caria in 334 BC, Ada adopted Alexander as her son and surrendered the city of Alinda to him. In return, Alexander bestowed on Ada the command of the Siege of Halicarnassus and, after its fall, made Ada queen of Caria.

Thaïs was an Athenian *hetaera* and companion to Alexander on his campaigns in Asia Minor; she is remembered for her role in urging Alexander at a symposium to burn down the palace of Persepolis in 330 BC, the main residence of the defeated Achaemenid dynasty. Thaïs made a speech which persuaded Alexander to raze the palace: Cleitarchus says that it was all done on a whim; Plutarch and Diodorus say that it was revenge for when Xerxes burnt down the old Temple of Athena on the Acropolis in 480 BC during the Persian Wars. This is how Diodorus describes the incident and Thais' role in it:

> When the king [Alexander] was inflamed by their words, they all leaped up from their couches and passed the word along to form a victory procession in honour of Dionysus. Promptly many torches were gathered. Female musicians were present at the banquet, so the king led them all out for the comus to the sound of voices and flutes and pipes, Thaïs the courtesan leading the whole performance. She was the first, after the king, to hurl her blazing torch into the palace. As the others all did the same, immediately the entire palace area was consumed, so great was the conflagration. It was remarkable that the impious act of Xerxes, king of the Persians, against the acropolis at Athens should have been repaid in kind after many years by one woman, a citizen of the land which had suffered it, and in sport.[23]

Thaïs was also the lover of Ptolemy I Soter, one of Alexander's generals, and may also have been Alexander's lover, if Athenaeus's statement that Alexander liked to 'keep Thaïs with him' means any more than he simply enjoyed her company. On Alexander's death, Thaïs married Ptolemy and bore him three children, two boys and a girl: Lagus, Leontiscus, and Eirene. Thaïs was never Ptolemy's queen, nor were their children heirs to his throne. Ptolemy, of course, had other wives: Eurydice of Egypt and Berenice I of Egypt.

The reputation of Thaïs endured into the Roman republic and early empire and beyond into the Middle Ages. The Roman comic playwright Terence casts a female protagonist who is a *hetaera* called Thaïs in his *Eunuchus,* and Cicero quotes Thaïs' words in *De Amicitia.* In Ovid's *Remedia Amoris* Thaïs' behaviour and mores are contrasted with Andromache's: Andromache is the epitome of the loyal and chaste wife, while Thaïs is the embodiment of sex and is, says Ovid, what his art (of love) is all about.[24] Thaïs is down there in Hell, in Dante's *Divine Comedy,* in the circle of the flatterers, immersed in an excrement-filled trench for having told her lover that she was 'marvelously' fond of him.[25] She emerges with Alexander conjured up by Faustus in Marlowe's *Doctor Faustus* and appears as Alexander's mistress in Dryden's *Alexander's Feast, or The Power of Music* (1697), in which Alexander is enthroned with 'the lovely Thaïs by his side' who sat 'like a blooming eastern bride'; the poem later became an oratorio, *Alexander's Feast,* by Handel. Robert Herrick (1591–1674) comes to the happy conclusion in his *What Kind of Mistress He Would Have* that Thaïs is the woman for him for spending the night with: 'she will neither famish me, nor overfill.'

Cleophis was the queen of Assacana, a city Alexander besieged in 326 BC, where he sustained an injury. With her people's best interests at heart, Cleophis surrendered the city to Alexander.[26] Quintus Curtius Rufus gossips that Cleophis placed her son or grandson on Alexander's lap and that Alexander showed her mercy because of her beauty; Justin goes a step further by alleging that Cleophis was able retain her kingdom and position by sleeping with Alexander and that she bore Alexander a son.[27]

9

'Not like us': Sex and the Historians

> This is how the enquiries [historie] of Herodotus of Halicarnassus look, [written] so that man's achievements are not erased over time, and that the glory of great and marvelous deeds, some the work of the Greeks, others by barbarians, does not fade. In particular, the purpose is to establish why they waged war against each other.[1]

Herodotus (484–425 BC) is the first Greek writer to attempt to separate the wheat of history from the chaff: he aims to present *ta genomena*, the facts, as opposed to myth, speculation and fantasy. Even if he does not always succeed and he is at the mercy of rumour, subjectivity and apocrypha, his reportage is still of great value.

Barbarians, from *barbaroi*, were non-Greek speakers and, therefore, non-Greeks – their name deriving from the onomatopoeic sounds of their speech, reminiscent of the bleating of sheep. Today, the word has come to mean 'uncivilised', but that was not what Herotodus understood by it. Indeed, he is often respectful of the barbarian and is at pains also to present their side of the events and issues he describes, showing a multifaceted world and conflicting sides of the war. That is why much of Herotodus is devoted to the non-Greek world; Plutarch, a Greek writer of the second century AD, indignantly criticises Herodotus for being *philobarbaros*, a barbarian lover.

That other great contemporaneous historian of ancient Greece, Thucydides, who wrote between 431 and at least 404 BC, is largely silent on the question of sexuality and any role it may have played in the history of his country. Apart from some stern advice to behave so that men have no cause to mention them for good or bad, and an incident of roof-top defensive tile-slinging at a besieging enemy, there is virtually nothing. We can put this down to Thucydides' professionalism and his desire to stay focused and produce a work of true lasting quality:

> Perhaps my work will seem less pleasurable to hear because it lacks the element of story-telling. However, if all those who wish to see clearly what has happened – and what is likely to happen again in the future in the same or similar way, since that is human nature – judge my work to be useful, that will be enough for me. This work is laid down to be a possession for all time rather than a performance for an immediate audience.[2]

To him, women have no role in a war.[3] As Hector says, war is man's work – despite Andomache's advice on tactics. And, by extension, history was very much the work of men, as much of extant ancient Greek history is concerned with the subject of war.

If Herodotus were to have his way then posterity would be convinced of the fact that it was women who were responsible for the way things panned out in the history of ancient Greece. Greeks, Phoenicians and Persians all implicate women in the causes of conflict between these three mighty Mediterranean powers. Women-snatching appears to have been at the root of all Greek history and nation building, as indeed it was at the heart of the Roman civilisation, when the Sabines lost the flower of their womenfolk to the emergent Romans. The day the mercantile Phoenicians landed on a beach in the then pre-eminent Argos to sell their wares to the native Greeks was pivotal. The goods obviously attracted the eye and interest of many a Greek woman who proceeded to browse and buy. Herodotus takes up the story:

> On the fifth or sixth day after their arrival, when their wares were almost all sold, many women came to the shore and among them especially the daughter of the king, whose name was Io (according to Persians and Greeks alike).[4]

The Phoenicians reciprocated by eyeing up the Greek women. They even abducted some, including Io, whom they shipped off to Egypt. The first blow had been struck. In retaliation, 'some Greeks' – Herodotus diplomatically suggests Cretans – landed at Tyre in Phoenicia and snatched *their* king's daughter, Europa, whence they sailed to Aea, a city of the Colchians; from there they carried off the king's daughter, Medea. Despite protests, the Greeks refused to return Medea because Io had never been returned to them. A de facto precedent had been set and so, some fifty years later, the Trojan Paris, son of Priam, was able to abduct Helen with what he thought would be impunity. The Greeks protested but were told that she was not going back because they had been denied when those Greeks had refused to return Medea. The result, of course, was a serious escalation into the ten-year-long Trojan War when the Greeks invaded Asia. Retribution was now loose in the world: in the words of W. H. Auden: 'Those to whom evil is done, Do evil in return.'

But the tragic denouement to this tangled series of international royal abductions was that, despite its apparent illegality, in the words of Herodotus:

> So far there had been nothing worse than women stealing on both sides ... to be anxious to avenge rape is foolish: wise men take no notice of such things. For clearly the women would never have been carried away, if they had not wanted to be.[5]

This is a refrain which was to ring down the ages, from Herodotus here via Ovid, who believed that women like a 'bit of rough' and really mean yes when they say no, to today, when it is cited as a lame attempt to justify rape.[6] Perhaps there was no physical violation involved in these abductions, but it is but a short, ambivalent step from Herodotus' words here to a defence for rape as we define it today. Even though it is as much a Persian sentiment as Greek, and the Greeks were accused by the Persians of overreacting in starting a war over a woman and thereby thus suggesting that 'rape' was of considerable significance and consequence, such a sentiment would have resonated with the readers of Herodotus, giving some the all-clear to treat their women as they wished.

Physical and sexual violence against women has been with us since the dawn of man. A 2,000-year-old adult female skeleton excavated in South Africa reveals that she was shot in the back with two arrows. A late Ice Age discovery from Sicily has unearthed a woman with an arrow in her pelvis. After all, for the Ancient Greeks rape – sexually motivated or otherwise – came with the sanction of the gods: as we have seen, Zeus raped Leda in the form of a swan, Europa in the guise of a bull. He raped Danaë disguised as the rain and Alkmen masquerading as her own husband. Zeus also raped Ganymede and Antiope. Additionally, Cassandra was raped by Ajax the Lesser; Chrysippus was raped by his tutor Laius; Persphone was raped by Hades; Medusa was raped by Poseidon; Philomela; raped by her brother-in-law; the daughters of Leucippus, Phoebe and Hilaeira, were abducted, raped and later married to Castor and Pollux, and so on.

The key issue in the abduction of Helen was a military issue in that it started a war, and Helen's role as a catalyst, willing or otherwise, became a cause of enduring enmity between Greek and Persian and Greek and Trojan. It was never that simple, though, as Herodotus reveals:

> The Phoenicians do not tell the same story about Io as the Persians. They deny that they carried her off to Egypt by force. She had sex in Argos with the captain of the ship. Then, when she discovered she was pregnant, she was ashamed to let her parents know, and so, lest they discover her condition, she willingly sailed away with the Phoenicians.[7]

The sexual customs and mores of 'barbarian' countries and civilisations feature prominently in Herodotus' ethnographical excursions around the Mediterranean. Herodotus mentions 375 women as individuals or in groups, seventy-six of which might be classified as being in an ethnographical context. Additionally, there are queens and regents, princesses and royal mistresses. Other mentions include sixty-seven professional women, all but seven of whom are priestesses, but the rest are, valuably, of the lower orders: nurses, bakers, prostitutes and the like. There are forty family women: mothers, wives, sisters and daughters; where there is a sexual dimension to these examples, we can discuss what Herodotus tells us about them. Three of the queens, Tomyris, Artemisia and Pheretime, exhibit excellent political and strategic military skills as good as any man's – much to the chagrin of many a man, no doubt.

An at times incredulous Herodotus found the wider world a very strange and wonderful place, full of strange and wondrous things. Apart from giant ants the size of foxes and amazing hippopotami, Libyan dog-headed men and men with no heads, their eyes in their breasts, the historian found even civilised Egyptians quite astonishing in some ways, not least because:

> The women go to market and men stay at home and weave [the exact opposite to Greek practice]. Women even urinate standing up and men sitting down.

The Egyptians stood the world on its head. Urine, or the wrong sort of urine, also played a big part in the cautionary tale of the adulterous wife of King Pheros:

> Pheros was a King of Egypt who went blind. After 10 years the oracle at Buto said he had served his punishment and would be cured if he washed his eyes out with the urine of a woman who had never slept with any man except her husband. So he tried his wife's urine ... it didn't work, then many other women until one worked and he could see again. All those women whose urine failed were collected together and burned. He then married the lady whose urine worked.

What was probably the most astonishing of Herodotus' observations about the Egyptians comes in his discussion of the Mendesians, who venerated the goat because of its association with Pan. Herodotus concludes by noting that, within his lifetime, a billy goat had intercourse with a woman there in full view of everyone – 'a most surprising incident'.[8] He then moves swiftly on to discuss pigs, which are 'unclean', making it impossible for pigherds to go into temples or intermarry within the community; they have to marry their own daughters instead.

Herodotus' aim as a historian is to prove that the Greek way of doing things, all things, is the right and proper way; all barbarians, even clever and sophisticated barbarians like the Egyptians, occasionally did things wrongly. Some of his episodes are undoubtedly fictitious, but that matters little; his objective is to establish the contrariness of the non-Greek, to expose the barbarian world in relation to the normative behaviour and customs of his fellow Greeks. He wanted Greeks to be glad to be Greek. And that, of course, applies to sexuality and women; about one third, twenty-five, of Herodotus' ethnographical excursions are concerned with sexual behaviour, and notably there are more allusions to female sexuality than male. It also gives the impression that non-Greeks were more asexual than Greeks. As an example, Herodotus tells us about the Lycians in Anatolia who are unique in two ways:

> In one of their customs, that of taking the mother's name instead of the father's, they are unique. Ask a Lycian who he is, and he will tell you his own name and his mother's, then his grandmother's and great grandmother's and so on. And if a free

woman has a child by a slave, the child is considered legitimate, whereas the children of a free man, however distinguished he may be, and a foreign wife or mistress have no citizen rights at all ...[9]

Herodotus is wrong on the first count; the Lycians did not use matronymics. We have no way of gauging the validity of the second.

To Herodotus the Libyans were particularly barbaric, especially the nomadic Ausoi and the desert-living Garamantes; Herodotus calls them bestial, not because they copulate with their beasts, but because they 'copulate promiscuously with their women', just as animals do, 'in the manner of flocks and herds'. Sex in public was presumably beyond the pale for most ancient Greeks.[10] Furthermore, when a Libyan girl reached adolescence she was subjected to a kind of regular beauty contest in which she became the property of the man whom he or she most closely resembled. The girls of the Ausoi and Machlyes played an ancient game in which they fought each other with sticks and stones; if any girls died in the fighting, and they obviously did, then this was proof that she was not a virgin.[11] Libyan Gindanes women were avid trophy hunters, parading the number of lovers they had enjoyed with leather anklets donated by those lovers.[12] Old-style Greek monogamy and adultery were of little consequence to the Nasamontes in the south of Libya and the Massagetae. If a man was having sex with a married women, one other than his wife, and, quite reasonably, did not want to be disturbed, he simply left his calling card at the door of her wagon: the phallic spear or quiver indicated quite clearly that she was busy and that he could take her 'without fear', fear, that is, of being interrupted by another chancer or by her husband who was, incidentally, quite relaxed about it all. By contrast, if that husband were an Athenian back home, he might legally kill the interloper. No such messy unpleasantness, though, amongst the free-loving Massegetae. Massagetae was a region in Scythia covering parts of modern day Turkmenistan, Afghanistan, Uzbekistan, and Kazakhstan.

Hesiod's *Catalogue of Women* gives us more information on the decidedly outlandish Massagetae and their even stranger neighbours:

[The Sons of Boreas pursued the Harpies] to the lands of the Massagetae and of the proud Half-Dog men, of the Underground-folk and of the feeble Pygmies; and to the tribes of the boundless Black-skins and the Libyans. Huge Earth bare these to Epaphus – soothsaying people, knowing seercraft by the will of Zeus the lord of oracles, but deceivers, to the end that men whose thought passes their utterance might be subject to the gods and suffer harm – Aethiopians and Libyans and mare-milking Scythians.[13]

The Nasamontes men certainly enjoyed their weddings. All male guests were permitted to have sex with the bride in a kind of 'gang – *droit du seigneur*'. Herodotus nonchalantly adds that in return for this multiple pleasuring the bride receives a present from each of her wedding night partners, 'something or other they have brought with them from home'. The Adyrmachidae were no less permissive:

> They are also the only tribe with whom the custom obtains of bringing all women about to become brides before the king, that he may choose such as are agreeable to him.[14]

Few, if any, would have left the king's bed a virgin on their wedding night.

Pheretima *(D. 515 BC)* was wife of the Greek Cyrenaean King Battus III and the last queen of the Battiad dynasty. Herodotus tells us that when Battus, the father of Pheretima and grandfather of Pheretima's son Arcesilaus, died in 530 BC, Arcesilaus III became king. He was defeated around 518 BC and exiled to Samos while Pheretima fled to the court of King Euelthon in Salamis, Cyprus. Arcesilaus, however, recruited an army in Samos, returned with it to Cyrene, and regained his regal position by murdering and exiling his political opponents, encouraged by Pheretima. When Arcesilaus left Cyrene for Barca, Pheretima took over control of the city; Arcesilaus was murdered by exiled Cyrenaeans intent on revenge. Pheretima went hot-foot to Arysandes, the Persian governor of Egypt, to get help in avenging the death of her son; Arysandes loaned her Egypt's army and navy. She marched to Barca and demanded the surrender of those Barcaeans responsible for the murder of Arcesilaus; when the Barcaeans ignored her, Pheretima laid siege to Barca for nine months. Amasis, her Persian commander, played a trick on the Barcaeans in which he ordered his soldiers to dig a large trench in front of the city camouflaged with wooden planks and earth; he then lured the Barcaeans out of the city with a promise of a well-rewarded armistice. They literally fell into the trap: Pheretima ordered her troops to cut off the breasts of the Barcaean wives, and enslaved the rest of the Barcaeans to the Persians.

So Pheretima avenged her son, returned to Egypt, and gave the army and navy back to the governor. However, while in Egypt Pheretima contracted a contagious parasitic skin disease and died in late 515 BC. Herodotus tells us that she was eaten alive by the worms – punishment by the gods for her butchery of the women of Barca.[15] She lives on in the name of the worm which infested her: Pheretima is a genus of earthworm now found in New Guinea and other parts of South East Asia; the worms are used as a medicine in China and carry biological agents efficacious in the treatment of epilepsy.

Another cruel, unusually militaristic and quite un-Greek woman was Queen Tomyris of the Massagetae, famous for slaying King Cyrus the Great, the founder of the Achaemenid Empire, when he invaded her country. Strabo, Polyaenus, Cassiodorus, and Jordanes, as well as Herodotus, all mention her.[16] She exemplifies for Herodotus the barbarity of barbarian women and, by implication, the weakness of barbarian man, himself lacking in essential Greek-style *andreia* to allow such a situation to exist. The gist is that the Massagetae are promiscuous as a result of being allowed too much political power; the maternal vengeance exacted by Tomyris would surely evoke comparisons with Clytemnestra's terrible actions in mythology.

Cyrus fooled Tomyris' army under the command of her son, Spargapises, into drinking copious amonts of wine which he, Cyrus, had left behind. Scythians were not accustomed to drinking wine, being much more partial to hashish and fermented mare's milk; accordingly, they drank themselves stupid and were successfully attacked by the Persians while under the influence. Spargapises was captured; he persuaded Cyrus to remove his bonds and, once free to move, promptly committed suicide. A vengeful Tomyris challenged Cyrus to a second battle, promising him his fill of blood. She won; Cyrus was killed and Tomyris had his head cut off and his corpse crucified before shoved his head into a wineskin full of human blood.

Search was made among the slain by order of the queen for the body of Cyrus, and when it was found she took a skin, and, filling it full of human blood, she dipped the head of Cyrus in the gore, saying, as she thus insulted the corpse, 'I live and have conquered you in fight, and yet by you am I ruined, for you took my son with guile; but thus I fulfil my threat, and give you your fill of blood.'[17]

To the Greeks, women and war simply did not mix. Herodotus' sensational reporting of these escapades was designed not just to illuminate what he saw as the perverted and bloodthirsty behaviour of barbarian women compared with the so-called civilised women of Greece, but to demonstrate just how far removed from Greek women they were – socially, politically and militarily. These embellished and slightly prurient descriptions of the permissive sexual mores of barbarian women are a manifestation of Greek man attacking the soft underbelly of his enemy by denigrating and slurring the sexual behaviour of their women. This insidious, demoralising tactic continued to be deployed to good effect well into the Roman period and beyond. It surfaces at the beginning of Herodotus' general description of the Massagetae, along with a description of their routine human sacrifice – anathema to a Greek:

> Each man has only one wife, but all these wives are held in common. Human life does not end normally with these people; but when a man grows very old, all his kinsfolk collect together and offer him up in sacrifice; offering at the same time some cattle too. After the sacrifice they boil the flesh and eat it; they who end their days like that are reckoned the happiest. If a man dies of disease they do not eat him, but bury him in the ground, bewailing his bad luck that he did not get to be sacrificed.[18]

Not all foreign women were condemned by Herodotus. In Halicarnassus (modern Bodrum in Turkey and birthplace of Herodotus) King Mausolos (r. 387–353) ruled in consort with his wife, Queen Artemisia, a woman whom Herodotus described as 'wondrous'. Decrees and laws were issued in joint names and honours were heaped on the them as an egalitarian regal couple. When Mausolos died, Artemisia ruled on her own for some years. Her expressions of grief for her husband were legendary; she is even reputed to have concocted and drunk a potion of her husband's bones and ashes. She organised poetry and oratory competitions to honour her husband and completed the building of his mausoleum, which became one of the Seven Wonders of the World, known as the Mausoleum of Halicarnassus. She embarrassed the people of Rhodes when she beat off their attack; the Rhodians found it hard to accept that they had been repelled by a woman.

Persian Xerxes made the mistake of 'falling in love' with his brother Masistes' wife; she, however, resisted his advances so Xerxes attempted to subvert this inconvenience by arranging a marriage between one of his sons, Darius, and her daughter.[19] Herodotus names her, Artaynte, but he does not name her chaste and respectable mother. Things became yet more 'Byzantine' when Xerxes then fell in love with Artaynte, his daughter-in-law – another woman of no little intelligence 'but doomed to come to a bad end along with all her house'. When told by Xerxes he would give her whatever she wanted in gratitude for her favours, she adroitly puts Xerxes on the spot by demanding he gives her the 'coat of many colours' – woven especially for him by his wife, Amestris. Appropriately, her name means 'strong woman'. A vacillating Xerxes offered her gold, cities and even an army to command by herself – there is no better present for a Persian. But she resolutely insisted on the coat and the coat was duly paraded on her back ...

An indignant Amestris ordered Artaynte's mother, the original object of Xerxes' lust, to be mutilated. The day of the slaughter was to coincide with the annual royal feast held on the king's birthday. On that day (and only that day) the king anointed his head and gave gifts to the Persians. Amestris then told Xerxes that Masistes' should be her gift – a request Xerxes was compelled by law to deliver. Despite desperate efforts to get Masistes to divorce his wife and marry Xerxes' daughter, Masistes would not relent and stormed out of the feast insisting that he was happily married already. Meanwhile, Amestris sent for Xerxes' guards and savagely mutilated Masistes' wife:

> She cut off the woman's breasts and threw them to dogs, and her nose and ears and lips also, and cut out her tongue. Then she sent the body home showing all the signs of the atrocity committed on her.[20]

Masistes fled to Bactria to fuel a revolt against Xerxes but Xerxes caught up with his force and destroyed it. So, Amestris exacted her vengeance while Herodotus succeeded in showing Persian Xerxes as weak, being not in control of his wife or mistresses, and the victim of yet another avenging woman. It also demonstrates the brutalising effect of royal courts, particularly on women: Clytemnestra, Medea and Cassandra are victims in one sense, Andromache, Penelope and Antigone in another. The queens and princesses of the Macedonian court were, we have seen, little more than pawns, married, divorced and forced to act as mistresses at a whim; they all anticipated the malevolent Livias, Messalinas, Poppaeas and Agrippinas of the maelstrom that was the early days of the Roman empire.

Amestris was acting in character: this was not her first atrocity for she was even implicated in child sacrifice if Herodotus is to be believed:

> I am informed that Amestris, the wife of Xerxes, when she had grown old, insured her own life with Hades by burying seven children of famous Persians on two occasions.[21]

Masistes, according to Herodotus, also had issues with the (confusingly named) general Artayntes:

> Masistes son of Darius, who happened to be at the Persian disaster, reviled the admiral Artayntes very bitterly, telling him (among other things) that his leadership made him look worse than a woman, and that no punishment was too severe to pay for the harm he had done the king. Now it is the greatest of all taunts in Persia to be called worse than a woman.

Artayntes reacted by attempting to cleave Masistes with his sword, but he was restrained. The incident exemplifies how much store Persians, like Greeks, set by their masculinity and their *andreia* – manhood and bravery. At the same time, it belittles the Persians by suggesting that one of their generals was no better than a woman. The deep insult would have resonated with Herodotus' readership because Greeks shared a similar infatuation with *andreia,* even to the extent where they imbued women with that quality when they acted bravely or exceptionally in any way. Such things were ordinarily the preserve of men.

Herodotus introduces the major role played by a woman in the Median royal succession when he describes the last Median king, Astyages (r. 585–550 BC). Astyages dreamt that his daughter, Mandane, urinated so much that she flooded the city of Nineveh and swamped all of Asia; the Magi eventually interpreted this as meaning that Mandane would give birth to a son who one day would destroy Astyages' empire. An alarmed Astyages married her off to a Persian, Cambyses I of Anšan, who was of a 'good family and quiet habits' and of no apparent threat. A second dream saw a vine growing out of Mandane's vagina and spreading all over Asia;

it received a similar interpretation. By now Mandane had given birth to a boy, Cyrus, so Astyages sent his general Harpagus (the 'Snatcher') to kill the child:

> Take the child that Mandane bore, and carry him to your house, and kill him; and then bury him however you like. [22]

Harpagus was extremely reluctant and in turmoil; after discussing the matter with his wife he gave the child to a cowherd, Mitridates:

> So saying, he sent a messenger at once to one of Astyages' cowherds, who he knew pastured his herds in the likeliest spots and where the mountains were most infested with wild beasts. The man's name was Mitradates, and his wife was a slave like him; her name was in the Greek language Cyno, in the Median Spako: for 'spax' is the Median word for dog.

The original plan was, of course, for Mitridates to expose the infant but, as it happened, his wife had just given birth to a stillborn child and implored him not to expose the infant Cyrus:

> Since I cannot convince you not to expose it, then, if a child has to be seen exposed, do this: I too have borne a child, but I bore it dead. Take this one and expose it but the child of the daughter of Astyages let us raise as if it were our own; this way, you won't be caught disobeying our masters, and we will not have plotted badly. For the dead child will have royal burial, and the living will not lose his life.

Mitridates and his wife proceeded to raise Cyrus as their own son, while Harpagus showed the stillborn to Astyages masquerading as the dead Cyrus to allay his fears. After ten years Astyages found Cyrus almost by accident but spared him on the advice of the Magi, returning him to his birth parents in Anšan. Harpagus, however, was cruelly punished when Astyages served up his own son for him at a banquet:

> But when Harpagus' son came, Astyages cut his throat and tore him limb from limb, roasted some of the flesh and boiled some, and kept it ready after he had prepared it ... Astyages and the others were served dishes of lamb's meat, but Harpagus that of his own son, all but the head and hands and feet, which lay apart

covered up in a wicker basket. And when Harpagus seemed to have eaten his fill, Astyages asked him, 'Did you like your meal, Harpagus?' 'Very much so,' Harpagus answered. Then those whose job it was brought him the head of his son and hands and feet concealed in the basket, and they stood before Harpagus and told him to open and take his pick.[23]

Cyrus succeeded his father in 559, and in 553, encouraged by Harpagus, understandably keen for revenge for being given the 'abominable supper', Cyrus rebelled against Astyages. After three years of conflict, Astyages' troops mutinied during the battle of Pasargadae, and Cyrus conquered the Median empire; he spared Astyages, who remained in Cyrus' court until his death.

Cambyses II was the unfortunate king of Persia from 530 to 522 BC. His troubles began when he entertained hopes of marrying a daughter of Amasis, who sent him a daughter of Apries instead; Cambyses reacted by declaring war. His greatest crime, though, was slaying the Apis bull, for which he went mad, turned to drink, and killed his brother Smerdis. He lost his empire and died from a gangrenous wound in the thigh, in the very same place in which he had wounded the sacred bull. His sister was also his wife; Cambyses had to change the law to allow him to do what was hitherto illegal under Persian law. He then compounded this by marrying his other, younger sister. This second sister-wife met an unfortunate death at the wrong end of Cambyses' insanity and temper. Herodotus takes up the story:

The Greeks say that Cambyses had set a lion cub to fight a puppy, and that this woman was watching too; and that as the puppy was losing, its brother puppy broke its leash and came to help, and the two dogs together got the better of the lion cub. Cambyses, they say, was pleased with this, but the woman wept: seeing this, Cambyses asked why she was crying, to which she replied that when she saw the puppy help its brother she was upset, remembering her brother Smerdis and knowing that there he would have no one to avenge him. Cambyses killed her for saying this. The Egyptians would have it that as the two sat at table the wife took a lettuce and plucked off the leaves, then asked her husband whether he preferred with or without leaves. 'With the leaves,' he said; whereupon she answered: 'Yet you have stripped Cyrus' house as bare as this lettuce.' An incandescent Cambyses attacked her, even though she was heavily pregnant; she miscarried and died of the wounds he inflicted on her.[24]

Herodotus calls it 'the savagery of a lunatic'. In the early Roman empire, a similarly disturbed and furious Nero was to inflict the same atrocity on his wife, Poppaea Sabina. Nero kicked Poppaea to death when she was heavily pregnant; she had complained of being ill and had the temerity to scold him for returning late from the races. Her body was not cremated according to Roman custom, but was stuffed with spices and embalmed in the oriental way.[25]

Phaidime played a crucial but dangerous role in the continuation of the Persian dynasty. She risked her life to end a palace coup: when Cambyses died he was replaced by a Magus usurper, Gaumata, who passed himself off as Smerdis, son of Cyrus. When Cambyses had a dream in which Smerdis would depose him, he had him murdered secretly.[26] One of the few that knew of Smerdis' death was Patizeithes, the steward of Cambyses' palace at Susa, who happened to have a brother who looked very much like Smerdis and whose name was also Smerdis, or Gaumata. Patizeithes then elevated his brother to the throne, pretending that he was Smerdis, the brother of Cambyses. The false Smerdis got away with it by not allowing anyone who knew the real Smerdis into his presence.[27] Otanes, a Persian nobleman, suspected this intrigue and became one of the seven conspirators who eventually killed Gaumata. One of the first things that Gaumata did was take on all of Cambyses' wives, one of whom was Phaidime, daughter of Otanes and widow of Smerdis. Otanes persuaded her to establish whether or not this Smerdis was, in fact, an imposter. According to Herodotus, Cyrus had Gaumata's ears cut off, so Otanes instructed his daughter to feel for 'Smerdis's ears next time they slept together' (Persian wives took it in turns to share the royal bed).[28] Phaidime had never seen the real Smerdis and could not swap notes with his other wives as they were all kept separate. Despite serious reservations, she was able to tell Otanes that this Smerdis had no ears, thus confirming that he was an imposter. With six others conspirators he slew 'Smerdis', allowing Darius to become king; Phaidime married Darius.

Sex with Darius led to the slaughter of virtually a whole family and an invidious decision for a woman who was a wife, mother and sister. The rule was that the seven conspirators mentioned above were always permitted an audience unannounced with Darius so long as he was not busy having sex with one of his wives. One of the seven, Intaphrenes, turned up,

but the gatekeeper and the messengers refused to allow him in, telling him that the king was having intercourse with one of his wives. Intaphrenes thought that they were lying so, drawing his scimitar, he cut off their noses and ears, then strung the body parts on his horse's bridle, hung it around the men's necks, and let them go.[29]

As soon as Darius was confident that the seven were not complicit in a plot and that Intaphrenes was acting alone, he imprisoned Intaphrenes and his entire family with a view to executing them. But Darius had not taken into account the impressive reasoning of Intaphrenes' wife and her compelling piety:

> Then Intaphrenes' wife started coming to the palace gates, weeping and lamenting; eventually persuading Darius to pity her by this. He sent a messenger to tell her, 'Woman, King Darius will let one of your imprisoned relatives live, whichever one you prefer.' After some thought she answered, 'If indeed the king gives me the life of one, I choose my brother from them all.' Darius was astonished when he heard her answer, and sent someone to ask her, 'Woman, the king asks what are you thinking of abandoning your husband and your children by choosing to save the life of your brother, who is not as close to you as your children and less dear than your husband?' 'Lord, she answered, 'I can get another husband, if a god is willing, and more children, if I lose these; but since my father and mother are no longer living, there is no way that I can have another brother; this is why I said what I did.'

Darius was most impressed by this; he released the brother, and the eldest son too for good measure. The rest were slaughtered.

Atossa, the daughter of Cyrus and wife of Darius, became embroiled in Persian foreign policy relating to the Persian invasion of Greece.[30] An enslaved Greek doctor, Democedes, cured Darius' seemingly incurable injured foot and was amply rewarded by him. Darius, of course, was anxious to keep him in his service although the doctor, for his part, was equally anxious to get home to Greece. Later, Atossa developed an abscess in her breast; when it deteriorated and burst, she summoned Democedes:

> He said he would cure her, but made her swear that she would repay him by granting whatever he asked of her, adding that he would ask nothing that would shame her.

Democedes duly cured Atossa, who was good to her word. Herodotus records the pillow talk between her and Darius:

My lord, although you are so powerful you are doing nothing to increase the power of the Persians. The right thing for a man who, like you, is both young and in control of great wealth, is to be seen to be doing something, so that the Persians know that they are ruled by a real man. It is in your interest to do this, not only so that the Persians know that their leader is a man, but also, if they are embroiled in war, they will have no time to plot against you. You should get to work on this now, while you are still young.

This is precisely what the doctor ordered: a flattering appeal to Darius' virility, his *andreia*, with sound and wise long-term domestic and foreign policy. Darius agreed and promised early action. Atossa disabused him of the misguided notion of attacking Scythia, diverting him on to Greece:

'Look,' Atossa said, 'let the Scythians go for now; you can take them whenever you like; I tell you, march against Hellas. I have heard about Laconian and Argive and Attic and Corinthian women, and would like to have them as servants. You have a man here who is fitter than any other to instruct and guide you in everything about Hellas: I mean the physician who healed your foot.'

Democedes was duly chosen as one of the spies to infiltrate Greece and gather intelligence, on strict orders that he is returned to Darius when the mission is accomplished. Unfortunately for Darius, after completing some surveillance of the Greek coastline the spies sailed for Tarentum in Italy, where sympathetic locals disabled the Persian triremes and arrested the Persians. Eventually, they caught up with Democedes in Croton but were forced to sail for home, without Democedes and despite threats of serious Persian reprisals. As a footnote, Herodotus adds:

Democedes gave them a message as they were setting sail; they should tell Darius, he said, that Democedes was now engaged to the daughter of Milo, the famous wrestler. Darius held the name of Milo the wrestler in high esteem; and, to my thinking, Democedes made this match and paid a lot of money for it to show Darius that he was a man of influence in his own country as well as in Persia.[31]

One story which Herodotus admits he does not believe involves Pharaoh Rhampsinitus who trapped one of the thieves who were systematically robbing his treasure. He had this thief decapitated and strung up, but later found to his horror that the corpse had vanished, on the instructions of the grief-stricken mother who wanted to apply burial rites for her son – so far, so very Greek.[32] To catch the criminal, Rhampsinitus, acting not very Greek:

> Put his own daughter in a brothel, telling her to take on all comers and, before having sex, to make each tell her the slyest and most irreligious thing he had done in his life; whoever told her the story of the thief, she was to seize and not let go.

Sure enough, the thief came calling, but he was wise to the plot:

> He cut the arm off a fresh corpse at the shoulder, and went to the king's daughter, carrying it under his cloak, and when asked the same question as the rest, he said that his most impious act had been when he had cut the head off his brother who was caught in a trap in the king's treasury; and his shrewdest, that after making the guards drunk, he had cut down his brother's hanging body. When she heard this, the princess grabbed him; but in the darkness the thief left her with the arm of the corpse; and clutching it, she held on, believing that she had the arm of the thief, but he was gone in a flash out the door.

The king exonerated the thief for his ingenuity and gave him his daughter's hand in marriage.

Other extraordinary gender and sex-related findings include men and women sharing equal authority; descendants of the Amazons having to kill in battle before they can marry;[33] auctions set up to ensure that all women find a partner; prostitution used to accumulate a dowry; athletic contests for virgin girls; freedom for girls and chaperoning for wives. Some of those Amazon descendants failed to register a kill and so died unmarried.

Candaules, also known as Myrsilos, was a king of Lydia from 735 to 718 BC. Herodotus says his name meant 'dog throttler'.[34] In telling this story he gives us another tale of caution in which a vengeful woman plays a central part. Candaules is murdered by his wife, Nyssia, due to his arrogance – he was in the habit of boasting about his wife's prodigious beauty to his bodyguard, Gyges:

> If you don't believe me when I tell you how lovely my wife is, a man always believes his eyes more than his ears; so do as I tell you – get a look at her taking her clothes off.

At first Gyges was outraged and refused, only too aware of the taboos surrounding nudity in Persian society and concerned how unpredictably Candaules might actually react if the deed was done.[35] Candaules eventually won him over by asserting that Nyssia lost all her shame when naked. He revealed a plan in which Gyges would hide behind a door in the royal bedroom to watch Nyssia undressing; Gyges would then steal away while the queen's back was turned. That night, Gyges took up his position and ogled as planned, but the queen glimpsed him and saw immediately that she had been betrayed and humiliated by her own husband. She swore revenge and formulated her own plan. The next day, Nyssia summoned Gyges and confronted him: 'One of you must die. Either my husband, or you, who have outraged convention by seeing me naked.' Eventually, Gyges quite sensibly chose to betray the king and save his own skin. Nyssia's scheme involved an element of *déjà vu*: Gyges hid behind the door of the bedroom armed with a knife provided by the queen, and slew Candaules in his sleep. Gyges married the queen and became king.

Candaules did not pay just with his life. He has the dubious privilege of lending his name to candaulism, a deviant sexual practice in which a man exposes his (usually) female partner, or images of her, to other people for their voyeuristic pleasure. The term is also applied to the practice of undressing or exposing a female partner's body to others or forcing her into having sex with a third person, into prostitution or pornography. Today the term is increasingly applied to the posting of revealing images of a female partner on the internet, or forcing her to wear sexually suggestive clothes for depraved and prurient public consumption.

Nyssia was obviously shrewd, a fact which for the average Greek makes Herodotus' story all the more disturbing, and urges him to be all the more careful to keep his women under wraps and shielded from the prying eyes of strangers. Nyssia defends the conventions that her husband spurned and proved him wrong when he asserted that women lose their shame when naked. She punished the violation and restored normality; in the end, only her husband had ever seen her naked, even if that took a change of husbands.

Herodotus is nearer to home when he reveals remarkable customs in *poleis* outside cosmopolitan Athens. He tells us why Ionian women do not eat with or address their husbands by name; why Spartan men and women mourn in equal measure; and that the polygamist wives of Thracians vie with each other to be buried with their husbands. The Thracian women, however, were not just indulging in a spot of long-term funeral planning; Herodotus exposes a much more conclusive and dramatic outcome:

> Each man has many wives, and at his death there is both great rivalry among his wives and eager contention on their friends' part to prove which wife was best loved by her husband. She who is judged to have that honour is praised by men and women alike and then slain over the tomb by her next of kin and then buried with the husband. The other wives are greatly unhappy at having lost out and feel deeply insulted.[36]

But that is not all. There seems to have been an unhealthy trade in child and sex-trafficking in Thrace, while girls intended as wives were bought from their parents at great expense:

> It is the custom to sell their children for export and to take no care of their virgins, allowing them to have intercourse with any man they wish. Their wives, however, they strictly guard, and buy them for a price from the parents.[37]

A young girl from Oaxus in Crete had a lucky escape after terrible treatment by her father and new stepmother:

> Etearchus became ruler. He was a widower with a daughter, Phronime, and he married a second wife. When the second wife came into his house, she thought fit to be the typical stepmother to Phronime, abusing her and inventing all sorts of malice against her; in the end she accused the girl of fornication, and persuaded her husband that it was true. So Etearchus planned a great sin against his daughter: to get rid of her.[38]

Etearchus enlisted the help of Themison, a Therean merchant, and made him swear to do his bidding whatever it be. He then ordered Themison to take Phronime out in a boat and dump her in the sea. Themison, however, was furious at having been duped so he took the order literally by dipping Phronime in the sea on the end of a rope and hauling her back on board, thus discharging his obligation under the oath. The couple then went to Thura where Phronime became the mistress of Polymnestus.

Some of the civilisations the Macedonians came into contact with had a history and reputation for sexual depravity. How far this served as salacious propaganda to undermine and diminish a potential enemy or a conquered victim it is hard to know, but the rumours are there and, as we know from our discussion of alleged Spartan sexual mores, 'mud sticks'.

One such civilisation was Babylon, first settled around 4,000 years ago. From a small city-state it grew to become a powerful and wealthy empire, thanks largely to Nebuchadnezzar II, who punctuated its walls with a hundred gates and created its Hanging Gardens which were to become one of the Seven Wonders of the World. Power and money, though, have a habit of corrupting and this is precisely what we are led to believe happened in Babylon, as exemplified by this 'most shameful custom' which can only be described as the cattle market to end all cattle markets; Herodotus gives us the details:

> Every woman born in the country must once in her life go and sit down in the precinct of Venus, and there have sex with a stranger. Many of the wealthier sort, who are too proud to mix with the others, drive in covered carriages to the precinct, followed by a goodly train of attendants, and there take their station. But the larger number seat themselves within the holy enclosure with wreaths of string about their heads ... and the strangers pass along them to make their choice.
>
> A woman who has once taken her seat is not allowed to return home till one of the strangers throws a silver coin into her lap, and takes her with him beyond the holy ground. When he throws the coin he says these words: 'The goddess Mylitta prosper thee.' (Venus is called Mylitta by the Assyrians.) The silver coin may be of any size; it cannot be refused, for that is forbidden by the law, since once thrown it is sacred. The woman goes with the first man who throws her money, and rejects no one. When she has gone with him, and so satisfied the goddess, she returns home, and from that time forth no gift however great will prevail with her. Such of the women as are tall and beautiful are soon released, but others who are ugly have to stay a long time before they can fulfill the law. Some have waited three or four years in the precinct.[39]

This description remained unquestioned by generations of scholars and passed into legend. Few questioned how far this was just the tabloid Herodotus spicing up and denigrating the questionable cultural history and mores of another barbarian civilisation. Similar set-ups were known in Cyprus and, according to Lucian, in Lebanon. In 331 BC, Babylon fell to Alexander the Great who would die there, in Nebuchadnezzar's palace, eight years later.

Christians later referred to the 'whore of Babylon,' an allegory of the Roman and Egyptian empires in the Book of Revelation (cc. 17 and 18) and 'Babylon the Great, the Mother of Prostitutes and Abominations of the Earth', destined surely to fall. She symbolises Sin and rides the first beast which is Death. It is Herodotus who probably had to answer for the following choice descriptions of Babylon, later repeated as the truth in Revelations:

17:2. With whom the kings of the earth have committed fornication, and the inhabitants of the earth have been made drunk with the wine of her fornication.

17:3. So he carried me away in the spirit into the wilderness: and I saw a woman sit upon a scarlet coloured beast, full of names of blasphemy, having seven heads and ten horns.

17:4. And the woman was arrayed in purple and scarlet colour, and decked with gold and precious stones and pearls, having a golden cup in her hand full of abominations and filthiness of her fornication.

17:6. And I saw the woman drunken with the blood of the saints, and with the blood of the martyrs of Jesus: and when I saw her, I wondered with great admiration.

They illustrate just how easily 'history' is manufactured, distorted and recycled. In the annals of ancient Greek women such misogyny was not uncommon, starting as we have seen with Hesiod in the eighth century BC.

The Etruscans had a reputation amongst the Greeks for depravity – so much so that the adjective 'Etruscan' became synonymous with harlotry in Roman times. Historians Theopompus of Chios (*c.* 380–*c.* 315 BC) and Timaeus (*c.* 345–*c.* 250 BC) can take much of the credit for this. First Timaeus:

Among the Etruscans who had become extravagantly luxurious, it is usual for the slave girls to wait on the men naked.

Then Theopompus, in whom it is difficult not to detect a whiff of envy:

Wife swapping is an established Etruscan custom. Etruscan women take particular care of their bodies and exercise often, sometimes along with the men, and sometimes by themselves. They are not ashamed to be seen naked. They do not share their beds with their husbands but with other men who just happen to be present, and they propose toasts to anyone they choose. They are expert drinkers and very attractive.

The Etruscans raise all the children that are born, without necessarily knowing who their fathers are. The children live like their parents, often attending drinking parties and having sex with all the women. It is no disgrace for them to do anything in the open, or to be seen having it done to them, to them it is a native custom. To them there is no disgrace – when someone asks to see the master of the house, and he is making love – in saying that he is 'doing so-and-so', calling the indecent action by its name.

When they have sex, either with prostitutes or with members of their family, this is what happens: after they have stopped drinking and are about to go to bed, while the lamps are still lit, servants bring in courtesans, or boys, or sometimes even their wives. And when they have enjoyed these they bring in boys, and make love to them. They sometimes make love and copulate while people are watching them, but most often they put screens woven of sticks around the beds, and throw cloths on top of them.

While they are keen on making love to women, they particularly enjoy boys and youths. The youths in Etruria are very good-looking, because they live in luxury and keep their bodies smooth. In fact all the barbarians in the West use pitch to pull out and shave off the hair on their bodies.[40]

The claims regarding outdoor sex are attested by wall paintings in the Tomba dei Tori and Tomba della Fustigazione, which show erotic couples and groups engaged in public copulation. It has been claimed that these people are participating in fertility rites using sympathetic magic: the couples performing intercourse are doing so to promote the fertility of the fields.

The boot is firmly on the other foot with Cornelius Nepos, the Roman biographer *(c.* 110–*c.* 25 BC), who interestingly compares Greek ways with Roman:

> No doubt there will be many, Atticus, who will think this kind of writing insignificant ... but these will mostly be unacquainted with Greek literature, who think nothing right unless it complies with their own customs ... For to Cimon, eminent among the Athenians, it was considered no disgrace to marry his half-sister, as his countrymen did the same; but such a union, according to our practice, is unlawful. In Greece it is considered an honour for young men to have as many lovers as possible. In Sparta there is no widow so noble that will not go upon the stage, if the money is right ... for what Roman is ashamed to bring his wife to a feast, or whose wife does not occupy the best room in the house, and live with everyone else? But in Greece it is very different because a wife is neither admitted to a feast, except if it is with relatives, and she only sits in the innermost room of the house, the gynaeconitis, and into which nobody goes who is not closely related to her.[41]

In the first century AD, Plutarch described the promiscuous lifestyle of the Persian kings in a section of the *Moralia* which goes by the name of *Advice on Marriage*; in so doing he draws parallels with and justifies adultery within Greek marriage:

> The Persian kings ... allow their married wives to dine with them; but when they feel like indulging in more amorous pursuits and getting drunk then they send their wives away and call in their concubines and their songstresses. They are right to do because they do not think it proper to debauch their wives with the tipsy frolics and dissolute extravagances of their intemperance. If then the man in the street here, swayed by the unruly motions of his incontinency, happens at any time to pay a call on an obliging mistress or his wife's slavegirl, the wife will not be irritated but will understand that it was his respect for her which made him not want her to suffer the follies of ebriety and foul intemperance. [42]

Plutarch's *Bravery of Women* is a catalogue of twenty-eight geographically organised groups of women, and individual examples from all around Greece. The following gives a taste of the catalogue and of the light it sheds on local culture and societies:

> It was a custom for the maidens of Ceos to go in a group to the public shrines and spend the day together while their suitors watched their sports and dances. In the evening they went by turns to each one's home and waited upon one another's parents and brothers, even washing their feet. Very often more than one youth would be in love with one maid, but their love was so orderly and so controlled by custom, that when the girl became engaged to one, the others ceased their attentions at once. The result of this orderly behaviour for the women was that no one could remember a case of adultery or seduction in that country for the space of seven hundred years.[43]

A less happy story is told of Micca from Elis:

> Philodemus ... had a beautiful daughter named Micca; one of the officers of the despot's mercenaries named Lucius ... took it on himself to make Micca his mistress and sent for her. Her parents, seeing the need, advised her to go, but the girl, being noble and high-minded, begged her father, embracing and beseeching him, that he would rather bear to see her dead than robbed of her virginity in such a shameful and lawless way. There was some delay, and Lucius himself, full of lust and drunk found Micca with her head on her father's knees; he ordered her to follow him. But, when she refused he tore off her clothes and whipped her naked body, while she bravely bore the painful lashes in silence ... but the barbarian, utterly crazed by rage and drink, killed the maiden.

Such is the picture the Greek historians, mainly Herodotus, give us of the sexual behaviour of their foreign, barbarian neighbours. They are clearly at pains to establish a difference with the 'other', graphically highlighting idiosyncrasies and what were often seen as perversions and deviant practice. Vilification, particularly in relation to women, was always a useful weapon in war. The Greeks, of course, were taken as the norm. Herodotus did try and offer a balanced and impartial perspective, but there was never any doubting who did things properly. But let the historian have the last word:

> I am obliged to record the things I am told, but I am certainly not required to believe them – this remark may be taken to apply to the whole of my account.[44]

10

The Benefits of a Small Penis: Sexuality and Beauty in the Visual Arts

Greek statuary and vase painting reflect the whole gamut of Greek life and culture. The quest for ideal beauty in men and women, sexual activity and sexual behaviour are all integral parts of that panoply and provide us with a fascinating view of how the Greeks liked to see themselves and how they conducted themselves in a sexual context.

The penis

The relatively small size of the penis possessed by gods and heroes as reflected on Greek statues has exercised, obsessed even, classics and fine art scholars and visitors to museums for centuries. The customary uncircumcised, diminutive penis was a sign of nobility and cultural superiority; big penises were vulgar and outside the cultural norm, something sported by the barbarians of the world. The small penis was consonant with Greek ideals of male beauty; it was a badge of the highest culture and a paragon of civilisation. Conversely, large organs and prosthetic phalluses were an object of fun and humour; on the comic stage any actor playing the 'fool' was immediately recognised by his prodigious phallus – the sign of stupidity, more of a beast than a man. Aristophanes tells us:

> **Chorus:** My comedy's a modest girl: she doesn't play the fool by bringing on a great thick floppy red-tipped leather tool to give the kids a laugh.[1]

The Chorus is claiming that demure Aristophanes never stoops to the lavatory humour and bawdiness to which other playwrights descend.

The repellent, rapacious satyr was recognised by his ever-erect penis. The penis was never a badge of virility or manliness in ancient Greece as it was in other cultures; potency came from the intellect needed to power man's responsibility to father children, prolong the family line and the *oikos*, and sustain the *polis*. A small penis meant a shorter distance for the sperm to travel on its journey of impregnatation. Ask Zeus: he had forty-five children all fathered using a decidedly unspectacular penis. Kenneth Dover, in *Greek Homosexuality*, says that the ideal penis was 'small, thin, and covered with a long, tapered foreskin'. Aristophanes describes the most desirable masculine features: 'a gleaming chest, bright skin, broad shoulders, tiny tongue, strong buttocks, and a little prick'.[2]

A good example of the modest member can be seen on a bronze statue of a victorious athlete touching the olive wreath on his brow, fished out of the Adriatic Sea near Fano, Italy in 1964. It was intended as a thoroughly serious piece of art reflecting not just the pinnacle of Greek sculpture but also a male in perfect physical shape, and a highly successful male at that. 'Zeus of Cape Artemision' hurling his thunderbolt – the epitome of male physique – is similarly less well endowed, as is 'The Hermes from Atalante'.[3]

This indifference to what we now consider an emblem of manliness extends into Greek views regarding public nudity, particularly in athletics where the ideal male body in action was there for all to see. However, only barbarians and slaves appeared in the nude so a *kynodesme* was worn. A *kynodesme* (κυνοδέσμη, 'dog leash') was 'a thin leather thong wound around the *akroposthion* that pulled the penis upward and was tied in a bow, tied around the waist, or secured by some other means' and worn by some athletes to conceal the penis. It was tied tightly around the *akroposthion*, the part of the foreskin that extends beyond the glans. It could either be attached to a waist band to expose the scrotum, or tied to the base of the penis so that the penis appeared to curl upwards. The public exposure of the penis head was regarded by the Greeks as immodest, dishonourable and shameless, something only seen in slaves and barbarians. We first learn of it from images of athletes on pottery, and later in the fifth century BC in the fragmentary satyr play *Theoroi* by Aeschylus. The Romans called it *ligatura praeputii*.

Some believe that the *kynodesme* had a valuable incidental benefit. In Greek and Roman medicine involuntary ejaculation was disapproved of and thought to compromise men's virility; it was also believed to affect the quality of the masculine voice, something of particular importance in a culture in which oratory was a paramount skill. This form of non-surgical infibulation was used by singers to preserve the voice. Others believe that:

> Tethering the *akroposthion* with the *kynodesme* is frequently confused with preputial infibulation, which had different objectives and was achieved by surgically piercing the prepuce and using the holes so created for the insertion of a metal clasp (fibula) in order to fasten the prepuce shut.

Celsus (*fl*. AD 14–37) criticises infibulation performed on adolescents 'for the sake of the voice, or for health's sake'.[4]

Athletes were not the only *kynodesme* wearers; numerous references to it in other more general contexts would suggest that it was in common use for anyone anxious to preserve their modesty, dignity and to avoid total nudity.

The foreskin, or prepuce, was particularly important: it could be impressively long, representing more than three-quarters of the length of the penis. Indeed, these are the proportions we sometimes see on vase paintings. Probably the best known such image is the Attic red-figure vase painting, attributed to the Sosias painter, in which Achilles bandages the wounded arm of Patroclus. Patroclus' penis is there for all to see, respendent with extensive foreskin. The long foreskin is celebrated in literature too, notably in Lucian's *Lexiphanes*:

> 'Surely,' I said, 'you don't mean that notable Dion, that lusty, low-scrotumed, cuntish, and mastic-chewing youth who masturbates and gropes whenever he sees someone with a large penis [πεωδη] and a long prepuce [ποσθωνα]?'[5]

The long prepuce is just as erotic as any big penis. This is evident from the *Thesmophoriazusae* of Aristophanes, where the randy father-in-law buries his face in a garment owned and worn by the young and handsome poet Agathon. He exclaims: 'By Aphrodite, this has a pleasant smell of a prepuce [ποσθη]!'[6]

In the ancient world generally, the penis was king, and masturbation was evidence of that regality. Ancient Iraqi poetry from the third millennium BC shows that the seminal creative force of the world was Enki or, more precisely, Enki's penis. It was his penis which dug the world's first irrigation ditches, created rivers, and introduced human sexual reproduction. After he fathered the first human baby, Enki exulted: 'Now let my penis be praised!' The ancient Egyptian god Atum jubilantly announced: 'I created on my own every being. My fist became my spouse. I copulated with my hand'. Atum's penis created all life, divine and mortal, through this gesture of sacred masturbation. In ancient Egypt, the penis was so powerful that it conquered death. Osiris flaunted his virility in the Underworld as King, declaring in the *Book of the Dead*: 'I am Osiris of the stiff penis, I am mightier than the Lord Terror; I copulate and I have power over myriads.'

Ancient Greek art features abundant penis worship by men. Athletes apart, men are generally depicted naked, even soldiers. Married or virtuous women, on the other hand, are portrayed clothed, even if depicted in the same artwork as their naked husbands. Prostitutes were generally naked with naked men.

While penises in later Greek art were on the small side, early Greek art from the fifth century BC and beyond tells a very different story, with oversized phalluses and even double penises abounding. Plants were penises growing in the ground; animals sported penis features, such as horses or birds with an erect penis for a head.

The penis was highly symbolic and possessed a religious function. The cult of Dionysus had a public parade every year in which the men carried the largest phallus manageable through the cities. The ass on which Hephaestus rides displays an erection. In Aphrodite's temple on the Acropolis, the altars were decked with phalluses. Small or large, the penis was a prime symbol of fertility. Dildos – the aforementioned *olisboi* – made from leather or polished wood and lubricated with olive oil were big business with Miletus, the dildo capital of the Mediterranean in terms of its production and exports. It would seem that Greek men liked to believe that many women envied their penises. Dildos were frequently depicted on artworks showing female homosexuality and masturbation.

Sex on vases

While sex was an extremely popular topic on vases, some subjects still remained taboo. One such taboo involved the illustration of the foreskin and exposure of the glans. There are very few vases depicting an exposed glans; one of the rare examples shows an attractive youth who is erect and about to engage in irrumation. Portrayals of irrumation by attractive, young males generally show the foreskin in its unretracted position. Irrumation, because it entails thrusting of the penis and is thereby penetrative, was acceptable, in contrast to its opposite, receptive fellatio where the mouth is penetrated.

Everything else was very much fair game for the painters. Every conceivable position of copulation and other sexual activity is depicted: vaginal, anal, contact on the thighs, male on female fellatio, cunnilingus, masturbation, use of dildos, troilism, soixante-neuf, sado-masochism, orgies, bestiality and so on.

Interestingly, the erotic illustrations of the sixth century differ from those of the fifth and fourth centuries BC, reflecting shifts in social acceptability. In the earlier period, the scenes depicted, initially on black-figure and later on red-figure vases, include only vaginal and anal intercourse while there are no scenes of oral sex and orgies. Of course, orofacial sex and group sex continued apace but they were obviously not considered appropriate for public consumption via vase and other ceramic painting.

By the end of the sixth century scenes of fellatio, cunnilingus and orgies began to appear on cups, *kylikes*, probably used in the *symposia* which were more private, tolerant and discreet. Represented on one of the most famous erotic artefacts, painted by Pedeius, is shown a *hetaera* tilted on a stool, taking a man's penis in her mouth while another man enters her from behind. Cunnilingus was frowned upon, as was fellatio, since it compromised male supremacy. To compensate, the artists often depicted women kneeling in submission. The missionary position is absent: women are usually shown on their knees, bent forward or on their backs with their legs resting on the man's shoulders. Also, because the genitals would be obscured, depictions of sexual intercourse in the missionary position would do nothing to arouse the observer who routinely visited *hetaerae* and looked at risqué vase paintings in order to see something they could not get from their wives. Anal intercourse is depicted.

Beauty

The pursuit of beauty was relentless; beauty was held in high regard. Thargelia the Milesian was so beautiful and accomplished that she was married to fourteen different husbands (as seen in Hippias, fr. 14). Anutis, the wife of Bagazus and sister of Xerxes, was the most beautiful and the most licentious of all the women in Asia. Timosa, the concubine of Oxyartes, surpassed all women in beauty; Xenopitheia, the mother of Lysandrides, was the most beautiful of all the women in the Peloponnese until the Spartans killed her and her sister Chryse. Pantica of Cyprus was also renowned to be a very beautiful woman; she was with Olympias, the mother of Alexander the Great, when Monimus asked for her hand in marriage, as she was a very licentious woman, Olympias said to him, 'O you wretch, you are marrying with your eyes, and not with your brain.' Some places boasted a plethora of beautiful women: Hesiod, in the third book of his *Melampodia*, and Theophrastus both call Chalcis in Euboea 'Land of fair women'. And Nymphodorus, in his *Voyage Round Asia*, says that there are nowhere more beautiful women than those in Tenedos, an island near Troy.[7] And then there was Helen of Troy, of course.

Ancient Greece was the venue of the first beauty contests, featuring both women and men. One famous winner was Herodice; the women contestants for such a title were called 'gold-bearers' (χρυσοφόροι). Theophrastus says that there is also a very serious beauty contest for men held amongst the Eleans. The victors receive weapons as their prize. In some places, Theophrastus adds, 'there are contests between the women for modesty and good management, as there are among the barbarians ... the honour paid to modesty ought to be higher.'[8]

Cosmetics

Roman playwright Plautus once quipped, 'A woman without paint is like food without salt,' a sentiment which held true for Greek as well as Roman women, no doubt, in the opinion of many men. For women, dress was often somewhat bland and unexciting; this was offset by flashy jewellery, fetching hair styles and striking make-up. The cult of Helen of Troy was, for obvious reasons, of special significance in Sparta. Excavations at sites where her cult was practiced have produced mirrors, eyeliners, combs, and perfume bottles, all underlining the importance of cosmetics to the ancient Greek woman. The word 'cosmetic' is significant: it comes from the Greek *kosmetikos,* denoting a sense of harmony, order and tranquillity, demonstrating how important make-up was in the general order of things. Mirrors literally reflect a concern about personal appearance and ancient burials have revealed numerous examples, particularly in the graves of women. Many are highly detailed and decorated; the Greeks also developed one of the first compacts, a box mirror made from two hinged metal disks.

The application of cosmetics was part of daily ritual and routine for better-off women and whores. Applying make-up was time consuming because cosmetics needed to be applied several times a day due to the warm weather conditions and poor quality of the products. In the Roman period some of the top 'brands' were imported from China, Germany and Gaul, and were so expensive that the sumptuary *Lex Oppia* was enacted in 189 BC in an effort to limit their use. These designer brands spawned cheap imitations, just as today, that were sold to poorer women. Cosmetics were applied in private, usually in a small room closed off to men.

Perfume was crucial in the pursuit of beauty. Women who smelled nice were presumed to be healthy. Due to the pungency of many of the ingredients used in cosmetics, women often soaked themselves in generous splashes of perfume.

It was not all good news for the woman, though. Cosmetics in ancient Greece were nothing short of industrial, with products resembling the contents of a chemistry laboratory more than anything else. As today amongst Asian women, light skin was craved, so women painted their faces with toxic white lead carbonate, called *fucus* (φῦκος), a life-shortening habit, or *cerussa* (ψιμύθιον). Where lead was not available chalk was used, but it was nowhere near as effective or enduring. Lead-based facial masks were applied to remove blemishes and impurities from the skin. Many Greek women died unknowingly from lead poisoning, after long-term application of this noxious substance. Pliny did not mince his words, pointing out 'it is useful for giving women a fair complexion; but like scum of silver, it is deadly poison'. Even when the health risks were known in Roman times, women continued to use it: such are the lengths to which the women of ancient cultures would go for the sake of beauty.

Less hazardous but equally repellent 'cosmetics' were used. Pliny recommended pigeon's dung for spots and pimples on the face; likewise crocodile dung was also efficacious in removing freckles. However, Dioscorides alerts us to the fact that the crocodile dung is often cut with starling droppings as a cheap adulteration.[9] Bull dung was recommended for a rosy glow to the cheeks. Galen and Dioscorides agreed with him on crocodile dung; Sextus Placitus (*fl.* AD 370) on the bull dung. Women smeared on creams made from honey mixed with olive oil added to make it shine to get a smooth foundation and moisturiser. Minoan women are said to have bathed in honey and milk. Cheeks were rouged with red-coloured pastes, *anchousa* (ἄγχουσα), obtained from the root of a plant; lipsticks were concocted with a dangerous combination of red iron oxide and ochre clays, or otherwise olive oil with beeswax; paints were used to produce the same pigment, *paideros* (παιδέρως), a vegetable dye, *sukaminon* (συκάμινον) and *fucus* (φῦκος). Pliny the Elder wrote that eyelashes fell out from indulging in too much sex – something of a trap for women who accordingly now found it especially important to keep their eyelashes long to demonstrate their chastity. Green eyeshadow came from poisonous malachite, while blue came from copper-based azurite, kuanos (χυανός: deep blue, the root of English cyan). Some men associated the application of make-up with witchcraft.

Xenophon's Ischomachus is known to us as the man looking for an 'airhead' of a woman whom he could mould and train as a wife according to his whim; he describes to Socrates how his wife is what today we might call 'tarted up':

> Ischomachus then said, 'One time, Socrates, I saw that my wife had clarted her face with white lead, so that she would seem to have a paler complexion than she really had, and put on thick rouge, so that her cheeks would seem redder than they really were, and high boots, so that she would seem taller than she actually was'.

Ischomachus is not too concerned about the embarrassing impression his wife may be giving, done up in such a way. On the contrary, he sees this as an opportunity to expound philosophically to his wife the difference between true beauty and the impression of beauty. Her painted appearance was presumably quite usual and normal, telling us perhaps how young Greek women routinely made-up and dressed to enhance their attractiveness.

Eubulus in 350 BC paints a sorry picture of the slap streaming down a *hetaera*'s face:

> By Zeus, we are not painted with vermilion, nor with dark mulberry juice, as you are often: and then, if you go out in the summer two streams of dark, discolored hue flow from your eyes, and sweat drops from your jaws and makes a scarlet furrow down your neck, and the light hair which straggles over your face seems gray, so thickly is it plastered on.

From Lysias' speech on the murder of Eratosthenes we learn that the errant wife made herself up before visiting her lover, a fact which did not go unnoticed by her husband. Apparently, red wine, beetroot and mastic, an aromatic resin, did the trick. Olive oil mixed with ground charcoal produced eyeshadow. The eyebrows and eyelids were stained black with kohl (στίμμι), stimmy – toxic antimony trisulfide, used more recently in safety matches ammunition, explosives and fireworks – or *asbolos* (ἄσβολος), made from soot. Dark powders were used to make the fashionable unibrow where the eyebrows are cosmetically joined up. The versatile and ubiquitous olive oil was also used as a moisturiser and a skin cleanser.

Depilation was done by epilation (plucking) and singeing to achieve glabrous, hair-free skin. In ancient Greece the removal of body and pubic hair was probably practiced by both men and women; it can be seen in red-figure pottery on which both men and women are depicted devoid of body or pubic hair.

Natural hair was held to be sacred: Greeks would often hang the hair of the dead on their doors before the burial, and mourners would cut their own hair to place on the corpse. Thicker hair was achieved by applying the urine of a young ass.

Oral hygiene was of a low standard, to say the least. White teeth were the hope for many Romans, and we can assume Greeks too, so false dentures, made from bone, ivory and paste, were popular. Ovid perceptively said: 'You can do yourself untold damage when you laugh if your teeth are black, too long or crooked.

Men too, especially in the elite classes, were concerned about their appearance. From about 400 BC, fashionable Greek men were going out and having their beards groomed, trimmed and oiled regularly. Clean-shaven faces became popular around 323 BC when Alexander the Great commanded that his soldiers shave their beards to stop their enemies grabbing them in close combat. The primitive razor was often a block of iron with one sharpened edge.

Women's underwear is mentioned in the *Odyssey* and the *Iliad* as well as by Herodotus, Aristophanes, and Lucian in the second century AD. Women wore a band of linen, the *zone,* around the waist and abdomen to give them shape and support. The *apodesmos* was a band, breast band, or girdle, and the *mastodeton* or *mastodesmos* was a breast band which flattened the breasts.

11

Sex in Greek Religion and in Philosophy

It is quite reasonable that men who are cowards or criminals
should be born again as women.

Plato, *Timeaus* 90e

Religion and Sex

In ancient Greece sex and religion were closely connected in a
number of ways. In antiquity men sometimes made a sacred pledge
by putting their hands on their testicles, as if to say, 'If I am lying
you can cut off my balls.' The practice of making a pledge on the
Bible is said to come from this dangerous gesture: men had to
squeeze their testicles while vowing to tell the truth, hence the Latin
word for witness is *testis* although *testis* probably comes from the
Greek for the number three τρία (m: τρεις, f: τρεις, n: τρία) – a
witness being a third observer of events.

Herodotus describes how, in some places, a woman is required
to spend the night alone in a temple. When describing the shrine at
Babylonian Is we learn that

no image has been set up in the shrine, nor does anyone sleep
there for the night, except one native woman, chosen from all
women by the god, as the Chaldaeans say, who are priests of this
god. These same Chaldaeans say (though I do not believe them)
that the god himself is accustomed to visit the shrine and rest on
the couch, as in Thebes of Egypt, as the Egyptians say (for there
too a woman sleeps in the temple of Theban Zeus, and neither the
Egyptian nor the Babylonian woman, it is said, has any recourse
with men), and as does the prophetess of the god at Patara in
Lycia, whenever she is appointed; for there is not always a place

of divination there; but when she is appointed she is shut up in the temple during the night.[1]

The cults of Demeter and Persephone championed female fecundity and world fertility with women taking a leading part in the festivals, the Thesmophoria, the Stenia and the Haloa. These and the Eleusinian Mysteries were noted for *aischrologia*, obscene jokes and insults traded between the women, along with the display of phalluses and female genitalia. Such sexual banter was a rare opportunity for women to project a voice in public and to bond with other women – phenomena which were thought to foster fertility. What the women actually said at these meetings was a secret then as it is now; their utterances were called *arrehta*, 'the unspeakable', violating social norms. A scholion of Lucian describes the 'male shapes' at the Thesmophoria, the phalluses:

> Here also are carried up unmentionable holy objects (ἄρρητα ἱερά) made from bread dough, representations of serpents and of male shapes (ἀνδρείων σχημάτων).[2]

He adds that the women can say whatever they want with total impunity – joking and mocking; shameful, *aiskhista,* and irreverent, *asemna.* Confrontational priestesses sidle up to them and plant thoughts of adultery in their minds. At the Stenia there was similar blaspheming and scoffing where again the abuse was exchanged just between women. At the festival of Demeter Mysia, men and male dogs were banned on the first night, but when men were admitted on the second night the ritual abuse took place between men and women.[3] The origin of the obscenities lies in the myth of Iambe, who was able to cheer up the disconsolate Demeter with what was presumably a risqué joke:

> Until assiduous Iambe ... moved the holy lady with many a quip and jest to smile and laugh and cheer her heart.[4]

An alternative version has Iambe, or Baubo as she is sometimes also known, exposing her genitals to Demeter and making her laugh that way. The sight of the human reproductive organs will have been welcome to the goddess of fertility:

> She lifted up her gown, and showed all those parts of her body which it is improper to name, and Baubo exposed her breasts; then the goddess laughed and laughed in her mind.[5]

Temple prostitution

Temple prostitution seems to have been rife in some places. Strabo, writing in his *Geographia*, written about AD 20, recorded:

> The temple of Aphrodite [at Corinth] was so rich that it owned more than a thousand temple slaves – prostitutes – whom both free men and women had dedicated to the goddess. And therefore it was also on account of these temple-prostitutes that the city was crowded with people and grew rich; for instance, the ship captains freely squandered their money, and hence the proverb, 'Not for every man is the voyage to Corinth.' [6]

He then tells the story of a lazy Corinthian prostitute who, when rebuked, tartly replies that she had already 'taken down three looms that day already'. The word for loom she used, *histos*, can mean anything that can be erected – all the more shocking because the whore appropriates the language of weaving and wool working – badges of virtue and of being an exemplary wife in Greece and Rome.

There may have been temple prostitutes in Egyptian Thebes. Strabo continues:

> For Zeus [Amon] who is held in the highest honour, they dedicate a very beautiful maiden of most illustrious family [such maidens are called 'pallades' (virgin-priestesses) or 'pallacide' (harlots) by the Greeks]; and she prostitutes herself, and has sex with whatever men she wishes until the natural cleansing of her body takes place [*synestin*, through menstruation]; after this she is married off to a man; but before she is married, after the time of her prostitution, a rite of mourning is celebrated for her ... before resuming normal, married life.[7]

If we are to believe Homer, the meeting between a Greek man and a temple prostitute could begin with a beating because she might not consent readily to the expected fellatio. In the first century BC, Diodorus Siculus described tombs of what he thought to be 'concubines of Zeus' (*ta pallakidas tou Dios*) saying they were approximately one mile from the monument of King Osymandyas – Rameses II – at Ramesseum.[8] They perhaps have their origins in the 'divine consort' (*hemet neter; hemet* means womb) of the 18th Dynasty; the most famous was Queen Hatshepsut (*c.* 1479–1458 BC) who was married to Amun and at the same time was the favourite wife of King Thutmose II. She also went by the name 'hand of the god' (*djedet neter*) and 'divine votaress' (*duat-neter*) with a role connected to the fertility of the god Amun-Min, implying that as 'the hand of god' Hatshepsut was quite literally acting as his masturbator.

Athenaeus tells us about other sacred connections to prostitution:

> I know, too, that there is a festival called the Hetaerideia, which is celebrated in Magnesia, not owing to the courtesans, but to another cause, which is mentioned by Hegesander in his Commentaries, who writes thus: 'The Magnesians celebrate a festival called Hetaerideia; and they give this account of it: that originally Jason, the son of Aeson, when he had collected the Argonauts, sacrificed to Zeus Hetaereius, and called the festival Hetaerideia. And the Macedonian kings also celebrated the Hetaerideia.'
>
> There is also a temple of Aphrodite the Prostitute (πόρνη) at Abydus, as Pamphilus asserts: 'For when all the city was oppressed by slavery, the guards in the city, after a sacrifice on one occasion (as Cleanthus relates in his essays on Fables), having got intoxicated, took several courtesans; and one of these women, when she saw that the men were all fast asleep, taking the keys, got over the wall, and brought the news to the citizens of Abydus. And they, on this, immediately came in arms, and slew the guards, and took possession of the walls, and recovered their freedom; and to show their gratitude to the prostitute, they built a temple to Aphrodite the Prostitute.'[9]

And:

> It is an ancient custom at Corinth (as Chamaeleon of Heracleia relates, in his treatise on Pindarus), whenever the city addresses any supplication to Aphrodite about any important matter, to employ as many courtesans as possible to join in the supplication; and they, too, pray to the goddess, and afterwards they are present at the sacrifices. And when the king of Persia was leading his army against Greece (as Theopompus also relates, and so does Timaeus, in his seventh book), the Corinthian courtesans offered prayers for the safety of Greece, going to the temple of Aphrodite. On which account, after the Corinthians had consecrated a picture to the goddess (which remains even to this day), and as in this picture they had painted the portraits of the courtesans who made this supplication at the time, and who were present afterwards.[10]

Cottina, evidently, was quite influential and affluent:

> But at Lacedaemon (as Polemon Periegetes says, in his treatise on the Offerings at Lacedaemon), there is a statue of a very celebrated courtesan, named Cottina, who, he tells us, consecrated a brazen cow; and Polemon's words are these: 'And the statue of Cottina the courtesan, on account of whose celebrity there is still a brothel which is called by her name, near the hill on which the temple of Dionysus stands, is a conspicuous object, well known to many of the citizens. And her votive offering is beyond the statue of Athene Chalcioecus – a brazen cow, and also the before-mentioned image.'[11]

Philosophy

Greek philosophers could be lukewarm when it came to expatiating on the subject of sex. Democritus *(c.* 460–*c.* 370 BC) believed that people derive as much pleasure from a good scratch as they do from having sex (Fragment 127). Empedocles *(c.* 495–430 BC), on the other hand, believed that love was one of the elemental aspects of life. With strife it was an essential catalyst of change; love *(philotes)* brought things together, strife repelled. Aristophanes parodied this in the *Birds* when the birds claimed Eros as one of their own:

> In the beginning there was only Chaos, Night, dark Erebus, and deep Tartarus. Earth, the air and heaven did not exist. Firstly, blackwinged Night laid a germless egg in the bosom of the infinite deeps of Erebus, and from this, after an eternity, sprang the graceful Eros with his glittering golden wings, swift as the whirlwinds of the tempest. He mated in deep Tartarus with dark Chaos, winged like himself, and thus hatched forth our race, which was the first to see the light. The gods did not exist until Eros had brought together all the ingredients of the world, and from their marriage Heaven, Ocean, Earth and the immortal race of blessed gods sprang into being. Thus our origin is very much older than that of the dwellers in Olympus. We are the offspring of Eros; there are a thousand proofs to show it. We have wings and we lend assistance to lovers. How many handsome youths, who had sworn to remain insensible, have opened their thighs because of our power and have yielded themselves to their lovers when almost at the end of their youth, being led away by the gift of a quail, a waterfowl, a goose, or a cockerel?

Aesara of Lucania was a Pythagorean philosopher and author of *On Human Nature*. Aesara taught that it is by the study of human nature and the human soul that we can understand the philosophical basis for natural law and morality: 'Human nature seems to me to provide a standard of law and justice both for the home and for the city.' She divides the soul into three parts: the mind which delivers judgement and thought, the spirit which contains courage and strength, and desire which provides love and geniality.

In Plato's *Symposium* we witness a sophisticated party game in which the symposiasts take it in turn to praise Eros. For Pausanias there are two Aphrodites, one representing earthly, heterosexual love, the other divine pederastic love, devoid of physical contact:

> The dual nature of Eros follows from the dual nature of Aphrodite: as there is an Aphrodite Urania and an Aphrodite Pandemos, so there is Eros Uranios and Eros Pandemos ... it follows that Eros is bad or good according to the kind of love-making which it prompts. The general characteristics of Eros Pandemos are that it is directed to women as well as boys, to the body rather than the soul, to unscrupulous satisfaction of lust; whereas Eros Uranios shuns females and seeks only such males as are noble and nearly mature both in mind and body. It is the followers of Eros Pandemos who have brought paederastia into disrepute.[13]

Some philosophers believed that sex for pleasure was unnatural, promoting instead the virtues of moderation, *sophrosune*, and self-control, *enkrateia*. In the *Laws*, Plato has one speaker declare that all sex should lead to procreation within heterosexual marriage.

Aristotle exhibited a deep insight into the nature of love:

> Those in love always get pleasure from talking, writing, or composing verses about the one they love; for they believe that in doing so they bring the object of their affection into sight. Love always begins this way: men are happy not only in the presence of the beloved, but also in his absence when they remember him. This is why, even when his absence is painful, there is some pleasure even in mourning and grief; for the pain is due to his absence, but there is pleasure in remembering and, as it were, seeing him and recalling his actions and personality.[14]

Despite some very restrictive thoughts chaining a wife to her husband and to their household, as outlined in the *Oikonomicus* from around 330 BC, Aristotle does not allow the husband to get off easily; he too has responsibilities to his wife and to their marriage and children. Fidelity is key; he must lead by example:

> Now a virtuous wife is best honoured when she sees that her husband is faithful to her, and has no preference for another woman; but before all others loves and trusts her and holds her as his own. And so much the more will the woman seek to be what he accounts her. If she perceives that her husband's affection for her is faithful and righteous, she too will be faithful and righteous towards him.

Aristotle wondered what all the fuss was regarding sex and asked:

> Why are people ashamed to admit that they want to have sexual intercourse, whereas this is not the case with drinking or eating or other such things? Is it because most of our desires are for things we must have, some of them actually being essential for life, whereas sexual desire is a non-vital indulgence?

Epicurus said that 'sexual intercourse has never done anyone any good, and we should be happy if it does us no actual harm'. He seems to have forgotten that he took a mistress, Leontion, who continued to enjoy sex when she joined the Garden community.[15] Zeno and the Stoics were with Plato on the benefits of pederasty (Athenaeus 363e). Stoic Chrysippus describes a painting of Hera giving Zeus fellatio as the reception of the seeds or order by the unformed matter of the universe.

Plutarch wrote seventy-eight treatises on all manner of Greek and Roman life, the *Moralia* (or Ἠθικά) *Ethika*; they include *Advice to Bride and Groom* (Γαμικὰ παραγγέλματα – *Coniugalia praecepta*); *Virtues of Women* (Γυναικῶν ἀρεταί – *Mulierum virtutes*); *Consolation to his Wife* (Παραμυθητικὸς πρὸς τὴν γυναῖκα – *Consolatio ad uxorem*); *Dialogue on Love* (Ἐρωτικός – *Amatorius*); and *Love Stories* (Ἐρωτικαὶ διηγήσεις – *Amatoriae narrationes*). An example, from the *Advice to Groom and Bride*:

> Men who do not like to see their wives eat in their company are thus teaching them to stuff themselves when alone. So those who are not happy in the company of their wives, nor join with them in fun and laughter, are thus teaching them to seek their own pleasures apart from their husbands.[16]

12

In Bed with a Witch: Erotic Magic

We have already mentioned that it was common practice in ancient Greece and Rome to vilify 'difficult' women by making insinuations regarding their chastity and sexual conduct. The same could be said about sorcery and witchcraft: if a woman needed to be denigrated or discredited then an effective means of doing this was to suggest that she dabbled in the dark arts. Drugs, magic, poison and potions were the armamentarium of the sorceress or witch, as described to us by the fifth-century-BC orator Antiphon in his *Against the Stepmother for Poisoning*.[1] Love, prostitution, abuse and intrigue were all involved and often inextricably tied up with witchcraft, or the suggestion of witchcraft.

Witches and witchcraft are not just about spells, potions, drawing down the moon and shape-shifting. There is often a sexual dimension to witches and their sisters, the bogeywomen, and nowhere is that truer than in the witches and bogeywomen of ancient Greece. Witches were a fact of life, in literature and in the real world. They were a manifestation of the ubiquitous superstition which pervaded ancient Greek culture.

Circe
The first Greek witch we meet is sexy Circe in the *Odyssey*, a witchy kind of a woman. Her sensuality is evident from the start to Odysseus and his men:

> And now they could hear Circe within, singing with her beautiful voice as she moved to and fro at the wide web that was more than earthly-delicate, gleaming, delectable, as a goddess' handiwork needs must be – a goddess or a woman, moving to and fro at her

wide web and singing a lovely song that the whole floor re-echoes with.

Circe was, on the face of it, hospitable. She put on a meal, but the food was drugged and changed the crew into pigs (and later back again) – the idea being to keep a ready supply of men to satisfy her voracious sexual appetite. Odysseus had taken precautions in the shape of a *molu*, an antidote with mystical properties, and escapes the transmogrification. Mercury, the provider, made it clear, though, that sex with Circe is inevitable:

> When Circe strikes you with the long wand she carries, draw the keen sword from your side, rush upon her and make as if to kill her. She will shrink back, and then ask you to sleep with her. At this you must let her have her way; she is a goddess; accept her bed, so that she may release your comrades and make you her cherished guest.

Odysseus duly succumbs to Circe's physical charms and the two begin a divinely approved, year-long torrid affair in Circe's 'sumptuous bed'.

Odysseus was not the only lover to be ensnared by Circe. Parthenius, a Greek mythographer from the first century BC, tells us how luckless Calchos fell under her uncompromising spell, literally and metaphorically, in his *Love Romances*. Circe is preparing to put an end to Calchos' stalking her:

> Calchos the Daunian [in southern Italy] was greatly in love with Circe. He handed over to her his kingship over the Daunians, and employed all possible blandishments to gain her love; but she had a passion for Odysseus, who was then with her, and loathed Calchos and forbade him to land on her island. However, he persisted and could talk of nothing else but Circe, and she, very angry with him, laid a trap and had no sooner invited him into her palace but she set before him a table covered with all manner of food. But the meats were full of magical drugs, and as soon as Calchos had eaten them, he went mad, and she drove him into the pig-sties. After some time, however, the Daunian army landed on the island looking for Calcos; she then released him from the spell but not before binding him by oath that he would never set foot on the island again, either to woo her or for any other reason.[2]

Ovid tells the tragic story of Circe's passion for Picus and the mystical lengths to which she goes to possess him in a myth which would have circulated in ancient Greek days. One day Picus was out boar hunting; Circe was nearby collecting strange herbs when she saw Picus and was smitten. She dropped the herbs and 'like blazing fire a thrill of ecstasy raced through her veins'. Because he rode so fast, Circe could not reach him, and cried, 'You won't get away,' calling on the powers vested in her herbs and spells. She conjured up an image of a boar which Picus pursued, thinking it a real boar. Then Circe prayed aloud. 'Oh, by your eyes, those eyes of yours,' she said, 'that captured mine, and by your beauty, loveliest of kings, that makes me here, a goddess, kneel to you, favour my passion ... and harden not your heart to Circe Titanis' love.' Picus, however, was unimpressed and declared his love for Canens, in response to which Circe repeatedly screamed: 'You'll pay for this, never again will Canens have you; now you will find out just what a wronged woman is capable of.' Picus fled but Circe turned him into a woodpecker, leaving nothing but his name, which is now the Latin for woodpecker.[3]

Ovid's Picus added uncontrollable jealousy to the witch's list of characteristics which already included desirable sexual attraction and deception. The metamorphoses she inflicted on men were interpreted as male emasculation by a vengeful woman.

Elsewhere, Circe purifies Jason and Medea after their murder of Apsyrtus and helps them to lay his ghost. When the Argonauts meet with Circe she is seductively washing her hair surrounded by congenitally malformed monsters:

> Here they found Circe bathing her head in the salt water. She had been terrified by a nightmare in which she saw all the rooms and walls of her house streaming with blood, and fire devouring all the magic drugs with which she used to bewitch her visitors. But she managed to put out the red flames with the blood of a murdered man, gathering it up in her hands; and so the horror passed. When morning came she rose from bed, and now she was washing her hair and clothes in the sea. A number of creatures whose ill-assorted limbs declared them to be neither man nor beast had gathered round her like a great flock of sheep following their shepherd from the fold ... The Argonauts were dumbfounded by the scene.[4]

Circe was responsible for turning Scylla into a monster when jealous of a rival. She poured the juice of poisonous herbs into the sea where Scylla used to bathe, changing her into the repellent monster we know.

Homer's Spartan Helen of Troy also exercised some magical skills when she concocted an aphrodisiac from a blood-dripping stone to keep Paris on the boil after their adulterous elopement to Troy.

Medea

For many, Medea is the archetypal witch; love, sex and passion are never far away. In the fifth century BC an obscure writer called Phercydes of Athens tells how Medea murdered her brother, Apsyrtus, to help the Argonauts against the Colchians, a version supported by Sophocles and Apollonius of Rhodes, although with Phrercydes it is Jason who deals the fatal blow. Pindar includes Medea in a scene in which Aphrodite, paradoxically, uses magic to help Jason win Medea's heart. Sophocles describes Medea in the *Rhizotomoi* as she harvests her roots naked, her hair in disarray.

It is the Apollonius Rhodius version which best illustrates Medea's superlative skills as a sorceress, a witch and a case study in what can go badly wrong when such a woman is scorned. Medea first got involved with Jason when he arrived at Colchis to claim his inheritance and throne by retrieving the golden fleece. Medea fell hopelessly in love with him and promised to help him on the condition that, if he was successful, he would take her away with him and marry her. Jason agreed. Medea's father, Aëtes, had his conditions too and promised to give Jason the fleece on completion of some very challenging tasks which Medea duly assisted him with. All went well, Jason took the fleece and sailed off with Medea, as promised.

Jason celebrated in Crete with the Golden Fleece; when the couple fled to Corinth Jason soon abandoned Medea for the king's daughter, Glauce. Horrified and distraught at this betrayal, Medea exacted her revenge when she sent Glauce a dress and golden coronet smeared with poison, killing both the princess and the king, Creon. Medea did not stop there but continued by butchering two of her own sons, Tisander and Alcimenes. It is probably this act – just one of many heinous deeds – that earns Medea the reputation as one of literature's most repugnant and reprehensible mothers. She had already unequivocally declared her hatred for her children early on in the Euripidean play that bears her name:

You accursed sons of a mother who know nothing but hate, damn you, your father and your whole house.[5]

Xanthus of Lydia (*fl.* 450 BC) mentions the reputation magicians, *mages,* had for incest, claiming that they had sex with their mothers, sisters and daughters, a charge later echoed by the Roman poet Catullus. Xanthus also reveals that female *mages* were shared by a number of husbands. Xenophon mentions incantations in the *Memorabilia* where he refers to love potions *(philtra).* He implies that the seductive song of the Sirens is a form of erotic magic which lured sailors to their doom; the unsuccessful efforts to divert Odysseus and his crew is, of course, the most famous example of the Sirens at work. Theocritus describes Simaetha's erotic magic and magical dolls; Simaetha's use of erotic magic is notable.

Diodorus tells the story of how Deianeira inadvertently killed her husband, Hercules, by means of a *philtron,* a love potion. Nessus, a centaur, had tried to rape Deianeira, but before he could do so he was killed with an arrow shot by Heracles. In his dying moments, Nessus gave Deianeira a 'love potion' which he vouched would keep Heracles faithful to her. When Deianeira smeared the *philtron* on Heracles' tunic it soon became apparent that the potion was poisonous. Heracles died in agony: blood, semen and olive oil turned out to be a lethal concoction for Hercules.

In the Roman era, the writer (and priest) Plutarch deals with superstition in his *On Deisidaemonia.* In the *Moralia* he explains the futility and dangers of *philtra* and other sorceries as administered by wives on their husbands. The ghost of Philinnion makes an appearance in the *Mirabilia* by Phlegon of Tralles. She visits Machates, the lodger in her parents' house, in the night, to have sex with him. Philinnion is annoyed that her parents seem to begrudge her this physical pleasure and inflicts on them more grief before she dies again. The grieving Machates commits suicide.[6]

Pasiphae, sister of Circe, was an active sorceress – that is when she was not having sex with a bull. She was a goddess that no promiscuous man would want to encounter: the fidelity charm she inflicted on Minos caused him to ejaculate serpents, scorpions, and centipedes from his penis, with the inevitable result that the poor concubine on the receiving end died a terrible death. How eye-wateringly painful this was for Minos as well is not recorded.

Other practitioners of the dark arts include Andromache, who, when she was forced into being Neoptomelus's concubine, gave potions to pregnant Hermione, Neoptomelus's wife, causing her to miscarry; the well-meaning, if bossy, nurse in Euripides' *Hippolytus,* who slyly recommends a love potion to a love-stricken Phaedra yearning for her stepson, Hippolytus; Simaetha, who chants an incantation ten times to draw the man she loves to her house; and Diotima, a philosopher and priestess who played a crucial role in developing the notion of Platonic love in the *Symposium*.

Herodotus leaves us an account of Melissa's *nekuomanteion* – an oracle in which the dead prophesy – and, as noted above, Periander's necrophilia.

Bogeywomen

Affiliated to witches and just as scarily malevolent was the bogeywoman – a sort of witch-lite. In ancient Greece she took the shape of Mormo, a monstrous donkey with the legs of a woman, either queen of the Lystraegones bereft of her own children and now vengefully murdering the children of others, or a child-eating Corinthian. Another was Empusa who appeared either as a cow, donkey or beautiful woman; yet another was Gello, a malevolent female spirit and child snatcher. Diodorus Siculus described Empusa as a beautiful, cannibalistic child-eater.[7]

Erotic Magic

Ancient Greek women could set themselves up as amateur witches, practicing a do-it-yourself form of witchcraft in the form of binding spells and curses, and in the deployment of voodoo dolls. These spells were usually perpetrated as acts of malicious, perverted revenge and spite and were sparked typically by thwarted love, failed lawsuits or commercial disputes. As well as often being on the receiving end of them, women handed them out as well with alacrity.

The popularity and ubiquity of this evil and sinister form of ancient hate mail is illustrated by the fact that 1,600 or so curse tablets alone – *defixiones* or *katadesies*, curse tablets or binding spells – have been found. *Katadesies* reach back as far as the fourth century BC in Greece. Fittingly, they traditionally were consecrated to the gods of the underworld. Mainly a practice of the lower classes, they gave vent to the curser's vengeful anger, malice and vindictiveness. Around one quarter of the tablets show erotic magic, deployed to wreak bitter revenge on duplicitous lovers, or to bind an object of desire to love and sex with the dedicator for the rest of his or her days. Here are some examples of women as both targets and as the curser; typical is the *defixio* which rains down every kind of disaster on the recipient, made all the more exotic with the addition of the usual inexplicable mumbo jumbo:

May burning fever seize all her limbs, kill her soul and her heart;
O gods of the underworld, break and smash her bones, choke

her, *arourarelyoth*, let her body be twisted and shattered, *phrix, phrox*.[8]

Curses were not exclusively heterosexual affairs. One from the second century AD describes a 'lesbian' curse where Heraias brings and binds the heart and soul of Sarapias. In another, Sophia attempts to inflame the heart, liver and spirit of Gorgonia through a corpse demon in an Egyptian curse.[9] This is edited down from sixty-six lines of torrid text:

> By means of the corpse-demon inflame the heart, the liver, the spirit of Gorgonia, whom Nilogenia bore, with love and affection for Sophia, whom Isara bore. Constrain Gorgonia to cast herself into the bath-house for the sake of Sophia; and you, become a bath-room. Burn, set on fire, inflame her soul, heart, liver, spirit with love for Sophia.

When a man named Apalo desired to attract a woman named Karosa for sex, this is what he cursed:

> Attract, inflame, destroy, burn, cause her to swoon from love as she is being burnt, inflamed. Goad the tortured soul, the heart of Karosa, whom Thelo bore, until she leaps forth and comes to Apalo ... do not allow Karosa, whom Thelo bore, to think of her husband, her child, drink, food, but let her come melting for passion and love and sex.

Tomb raiding was obviously taken very seriously. This stark warning was found at Agios Tychon, Cyprus: 'Anyone who does anything bad to my tomb, then the crocodile, hippopotamus, and lion will eat him.' But his was nothing compared with:

> I will seize his neck like that of a goose. His face will be spat at. A donkey will rape him, a donkey will rape his wife. He will be cooked together with the condemned.

One tablet addressed to a ghost reads:

> Seize Euphemia and lead her to me Theon, loving me with mad desire, and bind her with unloosable shackles, strong ones of adamantine, for the love of me, Theon, and do not allow her to eat, drink, obtain sleep, jest or laugh but make her leap out and leave behind her father, mother, brothers, sisters, until she comes

to me. Burn her limbs, live, female body, until she comes to me, and not disobeying me.

Physical violence was not always on the agenda. There are some examples of love *defixiones* where a lover will invoke underworld deities in a heartfelt bid to win the love of his life. We have already met Successus who dedicates his wife in a bid to see his love for her requited.

More typical, though, is the depravity evident in the sexually perverted, excessively malevolent curses projected at women:

I bind you, Theodotis, daughter of Eus, to the snake's tail, the crocodile's mouth, the ram's horns, the asp's poison, the cat's whiskers, the god's appendage, so that you may never be able to have sex with another man, not be shagged or be buggered or give a blow job, nor do anything that brings you pleasure with another man, unless I alone, Ammonion, the son of Hermitaris, am that man ... Make this erotic binding-spell work, so that Theodotis may no longer be penetrated by a man other than me alone, Ammonion, the son of Hermitaris, dragged in slavery, driven crazy, taking to the air in search of Ammonion, the son of Hermitaris, and that she may rub her thigh on my thigh, her genitals to my genitals, for sex with me for the rest of her life.[10]

For good measure this obsessive curse is complemented with a series of pictures which depict a god with a sceptre, a snake, a crocodile, a couple kissing, and a penis penetrating a vagina.

The wife of Aristocydes curses him and his lovers, cursing that he will never marry another woman ... nor a boy for that matter.

What these curses uniquely reveal are the inner secrets of the sex and social lives of women – both as the victims of perverted, paranoid lovers and insecure stalkers, and as the dispensers themselves of malicious and evil intent driven by wild jealousy and bitterness.

Voodoo dolls

Voodoo dolls were another popular yet deviant way of cursing the people the Greeks loved to hate; thirty-eight have been found. The dolls are accompanied by some sinister instructions, usually to inscribe magical words on a woman's head and other parts of her body, including the genitals; to stick a needle into her brain, and twelve others into other organs; to tie a binding spell written on a lead plate to the figures, dedicate it to the gods of the underworld and leave it at sunset near to the tomb of someone who has died violently or prematurely; to invite them to rise from the dead and bring X [the object of the charm], daughter of Y, to him and make her love him. There then follows a litany of evil instructions to deprive the girl of food and drink, sexual intercourse, sleep and health, all designed to make her have sex with the curser in perpetuity. Dehumanisation, subjugation, ritual abuse – physical, psychological and sexual – were the order of the day. 'Love' is very strange.

Osthanes had just the thing for any man looking to wreck a woman's sex life:

> If the genitals of a woman are smeared with the blood of a tick from a wild black bull, she will find sex repellant, [as Osthanes says] and love too, if she drinks the urine of the billy-goat, with spikenard [an aromatic plant] mixed in to disguise the disgusting taste.

There is more genital smearing with a lotion that, as far as fourth-century-AD Akarnachthas is concerned, has everything going for it: a guarantee of everlasting love and exclusive sex. The spell was excavated in Egypt; the very specific recipe comprises a crow's egg, the juice of a crowsfoot plant, and the bile of an electric catfish fished from the Nile. These are to be ground up with honey and smeared on the male's penis while chanting the following spell:

> Vagina of NN, open up and take the semen of NN and the unconquerable seed of ... let NN love me for all of her life ... and let her remain chaste for me, as Penelope did for Odysseus. And you vagina, remember me all my life because I am AKARNACHTHAS. Chant these words as you work the ingredients, and whenever you anoint your genitals, and so have sex with the woman you want. She will love only you, and no one but you will fuck her.

It is clear from these examples that the organs targeted were not incidental. Those tablets seeking to achieve erotic restraint and binding logically focus on the sexual organs of the target.

The Greeks and Romans ascribed to the evil eye a number of characteristics, chief among them envy; this was thought to be the catalyst for projecting the evil eye which, interestingly, was not confined to projection from the eye itself but could also be emitted via speech and breath. This eye was damaging to fertility and so particularly effective against women, children and crops. It was associated with people, especially women, who had double pupils and was often delivered by a sidelong glance. Paradoxically, it could derail magic, so sorcerers, working as they did in a world full of envy, were especially anxious. It could ruin blossoming love affairs but might be averted by spitting or by wearing a phallus, and in particular phallus amulets. The skin of the hyena was also an effective weapon. The conjunction of spitting and the phallus can be seen together in a Roman mosaic depicting a phallus ejaculating into a disembodied eye.[11]

Voces magicae were magical words with no obvious meaning, and yet their very mysteriousness gave them, and the magic people who uttered them, some considerable power. They were commonly used in curses, to which they added protective qualities, as illustrated by a fragment of Menander's which shows how they were used to ward off spells from newly married couples.[12]

13

Women's Sexual Medicine

Ancient Greek sexual medicine all started with Hesiod in the eighth century BC. Borrowing heavily from contemporary folk medicine, he repeated a belief which held that the effects of heat afflicted men more than women, diminishing men's performance and the production of semen from its sources, the head and knees:

> In the draining heat, when goats are plumpest and wine is finest, and women are on heat but men are weak.[1]

The Hippocratics and Galen later taught that the physiological function of producing semen literally drained a man, so man had to be careful not to overdo it sexually for fear of depleting his *pneuma*, his life spirit. A socially, and sexually, desirable element of male self-control was therefore *in situ* from the very beginning. Women, on the other hand, had cold and clammy bodies, incapable of producing the heat required to produce sperm; instead, they had menstrual fluid which contributed to new life. Aristotle championed the belief that the female body was inferior to the man's, and therefore women were considered inferior to men.

The *Hippocratic Corpus* is a cornerstone of ancient Greek medicine. It is a collection of medical treatises dating mainly from the fifth and fourth centuries BC which are the work of twenty or so authors covering sixty or so medical subjects. Gynaecology, and women's health generally, is reasonably well represented, with eleven gynaecological subjects covered – over 18 per cent of the total. They include *Semen* or *Generation* or *Intercourse; the Nature of the Child or Pregnancy; the Diseases of Women; Sterile Women; the Diseases of Young Women or Girls; Superfoetation; the*

Nature of Woman, and *Excision of the Foetus*. This proponderance may be accounted for by the anxiety felt by Greek men to ensure the biological function of women remained in good working order to produce those vital male heirs. Numerous other works of obstetrics and gynaecology were to follow down the years from various physicians, mainly Greek in origin.

In *On Generation* the Hippocratics believed that men got more pleasure from sex, although both men and women climaxed in the release of fluids.[2] Later, both Galen and Soranus were to teach that a woman could not conceive unless she felt pleasure during the sex act.

Herophilos (335–280 BC) produced nine medical books (now all lost) including a *Maiotikon,* a midwifery text; the aim of this book was to help midwives and doctors understand more fully the process of procreation and pregnancy. Herophilos is credited with teaching extensively on the physiology of the reproductive system. In his *Midwifery*, he digressed from the Hippocratics in that he believed the womb to be no different physiologically from other internal organs. He highlighted the analogous relationship between the male testicles and the female ovaries and takes credit for the discovery of the ovum. He believed that menstruation was the only physiological contribution women made to conception, and considered periods to be a cause of illness in women. He discussed phases and duration of pregnancy as well as causes of difficult childbirth and the anatomy of the genitalia.

One of the Hippocratics' core theories was that women's bodies were made up of flesh which was softer and more porous than men's,[3] an example being the female breast in which the woman's nourishment is converted into milk.[4] This porosity or sponginess was caused by the absorption of moisture in the form of blood, evacuated each month during the woman's period. The concept of porosity is linked to the sure knowledge that women leak, through the vagina, with menstrual fluid, sexual lubricant, locheal discharge and discharges from various infections.[5]

Blood clogging up the venous system in the breasts was a sure sign that a woman was going mad – a spurious physiological explanation for the age-old stereotype that women are naturally neurotic, erratic and prone to hysteria.

Menstruation
Menstruation and nosebleeds (*epitaxis*) were, then, a good thing as purging agents because they diminished the clogging. Women with

a heavy menstrual bleed lasting more than four days were thought to be delicate and to produce delicate embryos, while women with a light flow lasting fewer than three days were healthy and robust but somewhat masculine in appearance with diminished maternal instinct. *Amenorrhœa* (scanty menstruation) was a cause of all manner of physical and psychological illness; virgins were particularly prone, which went some way to explain their tendency to hang themselves or jump down wells to their deaths. Such was the stigma they had to endure when their condition made it difficult for them to find a husband.

Ancient Egyptians used softened papyrus as rudimentary tampons. Hippocrates noted that the Greeks used lint wrapped around wood. Aristophanes called the cloth that women used 'a pigpen'. Greek and Roman women, in common with women of other civilisations, used menstrual cloths; a sixth-century-AD philosopher and mathematician gathered some of her used ones up to put off an unwanted admirer. The alternative to cloths was to bleed into one's clothes, as described by Pliny.[6]

Menstruation caused all manner of anxiety amongst Greek males. The alleged mysterious, and tangibly alarming, qualities of menses, named after the Latin for month, had their origins in civilisations earlier than the Greek. The book of *Leviticus* refers to it as 'the flower that comes before the fruit of the womb', to mean a child. In the *Talmud*, men were advised not to go near a menstruating woman; if one walked between two men, one of the men would surely die. Persian women were banned from speaking to men or to even sit in water during menstruation. Hesiod warned that men should never wash in water that women had already used – just in case it was polluted by menstrual blood.

Dioscorides knew of over 100 agents which stimulated menstruation, while Pliny the Elder lists over ninety. Pliny describes the astonishing powers of menstruation: 'it would be hard to find anything that produces as many amazing effects (*magis monstrificium*) as menstrual discharge.' According to him, a period during a solar or lunar eclipse spelt disaster for the woman and for any man who copulates with her then. If a man with suicidal tendencies had sex with a menstruating woman he too would commit suicide. If a woman during her period walked naked through a field that is filled with pests, those pests will die as she walks past; Metrodorus of Scepsis is Pliny's source for this, claiming this happened in Cappadocia during a cantharid beetle plague and accounts for the fact that women there still walk in the fields with their dresses hitched up above their buttocks. Ironically, cantharidin was to become a popular aphrodisiac in the nineteenth century.

Sprinkling the ashes of menstrual blood onto clothing bleached them and spoilt purple dyes. A menstruating woman was not welcome in the kitchen or the garden: she would turn grape juice sour, make seeds sterile when touched by her, cause grafts to wither away, dry up garden plants and cause fruit to fall from the tree. Her reflection would cloud mirrors, blunt the edge of steel, and dull the sheen of ivory. If she looked at a swarm of bees, they would all drop down dead; brass and iron would instantly go rusty, and smell offensively; dogs which taste the discharge go mad, their bite then made poisonous and incurable. Josephus, the Romano-Jewish historian (AD 37–c. 100), revealed the heavy-duty industrial qualities of menstrual fluid:

> When they have filled the boats with bitumen, it is no easy task to decant their cargo, which owing to its tenacious and glutinous character, clings to the boat – until it is loosened by the monthly secretions of women and urine, to which it alone yields.[7]

Soranus describes the physiological changes that take place at the start of menstruation: lethargy, muscle aching, sluggishness, hot flushes and excessive yawning, nausea and lack of appetite. He sympathetically advises that each woman do what is best for her during her period: rest or light activity. Women approaching menopause should ensure that their periods cease gradually, extending them, if necessary, through the use of suppositories or injections. Soranus rejected the view that menstruation was a beneficial, healthy purgative, believing instead that its only use was in facilitating conception. For women in ancient Greece, the monthly period may have come as something of a relief, offering respite from the endless intercourse to produce endless babies, and a sign that she was not yet pregnant again.[8]

Childbirth
Giving birth was believed to cause the smaller vessels to break down and encourage blood flow; as such childbirth was encouraged along with the coitus that preceded it. There was, then, no place for celibacy; the fact that all of this gynaecology chimed with the male Greek concern to marry off daughters as soon as possible after puberty, in order to produce (male) children and further

the family line, was no coincidence. Cutting-edge medical science seems to have served social convention and expedience as much as the patient's health.

Estimates of population for Greece during the fourth century BC come in at 3.5 million on the Greek peninsula and 4 to 6.5 million in the rest of the entire Mediterranean Basin region, including all colonies such as those in Magna Graecia, Asia Minor and the shores of the Black Sea.

Multiple births were a contentious issue. Ancient medical writers and scientists came up with different theories to explain the phenomenon. The Hippocratics believed that multiple births were the result of an ideal fecundity; for Aristotle they were regarded as anomalies associated with monstrosity and excess. Aristotle wrote that multiple births were '*praeter naturam*', that is, 'outside nature's normal boundaries', or 'unnatural'. He believed that the largest conceivable multiple birth was five in one confinement – astonishing enough until he adds that the woman repeated the feat four times in her life. In fact, the first valid report of a woman exceeding five births did not come until 1888, when septuplets were born of an Italian lady. The report was promptly criticised for contradicting Aristotle's teachings.

Childbirth prescribed as a cure for all manner of maladies was not confined to the ancient world. Somerset Maugham's mother, Edith Mary (*née* Snell), had tuberculosis, a condition for which her physician prescribed childbirth. Sadly, it did not work; Edith's sixth son died on 25 January 1882, one day after his birth, on Maugham's eighth birthday, and Edith died of tuberculosis six days later at the age of forty-one.

The Hippocratics diagnosed several causes of miscarriage: carrying too heavy a weight, being physically abused, jumping up into the air (an occupational hazard for dancers), lack of food and fainting, fear, loud shouting, flatulence and drinking too much. There were numerous 'old-wives' tales' surrounding miscarriage. Aristotle describes women suffering from nausea in the early stages of pregnancy (*hyperemesis gravidarum*), which he said is worse if the baby was a girl. There were danger signs to watch for: diarrhoea was a bad sign in a pregnant woman; shrinking breasts means she will miscarry; if she is carrying twins and the right breast loses its fullness she will lose the male child, or if the left then the female. If she is underweight or in poor shape she is likely to miscarry. Doctors should not bleed a pregnant woman as this can lead to miscarriage, especially if the foetus is a large one. If the inside of the womb is too smooth a miscarriage may result because there is no traction to prevent the baby from simply dropping out.

Like Herophilos, some Greek writers such as Aeschylus and Aristotle minimised or dismissed the vital role played by the woman in pregnancy, relegating her to little more than a vessel temporarily accommodating the baby while it grows. Aristotle believed that pregnancy came about when semen and menstrual blood mixed in the womb. Most physicians, however, did acknowledge that a baby developed characteristics from both its mother and its father. However, when a woman failed to conceive, it was invariably the woman's fault, with never any suggestion that it might be the man who was infertile. Infertility in a woman was thought to be caused by a blockage of some sort: the standard fertility test involved wrapping her in a cloak and burning incense beneath her vagina. If the smell could then be detected in the woman's mouth she was fertile, indicating that she was, quite properly, hollow inside and ready to conceive. If there was no oral smell then there was a blockage, indicating infertility due to the inability of the semen to penetrate the inside of the womb. One treatment for this required the woman to sit all day in the sunshine outside her house while fumigations of myrrh, wormwood and garlic 'softened and opened the mouth of the womb', encouraging the flow of semen. It was probably one of the few times the wife got to relax and do nothing. An alternative treatment entailed going to the sanctuary of Asclepius at Epidaurus where patients would spend the night so that their dreams would cure them and lead to conception.

Overweight or obese women were thought to have difficulty conceiving because their fat blocked the entrance to the womb. Another myth said that a pregnant woman with a blooming complexion will deliver a male baby; poor colour brought with it the threat of a girl.

Midwives and local sagacious women performed most of the obstetrics. Mothers in confinement sat on a birth-friend's lap or on a birthing stool. Drugs were sometimes administered to induce labour or speed delivery; occasionally a woman might be shaken violently to encourage the birth. After a successful delivery, the new mother would visit the shrine of a suitable goddess, such as Artemis or Eileithyia, to give thanks for her baby. Artemis was a powerful mother goddess; a career virgin, she was something of an enigma – dispensing death one minute (her name means the one who slays) then assisting women in labour to deliver their babies the next. Mugwort, or artemisia, the herb used to induce troublesome deliveries, is named after her. The Temple of Artemis was one of the Seven Wonders of the World, such was her prominence in the worlds of men and gods.

Many babies and mothers did not survive what was a hazardous and traumatising experience both physically and psychologically.

Abstinence from sex and celibacy were considered bad for a woman's health as the womb dried out and could block menstruation which, if left untreated, might have fatal consequences.[9]

Empedocles (born *c.* 493 BC) believed that men were hotter than women.[10] Aristotle taught that men were more perfect than women; women were incomplete, deformed men because women were less capable than men of generating the heat that was vital for generation of the species due to the debilitating effect of menstruation. Aristotle championed the fallacy that the womb comprised two separate compartments; it was often used erroneously to explain the birth of twins whereby males were born from the right (hotter) chamber, and females from the colder left – with all the sinister implications which have endured down the centuries. Not only that, women were conceived with the left, ill-omened testicle while men came from the right and proper right.

Aristotle cautioned against having sex barefoot because bare feet made the body cold and dry when it needs to be warm and moist when we have sex. We have already mentioned how he taught that the eyelashes of people with a high sex drive fall out; this was because lust made the upper body cold, so depriving it of nourishment and causing hair loss.[11] Plutarch tells that the Cyrenaics recommend we should have sex in the dark, not in the light, so that the mind does not recall images of the sex act and fill us with desire when we remember them.[12] It seems that in Acadia many paid heed to this, because there was a temple of Black Aphrodite signifying the tendency to have sex 'with the lights out', as it were.[13] Plutarch also draws our attention to the athlete Cleitomachus who always got up and walked away whenever anyone started talking about sex; the belief was that sex was not good for athletic performance.[14] Pliny, though, thought the opposite, stating that 'when athletes are sluggish, sexual intercourse restores their performance.'[15]

Aristotle also rejected the Hippocratic belief that hysteria in women was attributable to the movements of the womb. He made tentative steps towards an understanding of the Fallopian tubes, largely unknown in antiquity. Some 600 or more years later Galen still subscribed to the temperature-based theory and the notion of the incomplete woman.

Contraception

There is little evidence relating to contraception in the ancient Greek world. Perhaps abortion, exposure or abandonment were adequate enough for most women's needs. Contraception was decidedly makeshift. Aristotle had advocated smearing cedar oil, white lead or frankincense on the female genitals, while the *Hippocratic Corpus* swore by drinking *misy*, dilute copper sulphate. The Hippocratics vowed not to use pessaries to effect an abortion, but some Hippocratic writings, in contradiction, prescribe them for that very same purpose. Herbs were commonly used to prevent conception or abort a child. The Pythagoreans were alone in opposing abortion on moral grounds.

The ancient Greeks would have been exposed to the methods of other cultures. The Egyptian *Kahun Papyrus* (1850 BC) recommends crocodile faeces either for preventing conception or as an abortifacient. In Arabic medicine, elephant faeces were frequently recommended. The *Ebers Papyrus* (1550 BC) contains several recipes that 'cause a woman to stop pregnancy in the first, second, or third period'. One recipe for a vaginal suppository comprises the unripe fruit of Acacia, colocynth, dates, and 6 or 7 pints of honey, and pouring the mixture onto a moistened plant fibre. Modern Arabic women still take colocynth as an abortifacient.

Probably the most effective contraceptive was silphium, or giant fennel, which had both contraceptive and abortifacient properties. Demand for silphium drove prices high in the fifth century BC, enabling Aristophanes to write nostalgically in *The Knights*: 'Don't you remember when a stalk of silphium sold so cheap?' It was cultivated in a limited coastal area of North Africa and eventually became extinct from overharvesting; the Greeks then turned to asafoetida. Other available contraceptives were Queen Anne's lace or wild carrot, pennyroyal, rue, artemisia, myrrh and pomegranate. Most have both contraceptive and abortifacient properties.

The ancient Greeks had some other interesting methods of birth control. Soranus prescribed water that had been used by blacksmiths to cool iron. Dioscorides was something of a birth control specialist: he knew of twenty-four contraceptive potions, three of which were magic, including an amulet made of asparagus. Others involved applying peppermint, honey, cedar gum, axe weed and alum in various concoctions to the genitals. Soranus is equally unromantic: his contraception of choice is stale olive oil, honey or the sap from a balsam or cedar tree applied to the entrance of the vagina – either on its own or (alarmingly) mixed with white lead and bunged up with wool. This has a coagulating and cooling effect which causes the vagina to close before sex, and acts as a barrier to the sperm. An alternative method, just as inelegant, involved the woman holding her breath when her partner ejaculates, pulling away so that his semen does not penetrate too deeply, then getting up straightaway and squatting and sneezing before wiping her vulva clean. Dioscorides also recommends using vinegar, olive oil, ground pomegranate peel and ground flesh of dried figs as vaginal suppositories; olive oil was still being advocated by the Marie Stopes Clinic as recently as 1931 along with other effective spermicides like lemon, alum and vinegar. Douches made from vinegar, alum or lemon juice were still used by the working classes in New York in 1947, and lemons were in use in 1970s Glasgow.

The Greeks also used *prostheta* or pesos. They were made from linen, sponge, or wool and rolled into a finger-like shape, coated with various drugs that could induce an abortion. Others were shaped like a small egg, nipple, or a tiny pencil or acorn. Hippocrates prescribed a pumpkin pessary, described as 'the inside of a pumpkin well crushed in cedar resin, wrapped into a cloth leaving its end bare, then inserted as deep as possible; after it is stained with blood, it is pulled out'.

The Egyptians developed the first diagnostic pregnancy test based on the detection of a unique substance in the urine of both women and domesticated animals. The best known Egyptian pregnancy test is the germination test. This requires the woman to urinate onto bags of wheat and barley. According to the *Berlin Medical Papyrus,* 'if the barley grows, it means a male child. If the wheat grows, it means a female child. If both do not grow, she will not give birth at all.' The *Berlin Medical Papyrus* also recommended that a woman should have her nipples and skin examined for unusual pigmentation, or that she should drink milk from a woman who has had a son: if she vomits she is pregnant. The *Kahun Medical Papyrus* suggests placing a woman in the daylight where pregnancy can be confirmed or ruled out by the colour of her skin. Another test involved grasping a woman's fingers and gripping her arm: if the veins in her arms pounded against your hand then she was pregnant. Several of these rudimentary pregnancy tests resurface in the Hippocratic Corpus under 'About the Barren Woman'.

Abortion

Debates over when life is thought to begin are ancient and enduring; there has never been complete agreement about when a foetus becomes a person, but the main view in ancient Hebrew, Greek, and Roman thought was that there could be no living soul in an 'unformed' and/or 'unquickened' body and, hence, the law of murder could not apply if a foetus was aborted before that time. However, other scholars, such as Basil, Bishop of Caesarea in Asia Minor *(c.* AD 330–379), called feticide murder at any point of development. Aristotle suggests that the foetus had a 'soul' after forty days from conception if a male, and ninety if female. There was no legislation against abortion in ancient Greece. Plato believed that the state should decree that all pregnancies in women over the age of forty should be terminated. For the ancients Greeks, life did not exist until birth, and thus no stigma or ethics were attached to abortion.

Ancient abortion techniques included applying ointments and creams topically on the abdomen or bruised corn boiled with vinegar, and boiled cypress leaves. Physicians such as Galen recommended hot baths, blood letting, strenuous exercise, leaping, riding in a shaky carriage, carrying heavy weights, emotional shock, body massages with hot oil, or being vigorously shaken by two strong men.

Surgical abortion was known in the ancient world though, due to lack of anaesthetics and antibiotics, it was highly dangerous and exceedingly painful. Celsus *(c.* 25 BC–AD 50) provides the most complete account of the dilatation and curettage (D&C) operation, which required placing one, sometimes two, hands into the uterus to straighten the foetus and then extracting the foetus with a hook. Hippocratic texts such as *Diseases of Women, Superfetation,* and *On the Excision of the Foetus* refer to a surgical tool called an *embruosphaktes* ('embryo-slayer'). It was deployed when manipulation failed to effect an embryotomy to evacuate the foetus as soon it was presumed dead, in order to save the mother. Hooked knives were used to dismember the foetus and thus ease delivery; likewise, decapitating instruments enabled the head to be delivered first.[16] Soranus recommended amputating parts of the foetus as they presented, rather than doing so internally, to avoid cutting the vagina with the blade.[17] Unusually large foetal heads were crushed with a cranioclast (a bowed forceps with teeth) or split with an embryotome; both instruments are still in use today. Traction hooks were also part of the instrumentation; samples have been found in Pompeii. Their use is described in Hippocrates, and further by Celsus and Soranus.[18]

Pliny the Elder (AD 23–79), Dioscorides *(c.* 40–90), and Pseudo-Galen (129–216) mention more 'superstitious' abortifacients, such as crossing over the root of a cyclamen, the egg of a crow, a viper, or a stone bitten by a dog. If a woman crosses the menstrual blood of another woman, she will abort.

Attempts to influence the sex of a baby also go back to ancient Greek times – naturally, all the hard work went towards trying to ensure a baby boy. Pliny the Elder teaches us that linozostis or parthenion was discovered by the god Mercury, and that many Greeks call it 'Hermes' grass: the male plant produces male babies and the female plant females. How does this happen? The woman should drink the juice of the plant in raisin wine, or eat the leaves decocted in oil and salt, or raw in vinegar. Some again decoct it in a new earthen vessel with heliotropium and two or three ears of corn until the contents become thick. This decoction should be given to women in food, with the plant itself given on the second day of menstruation for three successive days; on the fourth day, after a bath, the woman should have intercourse.

Hippocrates also recommends linozostis for uterine disorders, adding honey, or oil of roses or of iris or of lilies, also as an emmenagogue and to evacuate the afterbirth. Emmenagogues are herbs which stimulate blood flow in the pelvic region and uterus; some stimulate menstruation. He applied the leaves to fluxes from the eyes and prescribed a decoction of it with myrrh and frankincense for strangury – a blockage or irritation at the base of the bladder, resulting in severe pain and a strong desire to urinate – and other bladder troubles. For loosening the bowels, however, or for fever, a handful of the plant should be reduced down and drunk with salt and honey; it is even more powerful if the decoction has been made with a pig's foot or a chicken.

Malformation and disability
The Greek attitude to deformity and disability was alarmingly blunt and simple. Most deformed infants were simply abandoned or murdered.

Hipponax, himself noted for his ugliness and deformity, would have us believe that at the festival of Thargelia on the day of the sacrifice the two ugliest men that could be found were led along with strings of figs around their necks, and whipped on the genitals with rods of figwood and onion bulbs. They were then stoned to death, their bodies burnt, and the ashes scattered into the sea as a fertiliser. This is ironic not only on account of Hipponax's own ugliness but because a famous *hetaerae* called Thargelia was noted for her beauty. These scapegoated victims were called *pharmakoi*, their treatment supposedly effecting a purification of a city in peril. Interestingly, the same word denotes a magician, poisoner or, in its feminine form, a witch – all groups which suffered similar indignities down the ages.

Ugly people were victimised in this way in Greece because they were considered freaks, outside eugenicist nature, sent onto earth as a punishment to mankind by the gods. Their fellow men blamed them for any woes which befell the community. Deformity was, therefore, heaven sent. As earlier as Hesiod in the *Works and Days,* the euphemism for a 'normal' child was one who 'resembled his father'. Before the battle of Plataea in 479 BC the horrible consequences of not 'resembling your father' were quite clear from the battlefield oath:

> If I remain faithful to the inscribed oath, may women give birth to children who resemble their parents. If not, may they give birth to monsters.

This must have worked wonders for religious conformity and piety – not just amongst the soldiers that day but also with their womenfolk who must have been terrified of committing even the slightest misdemeanour relating to the taking of oaths.

Herodian (*c.* 170–*c.* 240 AD) supplies us with some interesting medical etymology: Labda was a daughter of the Bacchiad Amphion, and mother of Cypselus by Eetion. She got her name from the fact that her feet turned outward, making her look like the letter lambda (Λ), which, by all accounts, was originally pronounced labda.[19] As we know, girls were abandoned and exposed if they were deemed surplus to the requirements of the family, a burden on the *oikos.* The Athenian comic poet Posidippus put it well: 'Everyone, even a poor man, raises a son. Everyone, even a rich man, exposes a daughter.' The same hideous (by our standards) fate awaited the deformed and disabled, for whom death was often the only option. In eugenicist Sparta it was simpler still: the law officially required the abandonment of handicapped infants. In other parts of Greece mothers may have been less cold and brutal, if Plato's remarks in the *Theaetetus* are anything to go by. Referring to a 'lifeless phantom not worth rearing' he then asks:

> Or do you think your infant must be reared anyway and not exposed? Can you bear to see it examined and not be upset if it is taken away, even if it is your first-born?

This suggests that some Athenian mothers loved their disabled babies enough to raise them in the family. Aristotle is with Plato when, in the *Politics*, he advocates a law criminalising the rearing of deformed children.

In general, though, the subject of infant deformity seems to have been generally ignored at the time, presumably because of the quick and efficiently executed deaths the patients suffered or because of the social stigma. Garland makes the point that 'there is little discussion among Greek and Roman writers of genuine congenital abnormalities such as harelip or spina bifida, which today appear with monotonous regularity, even though these conditions are likely to have been no less prevalent in antiquity'. Hippocrates and his followers are as guilty as anyone else regarding the matter, although an exception comes with the *Seed*, in which the author explains deformity caused either by an external blow to the womb or to an internal growth within the uterus:

> When the child is deformed in the womb I consider that this occurs (a) as the result of a contusion. The mother has received a blow in the part where the embryo is, or has had a fall, or suffered some other violence. A deformity results in the place where the contusion occurred. When the contusion is extensive, the membrane enveloping the embryo is broken, and it is aborted. (b) Children may be deformed in another way: if there is some constriction in that region of the womb which is contiguous to the part in which the embryo is deformed, it must be the case that deformity occurs there as a result of the embryo's movement in the constricted space.

Other areas of women's medicine involved remedies made up from various concoctions and potions. Some of these were applied topically via salves and plasters; others were administered internally as fumigants, nasal clysters, enemas or pessaries. Fumigation involved the burning of agents such as human hair, medicinal herbs and bitumen in a pot; a lead tube from this was introduced into the woman's vagina. This, of course, was not without its hazards, if Soranus' warning about the dangers of burning the vagina is anything to go by.[20] Enemas were introduced for disorders of the bladder, rectum, vagina and uterus – vaginal douches via vaginal clysters were often deployed. Pessaries were inserted for a wide range of applications including inducing menstruation, reducing inflammation of the womb, expelling dead foetuses and relieving hysteria. Pessaries were also used in cases of prolapsed uterus while tents were administered to staunch uterine haemorrhage and suppurating wombs. Tents in a medical context are cylinders, usually absorbent, introduced into a canal or sinus to dilate it.

The 'wandering womb'

Much of Greek gynaecology was focussed on the womb, *hystera*, and its impact on a woman's ability to bear children. Hippocrates puts it succinctly: 'Of the so-called women's diseases, the womb is the cause of them all.'[21] Nowadays, hysteria is no longer recognised as a diagnosis or disorder and has been replaced by 'histrionic personality disorder', which is associated with conditions such as social anxiety and schizophrenia. Women have always been seen to be particularly prone, hence the cliché of 'female hysteria'. Up until the late nineteenth century the condition was inextricably linked to movements of the womb, presented as a lack of self-control caused by intense fear or anxiety often related to hypochondria or the imagined disease of a particular body part. First-line treatment was pelvic massage – a procedure in which the doctor stimulated the genitals until the woman achieved hysterical paroxysm, or orgasm.[22]

Hysteria was first noted around the time of and recorded in the Hippocratic writings, although the Hippocratics used the term *pnix* – suffocation. They believed that the womb dried up if a woman did not have frequent sexual intercourse; irregular penetrative sexual activity would cause the womb to gravitate towards moister organs such as the liver, heart, brain, diaphragm or bladder, at which point the woman would faint, lose her voice and become 'hysterical'. The administration of sweet-smelling odours often restored the womb to its rightful place. Where this failed, increasingly desperate measures involved binding the woman tightly beneath her breasts, palpating the affected organ, or hanging the woman upside down from a ladder. It was not until dissection became more prevalent – for many years it was only permitted in the medical school at Alexandria – that physicians learned that the uterus was fixed by ligaments and could not move about inside the body.

Plato believed that an animal living inside a woman's womb drove the maternal instinct to bear children; if deprived of sexual activity, the animal became restless and wandered throughout the body causing apnea (difficulty in breathing) and other conditions and diseases. Conveniently enough, sexual intercourse was the only cure; early marriage and the frequent sex that usually brought, then, was essential to a young girl's good health, the only way of taming the beast in her body.[23]

As already noted, hysteria was a particular occurrence in virgins and widows – both groups, of course, characterised by a relative absence of regular sex in their lives. Hippocrates warns that girls who marry late – beyond the age of fourteen, say – suffer nightmares from the onset of their first period. This can lead to asphyxiation as the blood in their womb cannot escape while the cervix is still intact and so flows back into the heart and lungs, driving the woman insane. Fever ensues, and the nightmares trigger thoughts of suicide, causing the women to jump down wells or to hang themselves, if indeed the reflux has not already choked them. Hippocrates' advice is for girls in such a condition to lose their virginity as soon as possible, and the only socially acceptable way of doing that is in the marital bed. They will be cured when they fall pregnant.[24] Widows, similarly, are cured by sex, or just by climaxing, so that the retained female semen is released. The inevitable conclusion amongst the best medical minds of the day was that, deprived of sex, a woman would go mad and eventually die, and the best way to preserve one's sanity and to live longer was to have sex, and to have it often.

So, the only real cure for the 'hysterical' woman was to become pregnant – thus conveniently enabling the woman to fulfil her childbearing role as a wife as well as satisfying husbands' needs for sexual gratification. Ironically, for some women hysteria may have provided a release from the tedium and the daily grind of being a good, compliant, wool-working, household-managing wife. Hysterical behaviour, though, was unseemly to the Greek male and so was medicalised with the prognosis that it could only be cured through regular sexual intercourse and childbirth A vicious circle for the Greek woman.

But the Greek woman had more than hysteria to worry about. Uterine dropsy, or hydrometra, is an accumulation of watery fluid in the cavity of the uterus resulting in fever, weak periods, swelling in the abdomen and withered breasts. Hippocrates recommended a complicated, rather undignified and unpleasant therapy: a laxative and immersion in a vapour bath of cow dung followed by the insertion of pessaries made from cantharid beetle and then bile; after three days a vinegar douche should be introduced. If the fever subsided and the stomach softened then the woman should have intercourse. She should drink samphire bark and eat dark peony berries with as much mercury plant, raw and cooked garlic as possible, and begin a diet of squid. If she eventually gave birth she was cured.

For uterine prolapse the *Hippocratic Corpus* advised a remedy that was even more exotic, and yet more meticulous and precise. Prolapse occurs when the uterus slips from its normal position into the vagina, the birth canal, the bowel or bladder. The woman should take garlic, undiluted sheep's milk, fumigation and a laxative, followed by another fumigation of fennel and absinthe and then two pessaries – one an onion, the other of opium poppies. If the woman's periods have stopped, then she should drink four cantharid beetles (with the legs, wings and head removed), and eat four dark peony seeds, cuttlefish eggs, parsley and wine. If her womb approaches her liver she will lose her voice, turn a dark colour and her teeth will chatter; a bandage should then be tied below her ribs and sweet wine poured into her mouth while malodorous vapours are burnt beneath her vulva. The Hippocratics believed that this condition particularly affected old women and widows.

We rarely hear of uterine cancer in ancient Greece, probably because the symptoms were difficult to differentiate from those of other conditions or diseases – vaginal bleeding and discharge, with periods stopping, for example. Plutarch mentions that cancer of the womb is particularly distressing. Philoxenus of Alexandria, in the mid-first century BC, was something of a cancer surgery specialist and was an exponent of surgical intervention in cervical cancer.

Breast diseases receive comparatively little attention, possibly because of the clinical obsession with the uterus. Hippocrates describes a case of breast cancer where the patient died after the bloody discharge from her nipple stopped. Breast cancer was one of the first cancers to be described by ancient physicians, when doctors in ancient Egypt described breast cancer more than 3,500 years ago. One surgeon described 'bulging' tumours in the breast for which 'there is no cure'. Around 400 BC, Hippocrates described breast cancer as a humoral disease caused by black bile or melancholia. He labeled cancer *karkinos,* meaning 'crab', because the tumors seemed to have tentacles which looked like the legs of crab.

Malaria (*plasmodium falciparum*) was widespread in many parts of the ancient Greek world. The female anopheles mosquito is thought to be attracted to certain chemical receptors found in the placenta of pregnant women. Empedocles blocked off a gorge in

Acragas, Sicily, because it was found to be a funnel for a southerly wind bringing in the deadly mosquitoes which introduced placental malaria.

Sexually transmitted infections would, of course, have plagued both men and women alike, particularly in a society which freely endorsed their men consorting with prostitutes, male and female. Discharges and ulcers are recorded but there is little on infection or contagion. The Hippocratics, using findings from a dissected inflamed urethra, along with Celsus and Galen all describe the symptoms of gonorrhoea, referring to it as 'strangury' (painful urination) caused by the 'pleasures of Venus'. The Hippocratics and Galen record oral sores which present during menstruation – possibly *herpes zoster*. In the Roman era, Martial and Galen mention anal warts and piles (*ficus*), Celsus and Galen genital warts. All of these conditions would have been common in ancient Greece.[25]

Agnodice and Salpe

Agnodice was the first professional gynaecologist and midwife of ancient Greece, practising around 500 BC. Her desire to study medicine was ignited when she saw all around her more and more women dying in childbirth or undergoing unnecessarily painful deliveries. One of the problems was that women, not unnaturally, disliked being treated by male doctors. In Hippocrates' day women were allowed to learn and practice obstetrics and gynaecology and midwifery, but when it was later discovered that some women were performing abortions, it was made a capital crime for women to practice medicine. Agnodice, however, was determined to help her fellow sex so she cut her hair and dressed as a man to pursue medical training. She then left Athens to study medicine in Egypt, where it was quite legal for women to study and practice medicine, studying at Alexandria under Herophilos, a leading anatomist of her day. Once qualified she continued to masquerade as a man in order to treat the women back in Athens.

However, Agnodice became the victim of her own success when she was rejected by female patients because (they thought) she was a man. Hyginus tells us how

> she heard a woman crying out in the throes of labour so she went to her assistance. The woman, thinking she was a man, refused her help; but Agnodice lifted up her clothes and revealed herself to be a woman and was thus able to treat her patient.

Agnodice was then tried as a man by the Areopagus on behalf of jealous husbands and rival doctors for seducing the women of Athens. To prove her true identity she again lifted up her tunic, only to be condemned on pain of death for deceit and false pretenses, allegations which she was able to disprove. Her opponents then condemned her for violating the law against women practicing medicine. She was saved by a group of influential Athenian women who protested and had the law repealed. Hyginus remarked again: 'you men are not spouses but enemies since you are condemning the woman who discovered health for us.'

Salpe is a first-century-BC midwife from Lemnos whose work was a major source for Pliny the Elder. Atheneus wrote that Salpe wrote *paignia*, or trifles. From Pliny we learn about Salpe's remedies for sunburn, stiffness, dog bites and sore eyes. There is also information on an aphrodisiac, a topical depilatory cream, and a procedure for stopping a dog from barking. Her pharmacopoeia included saliva and urine, which were believed to have both natural and supernatural powers. Salpe is often associated with Laïs, as both agreed on the magical powers of menstrual fluid against rabies and fever.

Neonatal Mortality

In antiquity, in both Greece and in Rome, the main causes of neonatal mortality – death within the first twenty-nine days of life – were insanitary conditions at the birth leading to infection, and trauma; infant deaths were also caused by intestinal disorders, particularly enteritis and dysentery. Celsus recorded that the latter was particularly virulent in children up to the age of ten and in their pregnant mothers, when the unborn baby was also lost. Overzealous swaddling – where the limbs are confined and the heartbeat slows down dangerously as a consequence – dirty laundry, and mastication of baby foods by wet-nurses who themselves might be carrying an infection will also have taken their toll. As, indeed, would the much-used goat's and cow's milk which contained infectious organisms and would have been used not just by reluctant breast-feeders but by poorer, undernourished women who were unable to feed and could not afford a wet nurse.

The earliest recorded female physician was Merit Ptah, a doctor in ancient Egypt who lived around 2700 BC. Many historians believe she is the first woman recorded by name in the history of all of the sciences. Ancient Greece could boast an impressive pedigree when it came to training and employing doctors. When Greek influence spread into regions dominated by Rome, Greek doctors were at the forefront of the migration. Physical examination and history taking are inarguably the cornerstones of good medical practice, accurate diagnosis and a good clinical outcome; whatever their shortcomings, Greek doctors, particularly those of the Hippocratic school, did encourage their colleagues to engage with their female patients to allay embarrassment and learn as much from their signs and symptoms as possible.

Hippocrates leaves several intriguing sexual case studies: a woman from Pheres suffered from idiopathic headache which persisted even after her skull was drained; during her period the headache was less severe. The headaches stopped completely when she fell pregnant. A chamber maid from Larissa suffered chronic pain during intercourse (dyspareunia); when she reached the age of sixty she suffered what seemed like severe labour pains every time she ate leeks. One day she stood up and felt something in her vagina, and promptly fainted; another woman nearby came to the rescue and pulled out what appeared to be a stone in the shape of a spindle whorl. A case of overzealous working of the wool? Hippocrates records that the woman made a full recovery; one wonders if the other woman ever did.

The Hippocratic case history of Phaethousa of Abdera is equally interesting. Having had a baby after her husband was exiled, Phaethousa stopped menstruating, grew a beard and eventually died. Some have argued that the story exemplifies the role of lust: as her husband was not around to satisfy her and she missed him so much, she came to resemble him. Others emphasize the fact that otherwise she was *oikouros*, a stay-at-home wife, and *epitokos*, highly fertile; in other words the model wife who was so good she had to become a man.[26] Finally, we hear of one of the most innovative forms of contraception: a patient presented to a gynaecologist complaining that vines were sprouting from her vagina. The doctor examined her and found that vines were indeed sprouting. When the doctor removed the object, she found that it was a potato that had sprouted vines. When asked why she had a potato in her vagina, the patient confessed to the doctor that her mother told her to put a potato in her vagina to stop her getting pregnant.

Aphrodisiacs

Galen believed that any food that produced flatulence also had aphrodisiacal qualities – a not altogether magical combination. This was believed until the eighteenth century. Pliny the Elder recommends 'a man's urine in which a lizard has been drowned' as an aphrodisiac. If there is no lizard to hand, 'the right section of a vulture's lung worn as an amulet in a crane's skin' did just as well. If all else failed a disappointing member might be activated by recourse to the dark arts. For an on-demand erection simply smear 'your thing' with crushed pepper in honey. (*GMP* 12, 36)

Theophrastus tells us about a big Indian man who had an inedible plant which when rubbed on his penis gave him sufficient erection to service as many women as he liked. Some users boasted they had managed twelve times, but the big Indian claimed he once had seventy women one after another. Admittedly, by the end, his semen was ejacualated in drops and was bloody, but seventy times all the same; women too became 'unusually eager for intercourse' when applying this drug. Sadly, Theophrastus omits to name the plant.[27]

The *Kyranides*, a compendium of dubious magico-medical works, compiled in Greek in the first century, includes an aphrodisiac to be worn as an amulet. It comprises lapis lazuli engraved with an ostrich holding a fish in its mouth. An orchid seed and a sliver of the gizzard are placed in the ostrich's stomach; wearing it ensures good digestion as well as an erection and 'fosters an interest in sex; especially good for old men and those who want sex often; it also makes the wearer seductive.'[28] Another from the same source requires a weasel's right testicle to be reduced to ashes and mixed with myrrh to form a paste, inserted into the woman's vagina before intercourse on a ball of wool; the result is immediate conception. The left testicle has the opposite effect as a contraceptive. The author invites sceptical readers to try it for themselves on a bird that is laying eggs.[29]

Anti-aphrodisiacs included nymphaea, a herb guaranteed to 'relax' the phallus for a few days. One writer even boasted that it would 'take away desire and even erotic dreams for forty days!' Pliny reveals that there was much confidence in animal body parts, especially those of the hippopotamus. Hippo parts were effective as antidotes for snakebite: all a victim had to do was swallow a coin-sized piece of hippo testicle with water. Hippos were the beast of choice for temporarily inhibiting sexual desire: simply take the hide from the left side of a hippo's forehead, then attach it firmly to the groin – the woman's groin, that is. If this was not repellent enough to stifle any residual passion it certainly made for an excellent barrier contraceptive. Pliny adds another:

A most powerful medicament is obtained by reducing to ashes the nails of a lynx, together with the hide ... these ashes, taken

in drink, have the effect of checking abominable desires in men
... and if they are sprinkled upon women, all libidinous thoughts
will be restrained.

Clitoridectomy

The oversized clitoris was dealt with very insensitively with
practices that attest to early evidence of female genital mutilation.
Physicians like Soranos, author of *Gynaikeia,* unceremoniously cut
the large clitoris out:

> Concerning an immensely great clitoris an uncouth size is present
> in certain clitorises and brings women into disorder by the
> deformity of the private parts. As most people say, these same
> women, affected by the lust (or erection) typical of men, take on
> a similar desire, and they approach sexual intercourse with men
> only under duress. If it comes to that [an operation], the woman
> is to be placed lying on her back and with thighs closed, lest the
> viscera of the vagina become distended. Then the excess part is to
> be held in place with a small forceps and cut back with a scalpel
> in proportion to its unnatural size.

The writer cautions against excising too much since there is
considerable blood loss. Paulus of Aegina, a later Greek writer with
a Christian axe to grind against so-called pagans, agrees with the
psychosexual theory and the procedure but also claims that womrn
with large clitorises generally lust after sex:

> An immensely great clitoris occurs in some women; the presenting
> problem is shameful impropriety. According to what some people
> report, some even have erections similar to men on account of the
> part and are eager for sexual intercourse.

14

Men's Sexual Medicine

In ancient Greek medicine male sexual health tends to be overshadowed by gynaecology and obstetrics but, obviously, it is just as important to the production line of male children in the various *poleis*.

Circumcision
Circumcision was deplored as were the barbarian countries who routinely practiced circumcision for cultural or religious reasons. The only exception was the surgical management of serious cases of penile gangrene. Celsus says:

> Sometimes through such an ulceration the penis is so eaten away underneath the foreskin that the glans falls off; in which case the foreskin itself must be cut away all round. It is the rule, whenever the glans or any part of the penis has fallen off, or has been cut away, that the foreskin should not be preserved, lest it come into contact, and adhere to the ulceration, so that afterwards it cannot be drawn back, and further perhaps may choke the urethra.[1]

Herodotus is the earliest Greek source for circumcision. He ascribes circumcision to the Colchians, Ethiopians, Phoenicians, Syrians, and Macrones, as well as to Egyptian priests. On the plus side, in their role as great civilisers, the Greeks persuaded the Phoenicians to abandon circumcision. Circumcision is one of the things which the contrary and annoying Egyptians do that is the opposite to everyone else:

> Everywhere else in the world, priests have long hair, but in Egypt they shave their heads ... other people, unless they have been

influenced by the Egyptians, leave their genitals in their natural state, but the Egyptians practise circumcision. Their concern for cleanliness also explains why they practise circumcision, since they value cleanliness more than comeliness.[2]

One cannot help sympathising with Herodotus when he marvels that the same people who set such store by genital cleanliness routinely handle dung and prepare food with their bare feet.

As an example of the Greek preference, the fifth-century-BC Attic red-figure *pelike* by the Pan painter depicts Heracles overthrowing Busiris, a mythological priest-king of Egypt; the Egyptians are shown with fat, ugly, wrinkled, circumcised penises with a bulbous externalized glans, in sharp contrast to Heracles' tidy penis with its elegantly long and tapered prepuce.

Later Greek writers, such as Strabo and Diodorus Siculus, wrote what must have been sickening and horrific accounts of the genital mutilation practiced by various primitive, sometimes cave-dwelling, tribes living around the Red Sea, as well as those of the Hebrews and Egyptians.[3] Some of these tribes cut off only the foreskin, others amputated the glans,[4] and still others amputated the entire penis.[5] According to Strabo in his description of the Hebrews and the descendants of Moses:

> In the first place, superstitious men were appointed to the priesthood, and then tyrannical people; and from superstition arose abstinence from flesh, from which it is their custom to abstain even today, and circumcisions and excisions [of females] and other observances of the kind.[6]

Apart from its associations with barbarians, primitiveness, backwardness, superstition and oppression, the circumcised penis is also linked in the Greek mind with slavery, as evidenced by a sixth-century Corinthian painted-clay tablet showing four slaves hard at work in a mine. One slave is clearly circumcised: his prodigious penis swings between his legs, the glans is exposed.

If we need further evidence of the anathema ancient Greeks felt towards the Hebrew practice of circumcision, we need go no further than Antiochus Epiphanies, a descendent of one of Alexander the Great's greatest generals. He, somewhat fanatically, ruled that the rabbis who performed circumcision should be 'stoned or fed to wild dogs. Mothers who permitted their sons to be circumcised shoud be garroted, their strangled infants strung about their necks, and then hanged upon crosses as terrible warnings to others.'

The penis

The Greeks believed that erections were 'inflated by the wind'. It was not until Leonardo da Vinci (1452–1519) dissected hanged men wth post-mortem erections that it was discovered that erections were caused by blood.

Trauma to the penis is vividly depicted on an Attic amphora where two of four naked honey thieves are battling against the swarm; the two are each stung on their penis – one of which is erect. A fitting punishment for the crime?

Trauma of a hugely symbolic kind was inflicted on the male genitalia in 415 BC, just before the launching of the Sicilian expedition, the largest and best-equipped fleet ever assembled by the Athenians. The aim was to sail to Sicily and subdue some of the island, if not all of it.[7] All over Athens at the time at people's front doors, at crossroads, at one corner of the Agora, for example, there were edifices called Hermai, life-size or larger stone apotropaic pillars with the messenger god Hermes' head carved at the top with genitals at the front. On the night before the expedition was due to sail, a person or persons mutilated many of these Hermai, defacing and castrating them. This iconoclasm, the Mutilation of the Hermai, remains unsolved to this day.

Hermes was originally a phallic god, associated with fertility, liminality, luck, roads and borders. The Hermai would habitually be rubbed or anointed with olive oil and adorned with garlands. Such superstition persists today, for example, with the Porcellino bronze boar of Florence, where the nose is rubbed shiny from being continually touched for good luck or fertility.

George Grote struggled to

> comprehend the intensity of mingled dismay, terror, and wrath, which beset the public mind on the morning after this nocturnal sacrilege, alike unforeseen and unparalleled ... This was, the mutilation of the Herma, one of the most extraordinary events in all Grecian History.[8]

Many believed the sacrilege compromised the success of the expedition – the work of saboteurs, either from Syracuse or Spartan sympathisers in Athens itself. One suspect was the writer

Xenophon. Enemies of Alcibiades took this opportunity to accuse him of other acts of impiety, including mutilations of other sacred objects and deriding performances of religious mystery ceremonies. As soon as he had left on the expedition, he was sentenced to death *in absentia*, both for the mutilation of the Hermai, and for profaning the Eleusinian Mysteries.

Peyronie's disease, also known as *induratio penis plastica* or chronic inflammation of the tunica albuginea (CITA), is a disorder of the connective tissue involving the growth of fibrous plaques in the soft tissue of the penis; today it affects an estimated 5 per cent of men. Specifically, scar tissue forms in the tunica albuginea, the thick sheath of tissue surrounding the corpora cavernosa, causing pain, abnormal curvature, erectile dysfunction, indentation, loss of girth and shortening.

Early evidence for Peyronie's disease has been found on an ancient Greek case has been discovered on a phallus votive limb, dedicated in a Minoan Peak Sanctuary, dated at the end of the third millennium BC. It is recognisable from the downward curvature of the glans in combination with the phallus in an erect form. We can reasonably conclude that the patient was seeking therapy here, hoping to be able to have sexual intercourse again.

15

Bad Language: Sex Manuals and Greek Sexual Vocabulary

Sex Manuals

It is often assumed that graphic sex manuals were a publishing phenomenon of the twentieth century. Not so. They existed, probably in some abundance, in ancient Greece and ancient Rome – simply another manifestation of the casual and enlightened attitude to all things sexual – be it painted on a wall, carved in the shape of a statue, written in a book, or scrawled in a brothel.

No actual sex manual survives from ancient Greece, but given that Ovid, for example, did not have to invent sex in order to find content for his *Ars Amatoria*, it is reasonable to assume that what was written about in the Roman era was all the rage in ancient Greece as well, that it was written down ... and then lost.

Xenophon called Nico of Samos a writer of 'lewd' books. Ovid, of course, wrote the gold standard, the *Ars Amatoria*, the *Joy of Sex* of its day. But women were at the forefront of the sex-manual industry: Pamphile was an erudite woman and wrote thirty-three books of historical memoirs, summaries of various histories, controversial treatises and books on sex. The *doctae puellae* courtesans Astyanassa and Elephantis also wrote 'pornography', both specialising in the elucidation of sexual positions; Astyanassa, according to the *Suda*, was a handmaiden to Helen of Troy. Martial mentions the sex books by Elephantis in his review of the work of Sabellus.[1] He recommends the books written by Sulpicia to women and men alike if they want the best advice on how to make the perfect marriage – on both sides of the bedroom door. Elephantis' famous book on sexual positions, *varia concubitis genera*, was a Roman *Kama Sutra*, no less; Paxamus could edify us with twelve positions in his *Dodecatechnon*. Suetonius records that gloomy, depraved Tiberius packed a copy of Elephantis when he left for his den of iniquity and depravity on Capri; Martial says it is '[a book] with intriguing new ways of making love'.[2] Apparently, it was something of a *'Rough Guide'* to the place, 'so that no one should lack a model for the execution of any lustful act he was ordered to perform' according to Suetonius. Philaenis astutely called her book *On Indecent Kisses,* with a good eye on the market.[3] If her chapter plan is anything to go by it was encyclopaedic: 'How to Make a Pass'; 'Cosmetics for Seduction Success'; 'The Use of Aphrodisiacs'; 'Abortion Methods'; and 'Sexual Positions'.

Bestselling author or not, a woman was unlikely to emerge unscathed from the vitriol that attended female success and popularity in Greece and Rome. The following describes Martial's reaction to Philaenis in the early Roman empire but it could just as easily have been written in ancient Greece – not so very far away in place and time and labouring under the same prejudicial attitudes towards women and 'lesbians'. At the same time it underscores the disgust with which fellatio and cunnilingus were held in ancient Rome, and Greece, no doubt, before that. Martial labels Philaenis a *tribas,* a 'woman who rubs', in the obscene diatribe in which he describes how she buggers the boys as vigorously as any man and performs cunnilingus on the girls. The sodomy was facilitated by the alleged size of her clitoris, deployed as a penis would be. As far as defamation goes, this was extreme and double edged: Philaenis was not only penetrating like a man, she was licking too – cunnilingus was seen by men as the last word in degradation. Bassa is a similar case; on first sight she appears as chaste as a Lucretia because she was never seen with a man, but she is really a *fututor* – a fucker, bringing together two *cunni,* pretending to be a man. Earlier, Catullus colourfully wrote that any woman who has sex with the repellent Aemilius would be just as likely to lick the anus of a hangman with diarrhoea. Martial seems almost obsessed with cunnilingus, with twelve epigrams referring to it. He excoriates Nanneius, an inveterate cunnilinguist suffering from lingual dysfunction after contracting a sexually transmitted disease of the tongue. He was so prolific a licker that prostitutes preferred to perform fellatio on him rather than kiss him – his comparatively redundant penis being much cleaner than his mouth.[4] Cunnilingus, like fellatio, indicated dubious oral hygiene, anathema to many Greeks and Romans who held the purity of the mouth in high esteem, because the mouth was the vehicle for oratory and declamation.

Elsewhere, women lend a helping hand when Martial recommends that Istantius Rufus has his girl masturbate him as he reads the salacious books, *pathicissimi libelli,* of Musaeus. Less instructive and more 'pornographic' were the works of Sabellus, Musaeus, Mummius, Sotades of Mantinea, Timon of Phlius, Botrys and Hemitheon, who wrote a homoerotic novel called *Sybaritica,* mentioned by Ovid, Martial and Lucian.[5] William Smith in his nineteenth-century dictionary entry calls Hemitheon 'a Sybarite of the vilest character, and the author of an obscene work'. Here is an extract from Lucian's book, to give a flavour of the *demi-monde* we are in here:

> Tell me, if Bassus your sophist, if Battalus the flute player, if the cinaedus Hemitheon of Sybaris who wrote for you such an elegant set of instructions on how to soften the skin, on waxing, on how to practise pederasty or have it practised on one ... a thousand things betray this lie; the walk, the look, the sound of the voice, the bent neck, the white lead, putty and paint which you use, in conclusion, as the proverb goes: 'It's easier to hide five elephants under your armpit than hide one cinaedus.'

Here is Ovid, moaning about the injustice of his exile, his fatal *error,* but at the same time usefully giving a snapshot of the ubiquity and prevalence of the risqué literature of the era:

> There's 'tragedy' too, involving obscene laughter, with many filthy words: it didn't harm one author to show an effeminate Achilles, belittling brave actions with his verse. Aristides associated himself with Milesian vice, but Aristides wasn't driven from his city. Eubius wasn't exiled, writer of a vile story, who described the abortion of an embryo, nor Hemitheon who's just written *Sybaritica.*

To this we can add Petronius' *Satyricon,* Apuleius' *Metamorphoses* and *Cupid and Psyche* which came out after Ovid. *The Priapeia,* too, an anthology of obscene verse celebrating phallic Priapus, and the *Milesian Tales, (Μιλησιακά).* This name derives from Aristides of Miletus who was active in the second century BC, a writer of obscene and amusing tales set in Miletus, a city notorious for its permissiveness and production of dildos. Lucian calls Aristides 'that enchanting spinner of bawdy stories'. Amusingly, Plutarch records that, following the defeat of Carrhae in 53 BC, copies of Milesian fables were found in the kit bags of the Parthians' Roman prisoners:

> Surena, calling together the senate of Seleucia, showed them certain obscene books, of the writings of Aristides, his Milisiaka; nor, indeed, were these forgeries, for they had been found among the baggage of Rustius, and were a good subject to supply Surena with insulting remarks about the Romans, who were not able even in a war to forget such writings and practices.[6]

Miletus lives on with us too in Chaucer's *The Miller's Tale*, Boccaccio's *Decameron* and the *Heptameron* of Margaret of Angoulême.

Sexual vocabulary

We can now review the 'bad language', the *aischrologia*, of the ancient Greeks as it related to sex and sexuality. Ancient Greek is a rich repository of sexual vocabulary, with manifold terms describing the whole gamut of sexuality and sex. Celsus, the Roman encyclopedist and physician, remarks that the Greek sexual vocabulary is superior to that currently in use in Latin:

> Next come subjects relating to the genitalia, for which the terminology employed by the Greeks is the best, and is now standard use, since it can be found in almost every medical book and discourse.[7]

Greek, then, was the *lingua franca* of medicine, even in Roman times. Some of these words shared a sexual connotation. Obscene language was permitted in certain religious festivals and encouraged in women – quite at odds with how women were usually expected to behave.

We have already noted that the cults of Demeter and Persephone promoted female fecundity and earthly fertility. The Thesmophoria, the Stenia, the Haloa and the Eleusinian Mysteries were notable for *aischrologia* – obscene jokes and scatalogical insults – along with the exhibition of phalluses and female genitalia. Their secret utterances were called *arrehta* – 'the unspeakable' – because they violated normal social conventions and conduct.

Homoerotic Obscenities

As we know, the Greeks, again in common with the Romans, had no vocabulary for our word 'homosexual'. Plato describes a woman who preferred other women as a *'hetairistria'* although, given the obvious connection with *hetaerae*, the word may mean prostitutes who had with sex with women. Lucian uses the same word in his *Dialogues of the Courtesans*.[8]

References to homosexuality were usually disparaging, often insinuating effeminacy and ways foreign to Greeks: *euryproktos* is used by Aristophanes to mean 'wide-arsed'. Similar is *chaunoproktos*: 'with a gaping arsehole'. Eubolos, an Athenian Middle Comic poet active around the late 370s, reveals that the Greeks never saw a *hetaerae* in all the ten years they spent outside Troy and, as a result, went home with arses wider than the gates of Troy.[9]

A slack anus was therefore suggestive of rampant anal sex; it was also the focus for a punishment for adultery, demonstrating just how reviled adultery and anal sex were. We have described how one of the punishments for, and a deterrent against, adultery with a married woman was to have a radish introduced forcibly into the rectum ('radish reaming') – a symbol of the erect male penis delighting in revenge; the verb is ῥαφανιδόω (*rhaphanidoo*) with an associated noun. It features in Aristophanes' *Clouds:* (l.1083): Τί δ᾽ ἢν ῥαφανιδωθῇ πιθόμενός σοι τέφρᾳ τε τιλθῇ (But what if he should suffer "the radish" through obeying you?)'. The scholion to Aristophanes' *Wealth* (168) adds helpfully that this humiliation rook place in the *agora* and was preceded by some eye-watering depilation of pubic hair by having hot ashes liberally scattered on the *mons pubis* and around the testicles. In the late Roman republic, Catullus picks up the theme in *Carmen 15* where he threatens *'percurrent raphanique mugilesque* (both radishes and mullets will run you through)' against those eying-up his boyfriend. In making the inserted objects as many and as prickly as possible, the aim was to torture the guilty party until he died of internal haemorrhaging.

An adulterer in Greek was known as a *moichos* where it attracted social stigma involving sex with another man's wife. An effeminate, or a man who allowed himself to be penetrated, was *malakos,* with its overtones of softness and weakness.[10] *Malaken phonen* was an 'effeminate voice'. *Androgunos* is a man-woman, used by Justin to describe effeminate male prostitutes 'who do unspeakable things … to practice this defilement.'[11]

The orator Demosthenes was afflicted by a speech impediment which won him the nickname Batalos, 'the stutterer'; unfortunately for Demosthenes, but apparently apt all the same, *batalos* can also mean 'arsehole', like *proktos*.[12]

Hipponax was an iambic poet whose verse reflected the vulgar side of Ionian society life in and around 540 BC. A deformity and disability may have influenced his acerbic wit and invective. Indeed, Hipponax had a reputation in antiquity for his obscenity; according to Demetrius of Phalermum:

> In his desire to abuse his enemies he shattered the metre, making it lame instead of straightforward, and unrhythmical, suitable for vigorous abuse.

Suda records that Hipponax describes one woman's 'opening of filth' (arse) to mean one who is impure, from *borboros* (βοϱβοϱος), filth, and a 'self-exposer' or 'flasher', from *anasuresthai* (ἀνασύϱεσθαι), to hitch up one's clothes. Elsewhere he destroys Mimnes, a painter, when he paints his own portrait of him as a sodomite: a wide-arse, or *euryproktos* (ευϱύπϱωϰτος), in this case gaping all the way up to the shoulders. Hipponax has no time for Bupalus the sculptor, as a fragment shows in which he calls Bupalus 'the mother-fucker', *metrokoites* (μητϱοϰοίτης), 'with Arete', which ironically means 'virtue'; elsewhere Hipponax tells us that Arete performs fellatio on him. *Messegudorpochestes* (μεσσηγυδοϱποχέστης) is a comic word coined by Hipponax and defined by Suetonius in his *On Defamatory Words*, as 'one who frequently leaves the table to defecate during a meal so that he may fill himself up again'. An eating disorder from antiquity?

Genitalia

Ta aidoia was a euphemism for genitals, as was *aischra*; the former could also mean anything that caused shame and was used as a neutral medical term for the genitalia. Herodotus calls temple prostitution *'aischistos'*.[13]

Krithe, barley, is a euphemism for penis. We meet it in Aristophanes' *Peace* (762–7) where a slave predicts that the female members of the audience will get their 'barley' that evening.

The second-century-AD grammarian Phrynichus Arabius defines *kynodesmai* as 'the thing with which the people of Attica who have their glans exposed bind their penis'. They call the penis *kyon*, dog. There is a vase which demonstrates the *cyon*, or the 'dog', from which the term 'dog-style' presumably comes, and which shows the woman on all fours with the man entering from the rear.

Peos means cock; Aristopanes uses it eighteen times.

We have seen how Strabo tells the story of an apparently idle Corinthian prostitute who, when admonished, tartly replies that she had 'taken down three "looms" that day already'.[14] The word for loom she used, *histos*, means anything that can be 'erected' – all the more shocking because the whore appropriates the language of weaving and wool working, the badges of virtue and of being a good wife in Greece and Rome.

Aristophanes uses the derogatory adjective *psolos* (ψωλος) which can simply mean 'having an erection', as in: 'He's come back here with an old man who's filthy, hunchbacked, wretched, wrinkled, bald, toothless, and, by God, I think he's *psolos* too!'[15]

Clitoris is from the Greek verb meaning 'to shut' – *kleiein* (κλείειν). Another name for it was *nymphi*, meaning 'bride' or 'lovely young woman'. The plural *nymphae* today refers to the labia minora in medical contexts.

The etymology of the word 'cunt' is uncertain. Some believe it derives from the Latin *cuneus*, 'wedge', or from the Proto-Indo-European *gwen*, which is the root of 'queen' and the Greek *gyne*, the word for 'woman'. In Aristophanes' *Acharnians* (750–818) the depilated daughters are described as smooth as piglets, *choiroi*, from cunt, *kysthos*.

What can only be described as dildo-like breadsticks, known as *olisbokollikes* (singular *olisbokollix*), were known in ancient Greece before the fifth century BC.

Masturbation was *anaphlasmos* with *anaphlao* as the verb. Aristophanes uses it in the *Lysistrata* to describe the Spartans masturbating. *Anaphlasmos* is also in Eupolis' *Autolycus* (*c.* 446–411 BC).[16] Another verb is *dephesthai* (as seen in Aristophanes *Peace* 290); *styesthai* means to get an erection.

The verb *lesbiazein* is used to refer to fellatio because the inhabitants of the island of Lesbos allegedly had a predilection for orofacial sex.

A fetishistic attraction to female or male buttocks is termed *callipygian*, 'with beautiful buttocks'. Pygela, a city in Ionia, got its embarrassing name after some of Agamemnon's men stopped off there with 'an ailment of the buttocks' – *pygae* according to Theopompus (Frag. 59). It was changed to Phygela when Pliny rewrote its etymology and thus its history when he recorded that the city was founded by fugitives, *phygades* (*NH* 5, 114). Similarly, Strabo advocated changing Pardosolene (*Geography* 13, 2) to Paroslen because Pardoselene meant 'fart moon'.

Meirax means a nubile young woman. The legal term for a wife is *damar* – its root means to subdue or tame, which socio-linguistically brings woman very close to a slave.

A word for virgin, *menandros* (μένανδρος), comes from μένω and ἀνὴρ, because the female is waiting for a man or husband, *andros*, and a pillar, μενεκράτης (from μένω and κράτος), which provided strong support.

Prostitute

Words for prostitute are legion. Perhaps the most graphic is *chamaitype* or *khamaitypês* (χαμαιτυπής), meaning 'ground-hitter', vividly describing the whore ground into the dirt as she plied her trade on her back. Dirt and prostitutes were often linked: Neaira, the fourth-century *hetaera*, is rubbed in the mud, *proupelakazeto*, by her lover, while another is *spodesilaura*, a pile of ashes, rubbish. Neaira is also described as *ergazomene ... toi somati*, 'a woman who works with her body'.[17]

A verb to describe a prostitute displaying herself was *proagogeuein*, which literally means 'to lead out', and is indicative of how a pimp or madam would display her human merchandise for all to see.[18]

We know that streetwalkers wore sandals which have been excavated with inscribed soles which left an imprint ΑΚΟΛΟΥΘΕΙ AKOLOUTHEI – 'Follow me!' St Clement of Alexandria says that some whores had erotic figures imprinted on the souls of their shoes.[19] The *pornai* (πόρναι) were the lowest rent whores, owned by pimps or a *pornoboskós* (πορνοβοσκός) working in brothels in 'red-light districts' such as Piraeus or Kerameikos, near the Acropolis. A brothel was a *porneion*.

Pallake denoted a concubine, usually a woman forced into sexual servitude as a prisoner of war or a bought slave.

Working girls had professional names and nicknames. Athenaeus tells us about two in an ancient version of 'pot calling the kettle black':

> Callisto once, who was nicknamed 'the Sow' (Ὗς), was fiercely quarrelling with her own mother, who also was nicknamed 'the Crow' (Κορώνη). Gnathaena settled the quarrel, and when asked what caused it, replied, 'What else could it be, but that one Crow was finding fault with the blackness of the other?'

There is also Nicion, a courtesan unflatteringly nicknamed 'the Dog-Fly', and Nico, 'the Goat'. A courtesan called Leme was nicknamed 'Parorama' (literally, an 'oversight'), because she used to let everyone she entertained pay two drachmas. There were 'Little Cows', 'Snails', 'Toads', 'Squids', 'Sows', 'Gazelles', 'Mosquitos',

'Bitches' and 'Bees'. One prostitute, Metiche, was nicknamed 'Waterclock' because she stopped performing as soon as the water ran out of the water jar by her bed.[20] According to Athenaeus, some prostitutes had some strange habits:

> Concerning Phanostrate Apollodorus, in his treatise on courtesans at Athens, says that she was called Phtheiropyle, 'Doorlouse', because she used to stand at the door (πύλη) and hunt for lice (φθεῖϱες).

He goes on to explain the etymology of the word for anchovies in a meretricious context:

> And again you have named, in the same manner, the animals called aphyae. Now, aphyae, besides meaning anchovies, was also a nickname for some courtesans; concerning whom Apollodorus says, 'Stagoniŏn and Anthis were two sisters, and they were called Aphyae, because they were white, and thin, and had large eyes.'

Lysias, in his speech against Medon for perjury, mentions a prostitute by the nickname of Antikyra – because she was in the habit of drinking with men who were crazy and mad; or because she was at one time the mistress of Nicostratus the physician, and he, when he died, left her a great quantity of hellebore and nothing else. Hellebore is a herb which grew near to Antikyra and was regarded as a cure for insanity.

Sexual Medicine

The word 'orgasm' is from the Greek word *orgasmos*, which is defined as 'to swell with moisture, be excited or eager', indicative of the physiological effects of orgasm. The word 'ecstacy' comes from the Greek *ekstasis*, which means to 'stand outside of oneself'.

A word for menstruation is *catamenia*, from the Greek *katamenia* (*kata* = by and *menia* = month). A 'catemenia cup' is a firm, flexible cup inserted in the vagina to collect menstrual blood. A girl's first menstrual period is called a *menarche* from the Greek word *men* (meaning month) and *arkhe* (meaning beginning).

The word 'hymen' occurs frequently in early Greek medicine. Aristotle refers to the hymen of the heart, a hymen of the intestines, and a hymen of the brain. To the Greeks, the hymen was membrane; it is named after Hymen, the Greek goddess of marriage, from whom it specifically refers to the membrane that partially covers the vagina.

'Syphilis' gets its name from a mythological Greek shepherd called Syphilus who was infected with a repellent disease as a punishment for insulting Apollo. Doctors in the late 1400s and early 1500s were so afraid of syphilis they would not write down its name, but used the Greek letter *sigma* as a symbol instead.

Love and passion

The Greeks were particular about what sort of love they were giving and getting. There are four distinct words for love in ancient Greek: *agápe*, *éros*, *philía*, and *storgē*. Here are their nuances:

Agápe (ἀγάπη) is brotherly love, or the love of God for man and of man for God. *Agápe* can be love for one's children and for a husband or wife, or partner, or for other famly members.

Éros (ἔρως) means sexual love and passion, or falling in love. To Plato, *eros* is love felt for a person which can graduate into an appreciation of a person's inner beauty, or even an appreciation of beauty itself. Plato does not see physical attraction as necessary for love to exist, hence the modern phrase 'platonic love' which means cerebral love, love without physical attraction. *Eros* can be destructive, 'limb loosening'; at the highest level, Zeus was overwhelmed by *eros* for Hera.[21]

Philia (φιλία) can be sexual and non-sexual; it means affection, friendship, or a dispassionate, virtuous love, as conceived by Aristotle. In his *Nicomachean Ethics*, *philia* is loyalty to friends, family, and community. *Philos* denotes love between family or friends, enjoyment of an activity or love between lovers; it can describe camaraderie between brothers in arms. Xenophon uses *philia* to describe the love between Ariadne and Dionysus, denoting mutual care and affection.[22] *Philotes* can be sexual love, as used by Hera when Zeus proposes they have sex out in the open on Mount Ida, 'where everything can be seen by anyone'.[23] The verb 'to kiss' is related: *kataphilein*, as used by Plutarch when he tells us that Pericles kissed Aspasia every day before he left the house and again when he returned.[24]

Storge (στοργή) is love and affection particularly of parents and children. It is rarely used in ancient Greek and then almost always as love within a family.

Pothos and *himeros* are 'desire', 'longing' and 'yearning'; *epithumia* is another word for 'lustful desire'. *Pathos* can mean 'passion' in a damaging or deviant context, while one of the meanings of *hubris* is 'uncontrolled, violent sex'. *Akrateia* or *akolasia* was 'unbridled passion'; however, 'self-control' was the aim, *enkrateia,* or *sophrosyne,* 'moderation'. This is what the Spartan soldiery exercised when it was separated from their wives and had to sneak home to have sex.[25] A bitter and twisted Hippolytus will trample women underfoot if they cannot learn *sophrosyne.*[26]

Rape

Rape can be seen as a demonstration of a lack of self-control. As in Latin, there is no specific word in Greek for 'rape'. *Harpazein,* like the Latin *rapere,* means 'to abduct' or 'carry off', with or without a suggestion of the sexual act as we understand it. Where the Greeks wanted to make it transparently clear that 'rape' in the sense of non-consensual sex is what is meant, they added *bia,* 'with force', to *harpazein* just as the Romans added *vi.* The subtle difference between rapists and seducers is demonstrated by the use of *tous biazomenous* for the former and *tous peithontas* for the latter, whom, Lysias tells us, 'function by corrupting the souls of their victims'.[27] Rape could also be denoted by the verb *hubrisein.*

Sexual intercourse

'Bed' was a euphemism for illicit sex, as in *eune* from Euripides' *Bacchae* (222–3) where Pentheus suspects the women of his family of debauchery; another such word is *lechos.* Words for sexual relations are *sunousia,* literally, 'being together', as well as *homilia,* 'intercourse', and *summixis* and *mixis,* 'mingling'. *Plesiazein* sounds apt, and means 'to have sexual relations with'. Aphrodite herself provides a word or two: *ta aphrodisia* is used to denote 'pleasures of sex', and *aphrodisiazein* to enjoy having sex. *Paschein* denotes the much vilified and socially ostracised passive role in male on male sex.

'Fuck' is *binein. Charizesthai* is to gratify sexually, as with Ischomachos' wife; compared to a slave, she is sexier because she is willing, while a slave girl is not necessarily so, compelled as she is to have sex.[28]

In pederastic relationships, *pederestaia,* we have noted that the older lover is the *erastes* while the youth is the *eromenos; paidika* can be used too to denote 'boyfriend', as in Plato's *Symposium* (183a).

In Aristophanes' *Lysistrata* (404–13) a jeweller is invited to mend a wife's necklace by inserting (*enarmotto,* meaning slot in) his safety bolt (*balanos*) in her hole (*trema*).

A female lover who was neither spouse nor prostitute was a *pallike* or *pallakis,* which equates to our modern usage of 'mistress', or 'concubine' if she is an accepted member of the *oikos.*

Coprophilia
'Coprophilia' comes from *kópros* (κόπρος), 'excrement', and *philía* (φιλία), 'liking'for': it is, then, the sexual arousal from faeces: *Skor* is 'shit'. *Peresthai* is 'to fart'; *Porde* meaning a fart can be found in Diogenes Laertius, 6, 94. *Kopros,* excrement, and its derivatives were popular for personal names, particularly for children found exposed on a dunghill, or for apotropaic reasons, to ward off evil spirits.

Other sexual words include:

ΑΝΑΣΕΙΣΙΦΑΛΛΟΣ: a permissive woman; one that jerks a penis [ανασεισίφαλλος = ανασείω + φαλλός] – *anaseisiphallos*

ΒΔΕΩ fart [βδέω = βρωμάω] – *bdeo, bromao*

ΓΛΩΤΤΟΔΕΨΕΩ suck off – *glottodepseo*

ΓΥΝΑΙΚΟΠΙΠΗΣ peeping Tom [γυναικοπίπης = γυναίκα + οπιπτεύω] – *gynaekopipes*

ΔΡΟΜΑΣ prostitute that walks the street [δρομάς = δρόμος] – *dromas*

ΕΣΧΑΡΑ a woman's genitalia [εσχάρα = από το ρήμα ίσχω (εμποδίζω)] – *escara*

ΗΔΟΝΟΘΗΚΗη: a woman's genitalia – edonopheke

ΕΥΠΥΓΟΣ a woman with a nice bum [εύπυγος = ευ + πυγή] – *eupugos*

ΚΑΣΣΩΡΙΣ whore [κασσωρίς = από το κάσις (αδελφός, εταίρος)] – *kassoris*

ΜΥΖΟΥΡΙΣ a woman that sucks a penis [μύζουρις = μυζάω + ουρά (πέος)] – *muzouris*

ΛΥΔΙΑ whore in Roman times – *Lydia*

ΛΟΧΜΗ: hirsute woman's genitalia [> λόχμη (θάμνος)] – *lochme*

ΣΠΟΔΗΣΙΛΑΥΡΑ: streetwalker [σποδή (καταβροχθίζω) + λαύρα (απόπατος)] – *spoderilaura*

ΧΑΛΚΙΔΙΤΙΣ: a very cheap whore – *chalkiditis*

Notes

1 In Bed with the Minoans

1. *Aegean Gender: Minoans, Mycenaeans, and Classical Greeks* http://chelsea-otoole.wikispaces.com/
2. Olsen, *Women, Children and the Family in the Late Aegean Bronze Age: Differences in Minoan and Mycenaean Constructions of Gender*
3. Molloy, 'Martial Minoans?'
4. Cornelius Nepos, *Praefatio*, 3–5
5. Aristotle, *Politics*, 2, 10
6. Strabo, *Geographia*, 10, 4, 21
7. Conon, *Narrations*, 16
8. Plato, *Laws*, 636B–D

2 Mythical Sex: Rape, Incest and Homoeroticism

1. Hyginus, *Fabulae*, 250, 3; 273, 11; Pausanias, *Guide to Greece*, 6, 20, 19
2. Antoninus Liberalis, *Metamorphoses*, 21
3. Homer, *Iliad*, 20, 233–235
4. Plato, *Laws*, 636D
5. Xenophon, *Symposium*, 8, 29–30
6. Conon, *Narrations*, 24
7. Pausanias, 9, 31, 7
8. Hesiod, *Theogony* 211 ff
9. Dio Chrysostom, *Discourses*, 6, 20
10. Footnote in the *Library by Apollodorus*, edited by E. Capps, p. 305
11. Hesiod, *Shield of Heracles*, 1ff
12. Homer, *Iliad*, 19, 95
13. Apollodorus, *Library*, 2, 8, 1

14. *Homeric Hymn to Apollo,* 306–348. Stesichorus, Fragment 239 (Campbell, pp. 166–167)
15. Orphic Fragment 58 Kern Athenagoras, *Apology* 20 (p. 397); van den Broek, p. 137 n. 20; Fowler 2013, p. 9
16. Nonnus, *Dionysiaca,* 18, 273 ff. (II pp. 82–83)
17. Herodotus, 4, 8–10
18. Hyginus *Fabulae,* 75; Apollodorus, *Library* 3, 6, 7; and Phlegon, *Mirabilia,* 4
19. Pausanias, 8, 25, 5
20. Hesiod, *Theogony* 270 ff; Ovid, *Metamorphoses,* 4, 786 ff
21. Hyginus, *op. cit.* 188
22. Ovid, *op. cit.* 2, 833–3, 2; 6, 103–107
23. Pausanias, 7, 17, 8
24. See A. Aggarwal, *Necrophilia: Forensic and Medico-legal Aspects,* p. 8
25. Nonnus, *Dionysiaca,* 12, 330 ff
26. For nymphomania see WHO *ICD-10;* Gourevitch, *Women Who Suffer.*
27. Pausanias, 1, 23, 6
28. Apollodorus, *op. cit.* 2, 13; Hyginus, *op. cit.* 169/a
29. Athenaeus, *Deipnosophistae,* 1, 23d
30. Justinus, *Historiae Phillippicae ex Trogo Pompeio,* 2, 4
31. Strabo, *Geographia* 11, 503
32. Ovid, *Fasti,* 6, 319ff
33. Plutarch, *De Cupiditate Divitiarum,* 8, 527 D. Athenaeus, *op. cit.* 5, 52
34. Csapo, *Riding the Phallus for Dionysus,* p. 260
35. Theocritus, *Idyll,* 13
36. Pindar, *First Olympian Ode* 71; Cicero, *Tusculanae Disputationes,* 2, 27, 67
37. See Aeschylus' *Bassarae;* Ovid, *Metamorphoses,* 10, 23; 11, 1–66
38. See Heinrich Wölfflin, *Drawings of Albrecht Dürer* (2013), pp. 24–25
39. Pausanias, 9, 30, 1
40. Apollodorus, 1 3, 3
41. Lucian, *Dialogues of the Gods;* Servius, commentary on Virgil *Eclogue* 3, 63; Philostratus, *Imagines,* 1, 24; Ovid *op. cit.* 10, 184
42. Apollodorus, *op. cit.*
43. Homer, *Iliad* 2, 594–600; *Scholia on the Iliad,* 595

3 Epic Sex, Tragic Sex and Comedic Sex

1. Cf. Aeschylus fragments 135, 136 Radt; Plato, *Symposium,* 179e–180b; Aeschines, *Against Timarchus* 133, 141–50
2. Homer, *Iliad,* 17, 411, 655
3. *Iliad,* 9, 663–669

4. Aeschylus, *Myrmidons*, fr. 135 Radt

5. *Iliad*, 19, 261–3

6. Homer, *Odyssey* 1, 354–361

7. *Iliad*, 22, 405ff

8. *Iliad*, 6, 425; 22, 470–72

9. *Iliad*, 6, 450–465

10. *Iliad*, 6, 485ff

11. *Iliad*, 6, 370–373; 6, 433–439

12. *Iliad*, 6,466–483

13. *Odyssey*, 7, 311f

14. Euripides, *Alcestis* 177

15. Euripides, *Hippolytus* 373–430

16. Apollonius Rhodius, *Argonautica*, 3, 126–8

17. Euripides, *Medea*, 214–6

18. Euripides, *Suppliants*, 990–1030

19. Euripides, *Helen*, 625–59

20. Homer, *Odyssey*, 6, 175–85

21. Thucydides, 2, 45, 2; Sophocles, *Ajax*, 293

22. Aeschylus, *Libation Bearers*, 123

23. Aeschylus, *Agememnon*, 1409

24. *op. cit.* 14

25. Aeschylus, *Eumenides*, 728–33

26. Aeschylus, *Libation Bearers* 166–68; 349–50; 158–64, 848–52, 863–66

27. Aeschylus, *Agamemnon* 1077; 1407

28. *op. cit.* 1619–20

29. *op. cit.* 1645; 1636; 1649

30. *op. cit.* 1645–6

31. Sophocles, *Antigone*, 47; 200; 61; 64

32. *op.cit.* 484; 480

33. *op. cit.* 463; 546–47; 83

34. *op. cit.* 917; 869

35. *op. cit.* 886; 1206; 939; 937

36. *op. cit.* 89–90

37. Michael Psellus, *Opusculum*, 32

38. Trans. Parker, *The Congresswomen of Aristophanes* http://courses.missouristate.edu/ecarawan/Congresswomen.htm

39. Aristophanes, *Thesmophoriazusae* 520ff; 785ff. Trans, adapted from *Aristophanes: Women at the Thesmophoria. The Complete Greek Drama, vol. 2.* (Eugene O'Neill, Jr. New York 1938)

40. *Idem*, 885ff.

41. *Idem*, 735–6. See also *Lysistrata* 113–4; 195–239; 395; *Thesmophoriazusae* 447–8; 556–7

42. Aristophanes, *Lysistrata*, 507–20; 160–2; 516; 519–20.

43. Aristophanes, *Peace*, 1127–58

44. Aristophanes, *Ecclesiazusae*, 311–; 323–6; 335–8

45. For women in Greek theatre generally and how they were marginalised, see this National Theatre film at http://www.nationaltheatre.org.uk/video/women-in-greek-theatre-1: 'This film explores the role of women in Ancient Greek society and the representation of female identity in Antigone, Women of Troy and Medea. Dr Lucy Jackson, Teaching Fellow at King's College London & Knowledge Exchange Fellow at the Oxford Research Centre in the Humanities (TORCH) looks back over these recent Greek productions at the National Theatre, featuring Helen McCrory and Jodie Whittaker'

4 Marriage, Love, the Wedding, Adultery and Rape

1. Hesiod, *Works and Days*, 699ff
2. Hesiod, *Theogony*, 590ff
3. Plutarch, *Advice on Marriage*, 16–18 = *Moralia* 140b–146a
4. *Palatine Anthology*, 7, 351, cited and translated by Douglas E. Gerber, Greek Iambic Poetry, Loeb (1999) p. 49. See Carey, *Archilochus and Lycambes*, 60–7
5. Musonius Rufus, *On the Goal of Marriage*, 13a
6. Papaspiridi, *Guide du Musée Nationale d'Athènes* (1927), 132 *c.* 340–320 BC. For Damasistrate, see Blake-Reed, Archedice, *FGE* 786–9 = Thucydides 6,59; Aspasia: *CEG* 167; Dionysia *IG* II, 11162.
7. *CEG* 530; 2; 135; 526
8. Plutarch, *Consolatio ad Uxorem*, 3
9. Menander, Fr. 258 K
10. Isaeus, *On the Estate of Aristarchus*, 10, 18–20
11. Athenaeus, *Deipnosophistae*, 13, 55
12. Macrobius, *Saturnalia*, 2, 5, 9-10: *Numquam enim nisi navi plena tollo vectorem*
13. Plutarch, *Dialogue on Love*, 749d–750a
14. Plutarch, *Cato Maior*, 17
15. Achilles Tatius, *Leucippe and Clitophon*, 37, 5ff
16. Athenaeus, *op. cit.* 13
17. *ibid.* 13, 66
18. *ibid.* 13, 67
19. *ibid.* 13, 56
20. Ibykos, fr. 286, *Poetae Melici Graeci*
21. *Greek Anthology*, 5, 210
22. *Greek Anthology*, 12, 50
23. Anacreon, fr 413 *PMG*; Ascelepiades, 5, 189; *Greek Anthology*, 5, 211
24. Fragment 31, *Lobel-Page*
25. *op. cit.* Fragment 47; 130
26. Euripides, *Hippolytus*, 175; 525–64

27. Plutarch, *Demetrius,* 38, 2ff
28. Homer, *Iliad,* 18, 190–496
29. *op. cit.* 3, 38–42
30. Homer, *Odyssey,* 8, 266–276
31. Plutarch, *Parallela Graeca et Romana,* 21
32. Stobaeus, *Anthology,* 4, 28
33. Plutarch, *Alcibiades,* 8
34. Parthenius of Nicaea, *Love Romances,* 18
35. Aristophanes, *Thesmophoriazusae* 395–7; see also 479–89; *Ecclesiazusa,* 225; 499–501
36. See the fragment relating to the regulation of a mystery cult of Methymna from the fourth century BC (*IG* 12, 2, 499)
37. Archilochus, Frag. 196a

5 Sex and Sexuality: Animal Lovers, Necrophilia, Dildos and Masturbation

1. Chrystal, *In Bed with the Romans,* especially chapter 5
2. Diodorus Siculus, 4, 6, 5
3. Isidore of Seville, *Eytmologiae,* 11, 3, 11; Pliny, *NH* 7, 33; 36; 51; 30; 23; Shrew: *NH* 30, 134; Diophantus Diodorus, 32, 10
4. Diodorus, 4, 11
5. *idem,* 32, 12
6. Pliny, *NH* 7, 33; 36; 51; 30; 23; Shrew, *NH* 30, 134
7. Phlegon, *Marvels,* 10, 28
8. Fragments 12, 15, 17
9. Sophocles, *Electra* 1–2; Athenaeus, *The Deipnosophists,* 13, 42
10. Athenaeus, *op. cit.* 13, 43; 13, 45; 13, 44;. 13, 42; 13, 84; 13, 85
11. Herodotus, 5, 92
12. Xenophon, *An Ephesian Tale,* 5, 1
13. Diodorus, 1, 92,6
14. A. Aggarwal, *Necrophilia: Forensic and Medico-legal Aspects,* p.8
15. Apuleius, *Florida,* 2, 49
16. Dio Chrysostom, *Discourses,* 5, 20
17. Artemidorus, *Oneirocritica,* 1, 45
18. *op. cit.* 1, 78
19. *op. cit.* 1, 80
20. *op. cit.* 1, 79

6 In Bed with the Boys and Girls

1. Aristotle, *Politics,* 2, 10
2. *Bisexuality in the Ancient World 2nd edition* (2002; trans. Cormac O' Cuilleanain).

3. Keuls, *Reign of the Phallus,* p. 291
4. Athenaeus, *The Deipnosophists,* 13, 80
5. *Ibidem,* 13, 82
6. Aristotle, *Problems,* 4, 26
7. Ovid, *Fasti,* 2, 303-358
8. Statius, *Achilleid,* 2, 167ff
9. Philostratus Junior, *Imagines* 1; Scholiast on Homer's Iliad, 19, 326; Ovid, *Metamorphoses,* 13, 162ff., Apollodorus, *Bibliotheca,* 3, 13, 8
10. Suetonius, *Julius Caesar,* 2, 45–53
11. Pausanias, *Description of Greece,* 5, 6
12. Aristotle, *Rhetoric,* 1398b
13. See Aristophanes, *Frogs,* 1308; *Wasps,* 1346; and *Ecclesiazusae,* 290
14. Tatian, *Address to the Greeks,* 33
15. Fragment 1, *The Louvre Papyrus*
16. Alcman, Fragment 3, 61–85
17. *PMG,* 358
18. Plutarch, *Lycurgus,* 18, 9

7 In Bed with a Whore: Pornai, Hetaerae and Other Prostitutes

1. Philemon, *The Brothers, PCG* 7, Fr 3
2. Alexis of Thurii, Kock *Com. Att* fragment 98
3. http://www.womenintheancientworld.com/ prostitutesandhetaeraeinancientathens.htm accessed 17 January 2016
4. For the considerable intellectual achievements of some *hetaerae* see my *Women in Ancient Greece;* Athenaeus, *Deipnosophists,* 13, 46; 13, 71.
5. Henry, *Prisoner of History,* 9
6. Aristophanes *The Acharnians,* 523–533
7. Lucian, *A Portrait Study,* 8
8. Plutarch, *De Pythiae Oraculis,* 14
9. Athenaeus, *op. cit.* 13, 59
10. Pausanias, *Description of Greece,* 10, 15, 1
11. Athenaeus, *op. cit.* 13, 54
12. Hippias frag. 14.
13. Athenaeus *op. cit.* 13, 55; 13, 83
14. *idem, op. cit.* 13, 87
15. See Hamel, *Trying Neaera: The True Story of a Courtesan's Scandalous Life in Ancient Greece*
16. Plato, *Symposium,* 176e
17. Athenaeus, *op. cit.* 13, 46; 13, 87
18. Xenophon, *Symposium,* 2, 1–3, 9–10

8 Spartan Sex and Power Sex in Macedon

1. Herodotus, 5, 39
2. *ibid,* 5, 40
3. Plutarch, *Advice on Marriage,* 18
4. Plutarch, *Lycurgus,* 15, 3
5. Arrian of Nicomedia, *op. cit.* 7, 4, 4–6. Translation by M. M. Austin. See also Arrian 7, 4, 4–8; Plutarch *Alexander* 70, 2; Diodorus 17, 107, 6; Justin, 12, 10; Athenaeus, *The Deipnosophists* 12, 538B; Aelian *op. cit.* 8,7; Plutarch, *Moralia* 329D–F
6. Athenaeus, 15, 6
7. Plutarch, *Amatorius,* 17
8. Athenaeus, 13, 40
9. Plutarch, *Alexander,* 21
10. Diodorus Siculus, 17, 77, 5
11. Arrian, *op. cit.* 2, 11, 9; Diodorus 35f; Plutarch, *Alexander* 20, 6–21; Quintus Curtius Rufus, *History of Alexander* 3, 11, 24–26
12. Curtius *op. cit.* 3, 12, 21; see also Plutarch *op. cit.* 21, 3; Athenaeus *op. cit.* 13, 603b-d; Diodorus 17, 38, 1; Justin 11, 9
13. Plutarch, *op. cit.* 29, 4; Curtius, *op. cit.* 4, 5, 1; Justin 11, 12
14. Arrian 4, 18, 4–19, 6
15. See Diodorus, 18, 2–4; Arrian, *De rebus successorum Alexandri* 9
16. Plutarch, *op. cit.* 77,4; Diodorus, 19,11
17. Diodorus, 19, 9-51; Justin, *op. cit.* 14, 6; Diodorus, 19, 52, 4; Justin, *op. cit.* 15, 2, 5; Diodorus, 19. 105
18. Plutarch, *op. cit.* 21
19. Justin, *op. cit.* 11, 10
20. Pliny the Elder, *NH* 35, 79–97
21. Plutarch, *op. cit.* 2, 1
22. Polyaenus, 8, 40; Plutarch, *op. cit.*
23. Diodorus Siculus, 17, 72
24. Ovid, *Remedia Amoris,* 383
25. Dante, *Inferno,* 18,133–136
26. *Metz Epitome,* 40–41
27. Curtius, 8, 10, 34–36; *Metz Epitome,* 45; Justin, 12, 7

9 'Not Like Us': Sex and the Historians

1. Herodotus, *Histories,* 1, 1
2. Thucydides, *A History of the Peloponnesian War,* 1, 22
3. But see Chrystal, *Women at War in Ancient Greece and Rome*
4. Herodotus, 1,1,3
5. *idem* 1, 4, 2
6. Ovid, *Ars Amatoria* 1, 663–668

7. Herodotus, 1, 205ff; 7, 99; 8, 68ff; 8, 87, 8.101; 4, 162ff, 206 ff
8. *idem*, 2, 46
9. Herodotus, 1, 173–4; trans G. C. Macaulay.
10. *idem*, 4, 180
11. *ibid.*
12. *idem*, 4, 176
13. Fragment 40A from Hesiod's *Catalogue of Women* found on Oxyrhynchus Papyri (1358 fr. 2)
14. *idem*, 4, 172, 2; 1, 216, 1
15. *idem*, 4, 205
16. Jordanes, *De Origine Actibusque Getarum*
17. Herodotus, 1, 214
18. Herodotus, 1, 206
19. *idem*, 9, 108
20. *idem*, 9, 112
21. *idem*, 7, 114
22. *idem*, 1, 108
23. *idem*, 1, 119
24. *idem*, 3, 31ff
25. Suetonius, *Nero*, 35, 3
26. Herodotus, 3, 30
27. *idem*, 3, 61
28. *idem*, 3, 68ff
29. *idem*, 3, 118
30. *idem*, 3, 133–134
31. *idem*, 3, 137
32. *idem*, 2, 121e ff
33. *idem*, 4, 144
34. *idem*, 1, 7, 2–13
35. *idem*, 1, 8, 2; 1, 10, 3
36. *idem*, 5, 5
37. *idem*, 5, 7
38. *idem*, 4, 154
39. *idem*, 1, 199ff
40. Theopompus, *Histories*, Book 43
41. Cornelius Nepos, *Lives of Eminent Commanders*, Preface 1–8
42. Plutarch, *Advice on Marriage*, 16–18, or *Moralia*, 140b–146a
43. Plutarch, *Bravery of Women*, 12
44. Herodotus, 7, 152

10 The Benefits of a Small Penis: Sexuality and Beauty in the Visual Arts

1. Aristophanes, *Clouds* 1, 2, 547
2. *ibidem*, 1010–19

3. The Getty *Victorious Youth* (School of Lycippus, 400–200 BC) in the Getty Villa. Poseidon (or Zeus) of Cape Artemision, National Archaeological Museum of Athens, Athens; The Hermes from Atalante, in the National Archaeological Museum in Athens. 'This second-century-BC statue represents a deceased youth in heroic nudity, after an original dating from the fourth century BC and inspired by the Lysippean style.' See also the so-called 'Sacred Gate kouros'. Marble, *c*. 600–590 BC; Kerameikos Archaeological Museum in Athens.
4. Celsus, *De Medicina*, 7, 25. See Hodges, *The Ideal Prepuce in Ancient Greece and Rome*, p. 381
5. Lucian, *Lexiphanes*, 12
6. Aristophanes, *Thesmophoriazusae*, 254
7. Athenaeus, *The Deipnosophists*, 13, 89
8. *ibidem*, 13, 90
9. Dioscorides, *Medical Material*, 2, 80

11 Sex in Greek Religion and in Philosophy

1. Herodotus, 1.181–2
2. Scholiast on Lucian, *De Meretricibus Dialogoi*, 2, 1
3. Pausanias, *A Guide to Greece*, 7, 27, 10
4. *Homeric Hymn to Demeter*, 200–204
5. Clement of Alexandria, *Exhortation to the Heathen*, 2, 17–18
6. Strabo, *Geographia*, 8, 6
7. *ibid*, 17, 46
8. Diodorus Siculus, 1, 47, 1
9. Athenaeus, *The Deipnosophists*, 13, 31
10. *ibid*, 13, 32
11. *ibid*, 34
12. Aristophanes, *Birds* 693–707
13. Plato, *Symposium*, 180c–181c
14. Aristotle, *Rhetoric*, 1370b
15. Epicurus, *Sententiae Vaticanae*, 51
16. Plutarch, *Advice to Bride and Groom*, 15

12 In Bed with a Witch: Erotic Magic

1. Antiphon, *Against the Stepmother for Poisoning*, 1, 14–20
2. Parthenius, *Love Romances*, 12
3. Ovid, *Metamorphoses* 14. 308 ff; Virgil, *Aeneid*, 7, 187 ff
4. Apollonius Rhodius, *Argonautica*, 3, 475–80; 533; 1026–62; 1191–1224; 1246–67; 4, 123–66; 445–81; 1636–91
5. Euripides, *Medea*, 112f

6. Phlegon of Tralles, *Mirabilia*, 1. The story forms the basis of Goethe's *Bride of Corinth*
7. Plutarch, *Moralia*, 138a–146a; *idem, de Superstitione*. Pliny, *NH* 28, 47 and 104; Plato *Laws*, 7, 808d. Translation is by T. J. Saunders. Mormo: Plato, *Crito* 46c; Lucian, *Vera Historia* 139; Empusa: Aristophanes, *Frogs* 285–295; Gello: Sappho *frag* 178; Diodorus Siculus, 20, 41
8. *CIL* 8, 12507; *PGM* 36, 283–294; 1, 83–87; 1, 167–168; 32. Sophia and Gorgonia *SGD* # 151
9. Ziebarth, 24, 1–4, pp. 1042ff
10. *SGD*, 161
11. Pliny, *NH* 28, 256
12. Menander, F313 Korte

13 Women's Sexual Medicine

1. Hesiod, *Works and Days*, 582–588
2. Hippocrates, *On Generation*, 4, 1–3
3. Hippocrates, *Diseases of Women*, 1, 1
4. Hippocrates, *Glands*, 16
5. Carson, p. 153
6. On menstrual cloths, see Croom, *Running the Roman Home* 96–97; Pliny, *NH* 28, 23
7. Josephus, *Jewish Wars*, 4, 8, 4
8. Soranus, *Gynaecology*, 1, 24
9. Hippocrates, *Diseases of Women*, 1
10. *Frag* A81, B65, B67
11. Aristotle, *Problems*, 877a; 878b
12. Plutarch, *A Pleasant Life is Impossible on Epicurean Principles,* 1089a
13. Pausanias, *A Guide to Greece*, 8, 6
14. Plutarch, *Table Talk*, 170e
15. *NH* 28, 58
16. Celsus, *De Medicina*, 7, 29, 7
17. *Gyn*, 4, 2
18. Celsus, *op. cit.* 7, 29, 4–5; Soranus, *Gyn*, 4, 12
19. Aelius Herodianus, 5, 92
20. Soranus, *Gyn*, 4, 14–150
21. Hippocrates, *Places in Man*, 47
22. See *Maines, The Technology of Orgasm*
23. Plato, *Timaeus*, 91a–c
24. Hippocrates, *On Virgins*, 8, 466–70
25. Celsus, 4, 28; Galen, *Nat. Mul.* 109; *Epid.* 3, 7. Martial, 1, 65, 4; 7, 71
26. Hippocrates, *Epidemics*, 6, 8, 32

27. Theophrastus, *Enquiry into Plants,* 9, 18
28. *Kyranides,* 1, 18
29. Theophrastus, *op. cit.* 2, 7

14 Men's Sexual Medicine

1. Celsus, 6, 18, 3b
2. Herodotus, 2, 104
3. Strabo, *Geography,* 16, 2, 37; Diodorus Siculus, 1, 28
4. Strabo, *op. cit.* 16, 4, 5
5. Diodorus Siculus, 3, 32
6. Strabo, *op. cit.* 16, 2, 37 See Strabo's observation that Jews practiced female circumcision at 16, 4, 10
7. Thucydides, *History of the Peloponnesian War,* 6, 27
8. George Grote (1794–1871), 'The Mutilation of the Herma' from his *History of Greece*

15 Bad Language: Sex Manuals and Greek Sexual Vocabulary

1. Martial, 10, 35
2. Suetonius, *Tiberius* 43, 2; Martial 43, 1–4
3. A large number paprus fragments have been found, indicating its popularity: *Oxyrhynchus Papyrus* 2891
4. Martial 7, 67; 1, 90; see also 7, 70; Catullus, 97; Martial, 11, 61
5. Ovid, Tristia 2, 417; Lucian, *Adversus Indoctum,* c. 23; Martial, 12, 95
6. Plutarch, *Crassus,* 32
7. Celsus, *On Medicine,* 6, 18, 1
8. Plato, *Symposium* 191e; Lucian, *Dialogues of the Courtesans,* 5, 2
9. Fragment 120
10. e.g. Aristophanes, *Clouds,* 979
11. Justin Martyr, *Apology,* 1, 27, 2
12. Plutarch, *Demosthenes,* 4
13. Herodotus, 1, 99
14. Strabo, *Geographia* 8, 20, 6
15. Aristophanes, *Birds* 502–9, 74; scholia to Aristophanes, *Wealth* 267–75
16. Aristophanes, *Lysistrata,* 1099; Eupolis, *Autolycus,* 21
17. Demosthenes, *Against Neaera,* 59, 22
18. Justin Martyr, *Apology* 1, 27
19. St Clement of Alexandria *Paedogogus,* 2, 11, 116
20. Athenaeus, *Deipnosophistai,* 576c; 13, 45; 47; 70
21. Homer, *Iliad,* 14, 315–6
22. Xenophon, *Symposium,* 9, 6
23. Homer, *Iliad,* 14, 331–2

24. Plutarch, *Pericles*, 24, 6
25. Plutarch, *Lycurgus*, 15, 5
26. Euripides, *Hippolytus*, 667–8
27. *On the Murder of Eratosthnes*, 1, 32–3
28. Xenophon, *Economics*, 10, 12

Primary Sources Cited

Achilles Tatius (*fl.* second century AD); *Leucippe and Clitophon*
Aelian (*c.* 175–*c.* 235 AD); *Varia Historia*
Aeschylus (*c.* 525–*c.* 456/455 BC); *Agamemnon; Libation Bearers; Eumenides; Bassarae; Fragments; Myrmidons*
Aeschines (389–314 BC), *Against Timarchus*
Alexis of Thurii (*c.* 375–*c.* 275 BC); comic poet
Alcman (*fl.* seventh century BC); lyric poet
Anacreon (b. 575 BC); lyric poet
Antiphon (480–411 BC), *Against the Stepmother for Poisoning*
Antoninus Liberalis (*fl.* AD 100–300); *Metamorphoses*
Apollodorus (AD 100–200); *Bibliotheca*
Apollonius Rhodius (b. AD 295); *Argonautica*
Apuleius (second century AD); *Metamorphoses, Florida*
Archilochus (*c.* 680–*c.* 645 BC); *Fragments*
Aristophanes (*c.* 446–*c.* 386 BC); *Thesmophoriazusae; Lysistrata; Ecclesiazusae; Frogs; Clouds; Birds; Acharnians; Wasps; Plutus*
Aristotle (385–22 BC); *Politics; Generation of Animals; Problems; Rhetoric*
Arrian, Indica (*c.* AD 95–175); *Anabasis Alexandri; De Rebus Successorum Alexandri*
Artemidorus (second century AD); *Oneirocritica*
Ascelepiades (*c.* 124/129–40 BC)
Athenaeus of Naucratis (*fl.* second century AD); *Deipnosophistae*
Athenagoras (*c.* AD 133–*c.* 190); *Apology*
Catullus (84–54 BC)
Celsus (first century AD); *De Medicina*
Cicero (106–43 BC); *Tusculanae Disputationes* 2, 27, 67
CIL *Corpus Inscriptionum Latinarum*, Berlin 1863

Clement of Alexandria (*c*. 150–*c*. 215); *Exhortation to the Heathen*
Conon (before 444– after 394 BC); *Narrations*
Demosthenes; *Apollodorus Against Neaera*
Dio Chrysostom (*c*. 40–*c*. 115); *Discourses*
Diodorus Siculus (*fl*. 60–30 BC); *Bibliotheca Historica*
Dioscorides (first century AD); *Medical Material*
Epicurus (341–270 BC); *Sententiae Vaticanae*
Euripides (*c*. 480–406 BC); *Andromache; Medea; Electra; Bacchae; Hippolytus; Cretans; Chrysippus; The True-Hearted Wife; Alcestis; Suppliants; Helen*
Herodas (*fl*. 300 BC); *Mimes*
Herodian (*c*. AD 170–*c*. 240); *History of the Empire from the Death of Marcus*
Herodotus (484–425 BC); *Histories*
Hesiod (*fl*. 750–650 BC); *Works and Days; Catalogue of Women* or *Ehoiai; Theogony; Shield of Heracles*
Hippias (late fifth century BC); *Fragments*
Hippocrates (*c*. 460–*c*. 370 BC); *Epidemics; Airs, Waters, Places; On Generation; Diseases of Women; Glands; Places in Man*
Hipponax (541–487 BC); iambic poet
Homer (*c*. 850 BC); *Odyssey; Iliad*
Homeric Hymn to Apollo
Homeric Hymn to Demeter
Hyginus (*c*. 64 BC–AD 17); *Fabulae*
Ibykos (*fl*. sixth century BC); *Poetae Melici Graeci*
Isaeus (*fl*. early fourth century BC; Attic orator; *On the Estate of Aristarchus*
Isidore of Seville (*c*. AD 560–636); *Etymologiae*
Jordanes (sixth century AD); *De Origine Actibusque Getarum*
Josephus (AD 37–*c*. 100); *Against Apion; Jewish Wars*
Justinus (second century AD); *Historiae Phillippicae ex Trogo Pompeio*
Juvenal (AD 55–138); *Satires*
Louvre Papyrus
Lucian (*c*. AD 125–180); *In Praise of a Fly; Vera Historia; Dialogues of the Gods; A Portrait Study; Lexiphanes; Adversus Indoctum; Dialogue of the Courtesans*
Lysias (*c*. 400 BC); *Against Eratosthenes*
Macrobius (*fl*. AD 400); *Saturnalia*
Martial (AD 41–104); epigrammist
Menander (*c*. 342/41–*c*. 290 BC); *Epitrepontes; Fragments*
Metz Epitome; *Liber de Morte Alexandri Magni Testamentumque*

Michael Psellus (AD 1000); *Opusculum*
Musonius Rufus (AD 100); Stoic philosopher; *On the Goal of Marriage*
Nepos, Cornelius (*c.* 110–*c.* 25 BC); *Excellentium Imperatorum Vitae Praefatio*
Nonnus (fifth century AD); *Dionysiaca*
Ovid (43 BC–AD 17); *Metamorphoses; Remedia Amoris; Ibis; Heroides; Fasti; Amores; Ars Amatoria*
Palatine Anthology: the collection of Greek poems and epigrams discovered in 1606 in the Palatine Library in Heidelberg. It comprises material from the seventh century BC to AD 600 and later formed the main part of the Greek Anthology.
Parthenius (first century BC–14 AD); *Erotica Pathemata*
Pausanias (*c.* AD 110–*c.* 180); *Description of Greece*
PGM: K. Preisendanz, *Papyri Graecae Magicae*, Leipzig 1928
Philemon (*c.* 362 BC–*c.* 262 BC); *The Brothers*
Philostratus (third century AD); *Imagines*
Phlegon of Tralles (second century AD); *Mirabilia*
Pindar (*c.* 522–*c.* 443 BC); *Pythian Ode; Hymn to Fates*
Plato (428–348 BC); *Theaetetus; Laws; Crito; Symposium; Timaeus*
Pliny the Elder (AD 23–79); *Historia Naturalis*
Plutarch (*c.* AD 45–125); *Moralia; Lycurgus; Alcibiades; Alexander; Demetrius; Coniugalia Praecepta; De Superstitione; On Deisidaemonia; De Cupiditate Divitiarum; Consolatio ad Uxorem; Dialogue on Love; Cato Maior; Parallela Graeca et Romana; De Pythiae Oraculis; Bravery of Women; A Pleasant Life is Impossible on Epicurean Principles; Table Talk; Crassus; Pericles; Demosthenes*
Polyaenus (second century AD); *Strategems*
Quintus Curtius Rufus (first century AD); *History of Alexander*
Sappho (b. 630/612 BC–*c.* 570)
Scholia on the Iliad
Scholiast on Lucian *De Meretricibus Dialogoi*
Scholion to *Argonautica*
Semonides (seventh century BC); *Types of Women*
Servius, *commentary on Virgil's Eclogue*
Sophocles (*c.* 497–406 BC); *Ajax, Antigone; Tereus; Trachiniae; Elektra*
Soranus (*fl.* AD 100); *Gynaikea; Leonidas*
Statius (*c.* AD 45–*c.* 96); *Thebaid; Achilleid*
Stesichorus (*c.* 640–555 BC); lyric poet
Stobaeus, Joannes (*fl.* fifth century AD); from Stobi in Macedonia

Strabo (64 BC–*c*. AD 24); *Geographia*

Suda: a huge tenth-century Byzantine encyclopedia of the ancient Mediterranean world

Suetonius (*c*. 69–after AD 22); *Julius Caesar; Nero; Tiberius*

Tacitus (*c*. AD 56– after 117); *Dialogus*

Tatian (AD 120–180); *Address to the Greeks*

Theocritus (*fl*. 270 BC); *Idylls*

Theophrastus (*c*. 371–*c*. 287); *Enquiry into Plants*

Theopompus of Chios (*c*. 380–*c*. 315 BC); *Histories*

Thucydides (460–395 BC); *History of the Peloponnesian War*

Virgil (70–19 BC); *Aeneid*

Xenophon (*fl*. 371 BC); *Oeconomicus An Ephesian Tale*

Abbreviations

AJP = *American Journal of Philology*
Anc Soc = *Ancient Society (Louvain)*
BHM = *Bulletin of the History of Medicine*
C&M = *Classica et Mediaevalia*
CB = *Classical Bulletin*
CJ = *Classical Journal*
Cl. Ant = *Classical Antiquity*
CA News = *Classical Association News*
CP = *Classical Philology*
CQ = *Classical Quarterly*
CR = *Classical Review*
CW = *Classical World*
DSM = *The Diagnostic and Statistical Manual of Mental Disorders*
EMC = *Echos du Monde Classique*
G&R = *Greece and Rome*
GRBS = *Greek, Roman and Byzantine Studies*
HSCP = *Harvard Studies in Classical Philology*
JHS = *Journal of Hellenic Studies*
JRS = *Journal of Roman Studies*
JWAG = *Journal of the Walters Art Gallery*
PCPS = *Proceedings of the Cambridge Philosophical Society*
SO = *Symbolae Osloensis*
SHPBBS = *Studies in History & Philosophy of Biological & Biomedical Sciences*
TAPA = *Transactions of the Proceedings of the American Philological Asscn*
WHO = *ICD: International Classification of Diseases (10th version, Geneva 2010)*

Bibliography

Aggarwal, A. *Necrophilia: Forensic and Medico-legal Aspects* (Boca Raton, FL: 2011)

Aggleton P. '"Just a snip?": A Social History of Male Circumcision', *Reproductive Health Matters,* 15 (2007), 15–21

Aguirre, C. M. 'Expressions of Love and Sexual Union in Hesiod's Catalogue of Women', *CFC (G): Estudios griegos e indoeuropeos,* 192 (2005), 19–25

Alden, M. 'Ancient Greek Dress', *Costume* 37 (2003)

Alexiou, M. *The Ritual Lament in Greek Tradition* (New York: 2002)

Allen, (Sister) P. *The Concept of Woman: the Aristotelian Revolution, 750 BC–AD 1250* (Montreal: 1985)

Allen, P. L. *The Wages of Sin: Sex and Disease, Past and Present* (Chicago, IL: 2000)

American Psychiatric Association, *Diagnostic and Statistical Manual of Mental Disorders IV* (Arlington: 1994)

Amunsden, D.W. 'The Age of Menarche in Classical Greece and Rome', *Human Biology,* 42, (1970), 79–86

Anderson, J. E. 'Two Sides to Every Story: A Tale of Love and Hate on a Lakonian Stele', *ΣPARTA: Journal of Ancient Spartan and Greek History,* 3

Anderson, Ø. 'The Widows, the City, and Thucydides', *SO,* 62 (1987), 33–50

Androutsos, G. 'Sexual Mutilations through the Ages', *Rev Med Brux.* 33 (2012), 556–61

'Hermaphroditism in Greek and Roman Antiquity', *Hormones* 5 (2006), 214–217

Angel, J.L. 'The Length of Life in Ancient Greece', *Journal of Gerontology* 2 (1947), 18–24

Angeloglou, M. *A History of Make-up* (London: 1970)

Ankerloo, B. *Witchcraft and Magic in Europe Vol 2: Ancient Greece and Rome* (London: 1998)

Annas, J. 'Plato's Republic and Feminism', in Osborne (ed), *Woman in Western Thought*, 24–33

Archer, L. J. (ed.) *Women in Ancient Societies: An Illusion of the Night* (London: 1994)

Aristophanes and Menander: *Women in Power; Wealth; The Malcontent; The Woman from Samos* (London: 1994)

Arkins, B. 'Sexuality in Fifth-Century Athens', *Classics Ireland* 1 (1994)

Arnott, W. G. *Menander, Plautus and Terence* (Oxford: 1975)

Arthur, M. B. 'Early Greece: The Origins of the Western Attitude toward Women', in J. Peradotto, *Women in the Ancient World: The Arethusa Papers*, (Albany: 1984), 7–58

Ashari, D. 'Laws of Inheritance, Distribution of Land and Political Constitutions in Ancient Greece', *Historia: Zeitschrift für Alte Geschichte* 12 (1963), 1–21

Atchity, K. 'Greek Princes and Aegean Princesses: The Role of Women in the Homeric Poems', in *Critical Essays on Homer*, ed. Kenneth Atchity, (Boston: 1987), 15–36

Augoustakis, A. *Motherhood and the Other: Fashioning Female Power in Flavian Epic* (Oxford: 2010)

Ault, B. A. *Ancient Greek Houses and Households: Chronological, Regional, and Social Diversity* (Philadelphia: 2005)

Austin, N. *Helen of Troy and Her Shameless Phantom* (Ithaca, NY: 1994)

Badian, E. 'ROXANA', Encyclopædia Iranica, online edition, 2015: http://www.iranicaonline.org/articles/roxana [accessed on 31 January 2016]

Bagnall, R. S. *Women's Letters from Ancient Egypt, 300 BC–AD 800*, (Ann Arbor, MI: 2006)

Bahn, P. G. *Ancient Obscenities: Or Things You Shouldn't Know About the History of Mankind* (London: 2003)

Bahrani, Z. *Women of Babylon: Gender and Representation in Ancient Mesopotamia* (London: 2001)

Baird, J. *Ancient Graffiti in Context* (London: 2010)

Bakker, E. J. (ed.) *Brill's Companion to Herodotus* (Leiden: 2002)

Barber, E.W. *Women's Work: The First 20,000 Years – Women, Cloth and Society in Early Times* (London: 1996)

Barcan, R. *Nudity: A Cultural Anatomy* (New York: 2004)

Bardi, U. *The Sex Life of the Sphinx* (2005) http://www.
surfchem.unifi.it/solid/bardi/chimera/sexlifeofthesphinx/
sexlifeofthesphinx03oct05.htm.

Bardis, P. D. 'Selected Aspects of Sex Life in Ancient Greece',
Indian Journal of Social Research 7 (1966), 57–63

Barnes, C. *In Search of the Lost Feminine: Decoding the Myths
That Radically Reshaped Civilization* (2006)

Barras, V. *Galen's Psychiatry,* in Hamanaka, 3–8

Bayon, H. P. 'Ancient Pregnancy Tests in Light of Contemporary
Knowledge', *Proceedings of the Royal Society of Medicine*
32(1939), 1527–39

Beard, M. *Pompeii: The Life of a Roman Town* (London: 2008)
'"With this body I thee worship": Sacred Prostitution in
Antiquity', in Wyke, M. *Gender and the Body in the Ancient
Mediterranean* (Oxford) 56–79

Beard M. R. *Woman as Force in History: A Study in Traditions and
Realities* (1946)
On Understanding Women (1931)

Bell, L. A. *Visions of Women: Being A Fascinating Anthology With
Analysis Of Philosophers' Views Of Women From Ancient To
Modern Times* (London: 2003)

Bell, R. *The Oxford Handbook of Childhood and Education in the
Classical World* (Oxford: 2014)

Bell, R. E. *Women of Classical Mythology: A Biographical
Dictionary* (Oxford: 1993)
'Cassandra in the Classical World', in Bell, *Women in Classical
Mythology*

Bertman, S. *The Conflict of Generations in Ancient Greece and
Rome* (Amsterdam: 1976)

Betz, H. D. *Greek Magical Papyri in Translation 2/e* (Chicago: 1997)

Bicknell, P. 'The Witch Aglaonice and Dark Lunar Eclipses in
the Second and First Centuries BC', *Journal of the British
Astronomical Association* 93, 160–163

Blair, E. *Plato's Dialectic on Woman: Equal, Therefore Inferior*
(London: 2012)

Blake-Reed, J. S. *Manchester Guardian* 23 Feb 1922

Blanshard, A. J. L. 'Roman Vice', in *Sex: Vice and Love from
Antiquity to Modernity* (Oxford: 2010), 1–88

Bloch, E. 'Sex Between Men and Boys in Classical Greece: Was it
Education for Citizenship or Child Abuse?', *Journal of Men's
Studies* (2001)

Blok, J. 'Virtual Voices: Towards a Choreography of Women's Speech in Classical Greece', in André Lardinois ed. *Making Silence Speak: Women's Speech in Ancient Greece* (Princeton: 2001), 95–116

'The Appointment of Priests in Attic Gene', *Zeitschrift für Papyrologie und Epigraphik* 169 (2008), 95–12

(ed.) *Sexual Asymmetry: Studies in Ancient Society* (Amsterdam: 1987)

'Women in Herodotus' Histories', In Bakker (2002), 225–242

Blondell, R. *Ancient Sexuality: New Essays* (Columbus, OH: forthcoming)

Women on the Edge: Four Plays by Euripides (New York: 1999)

Bluestone, N. H. *Women and the Ideal Society: Plato's Republic and Modern Myths of Gender* (Massachusetts: 1988)

Blundell, S. *The Sacred and the Feminine in Ancient Greece* (London: 1998)

Women in Ancient Greece (Cambridge, MA: 1995)

Blyth, J. M. 'Women in the Military: Scholastic Argument and Medieval Images of Female Warriors', *History of Political Thought* 22 (2001); also at www.imprint.co.uk/hpt/179.pdf

Bodel, J. *Epigraphic Evidence: Ancient History from Inscriptions* (London: 2001)

Boehringer, S. *L'Homosexualite Feminine dans l'Antiquite Greque et Romain* (Paris: 2007)

Homosexualite: Aimer en Grece et Rome (Paris: 2010)

'Sex, Lies and (Video) Trap: The Illusion of Sexual Identity in Lucian's Dialogues of the Courtesans', in Blondell, *Ancient Sex Des Femmes en Action: L'individu et la Fonction en Grèce Antique* (Athens: 2013)

'Female Homoeroticism', in Hubbard, T. K. *A Companion to Greek and Roman Sexualities* (Chichester: 2014), 150–163

Boer, R. 'From Horse Kissing to Beastly Emissions: Paraphilias in the Ancient Near East' In Masterson, M. *Sex in Antiquity: Exploring Gender and Sexuality in the Ancient World.* (London: 2014) 69ff

Booth, C. *In Bed with the Ancient Egyptians* (Stroud: 2015)

Bosman, P. (ed.) *Mania: Madness in the Greco-Roman World* (Pretoria: 2009)

Boswell, J. *The Kindness of Strangers: The Abandonment of Children in Western Europe from Antiquity to the Renaissance,* (New York: 1998)

Bouvrie, S. des *Women in Greek Tragedy* (Oslo: 1990)

Bowden, H. *Classical Athens and the Delphic Oracle: Divination and Democracy* (Cambridge: 2005)

Bowman, L. 'Nossis, Sappho and Hellenistic Poetry', *Ramus* 27 (1998), 39–59

Boys-Stones, G. *The Oxford Handbook of Hellenic Studies* (Oxford: 2009)

Brashear, W. M, 'The Greek Magical Papyri: "Voces Magicae"', *Aufstieg und Niedergang der Römischen Welt* II, 18 (1995), 34–5

Bremmer, J. 'Greek Pederasty and Modern Homosexuality', in Bremmer, *From Sappho to De Sade*, 1–14
From Sappho to De Sade: Moments in the History of Sexuality (London: 1991)

Brisson, C. *Sexual Ambivalence: Androgyny and Hermaphroditism in Graeco-Roman Antiquity* (Berkeley: 2002)

Brisson, L. 'Women in Plato's Republic', *Etudes Platoniciennes* 9 (2012), 129–136

Brooten, B. J. *Love between Women: Early Christian Responses to Female Homoeroticism* (Chicago: 1996)
'Lesbian Historiography before the Name?' *GLQ: A Jnl of Lesbian and Gay Studies* 4 (1998), 606–630

Brosius, M. *Women in Ancient Persia, 559–331 BC* (Oxford: 1996)

Brown, P. G. M. 'Love and Marriage in Greek New Comedy', *CQ* 43 (1993) 189–205

Brule, P. *Women of Ancient Greece* (Edinburgh: 2003)

Brumfeld, A. 'Aporetta: Verbal and Ritual Obscenity in the Cults of Ancient Women', in Hagg, R. (ed.), *The Role of Religion in the Early Greek Polis* (Stockholm: 1996) 67–74

Budin, S. *The Myth of Sacred Prostitution in Antiquity* (Cambridge: 2008)

Buis, E. J. 'Mythology' in *Encyclopedia of Rape*. ed. Merril D. Smith (Westport: 2004), 132–134

Bunchan, B. *Women in Plato's Political Theory* (New York: 1999)

Burg, B. R. *Gay Warriors* (New York: 2002)

Bushnell, R. W. *A Companion to Tragedy* (Chichester: 2005)

Butrica, J. L. 'Some Myths and Anomalies in the Study of Roman Sexuality', in *Same-Sex Desire and Love in Greco-Roman Antiquity*, 218–224

Bryk, F. *Circumcision in Man and Woman: Its History, Psychology and Ethnology* (Honolulu: 2001)

Cahill, J. *Her Kind: Stories of Women from Greek Mythology* (Peterborough, Ont: 1995)

Cairns, D. *Body Language in the Greek And Roman Worlds* (Swansea: 2005)

Calame, C. *The Poetics of Eros in Ancient Greece* (Princeton: 2013)

Caldwell, J. M. *Religion and Sexual Violence in Late Greco-Roman Antiquity*. (PhD thesis, Syracuse University, 2003)

Calimach, A. *Lovers' Legends: The Gay Greek Myths* (New Rochelle: 2002)

Cameron, A. (ed.) *Images of Women in Antiquity* (London: 1983)
'Love (and Marriage) Between Women', *GRBS* 39 (1998), 137–156

Cantarella, E. 'Gender, Sexuality, and Law', in Gagarin, M. *The Cambridge Companion toAncient Greek Law* (Cambridge: 2011) 236–253
Bisexuality in the Ancient World (London: 2002)
Pandora's Daughters: The Role and Status of Women in Greek and Roman Antiquity (London: 1987)

Carey, C. 'Apollodoros' Mother: The Wives of Enfranchised Aliens in Athens', *CQ*41 (1991), 84–89
'Archilochus and Lycambes', *CQ* 36(1986), 60–67

Carney, E.D. *Olympias: Mother of Alexander the Great* (London: 2006)
'Women and Dunasteia in Caria', *AJP* 126 (2005), 65–91
Women and Monarchy in Macedonia, (Norman, OK: 2000)

Carpenter, T. A. (ed.) *Masks of Dionysus* (Ithaca, NY: 1993)

Carroll, M. *Woman in All Ages and in All Countries* Vol. 1 1907. (Reprint. London: Forgotten Books, 2013)

Carson, A. 'Putting Her in Her Place: Woman, Dirt, and Desire', in Halperin (ed.), *Before Sexuality: The Construction of Erotic Experience in the Ancient Greek World* (Princeton: 1990), 135–69

Cartledge, P. 'Alexandria the Great', *History Today* 59 (2009)
The Spartans: An Epic History, 2nd edition (2003)
The Greeks. A Portrait of Self and Others (Oxford: 1993)
'Engendering History: Men v Women' in Cartledge, *The Greeks: A Portrait of Self and Others* (Oxford: 1993)
'Spartan Wives: Liberation or License?', *CQ* 31 (1981)
'The Politics of Spartan Pederasty', *PCPS* 27 (1981), 17–36

Chandezon, C. 'Dream Interpretation, Physiognomy, Body Divination', in Hubbard (2014), 297–313

Chrystal, P. *Women in Ancient Greece: Seclusion, Exclusion, Illusion* (Stroud: 2016)
Ancient Greece in 100 Facts (Stroud: 2016)

Women at War in Ancient Greece and Rome (Barnsley: 2016)

Roman Women: The Women Who Infuenced the History of Rome (Stroud: 2015)

In Bed with the Romans (Stroud: 2015)

Women in Ancient Rome (Stroud: 2014)

Differences in Attitude to Women as Reflected in the Work of Catullus, Propertius, the Corpus Tibullianum, Horace and Ovid (MPhil thesis, University of Southampton, 1982)

Chugg, A. M. *Alexander's Lovers*, 2nd edition (2012)

Cilliers, L. *Mental Illness in the Greco-Roman Era* in Bosman (2009), 130–140

Clark, G. *Women in the Ancient World* (Oxford: 1989)

Clarke, W. M. 'Achilles and Patroclus in Love', *Hermes* 106 (1978), 381–396

Clauss, J. J. (ed), *Medea: Essays on Medea in Myth, Literature, Philosophy and Art* (Princeton: 1997)

Cohen, B. 'Exposing the Female Breast of Clothes in Classical Sculpture' in A. G. Koloski-Ostrow (ed), *Naked Truths. Women, Sexuality and Gender in Classical Art and Archaeology*, (London: 1997), 66–92

(ed.) *The Distaff Side: Representing the Female in* Homer's Odyssey (Oxford: 1995)

Cohen, D. 'Law, Sexuality, and Society The Enforcement of Morals in Classical Athens' (Cambridge: 1991)

'Seclusion, Separation and the Status of Women' in McAuslan, I. *Women in Antiquity*, 134–145

'Law, Society and Homosexuality in Classical Athens' in Golden (ed.) *Sex and Difference in Ancient Greece and Rome*

'Consent and Sexual Relations in Classical Athens', in A. E. Laiou (ed.), *Consent and Coercion to Sex and Marriage in Ancient Societies* (Washington, DC: 1993), 5–16

Cohen, E. E. 'Sexual Abuse and Sexual Rights: Slaves' Erotic Experience at Athens and Rome' in Hubbard (2014), 184f

'Whoring Under Contract: The Legal Context of Prostitution in Fourth-Century Athens', in Hunter, V. ed., *Law and Social Status in Classical Athens* (Oxford: 2000) 113–47

'Written Contracts of Prostitution in Fourth-century Athens', in Triantaphyllopoulos, M.I (Komotini, 2000) 109–22

Cohen, I.M. 'The Hesiodic Catalogue of Women and Megalai Ehoiai', *Phoenix* 40 (1986), 127–42

'Traditional Language and the Women in the Hesiodic Catalogue of Women', *Studia Classica Israelica* 10 (1989), 12–27

Cole, S. 'Greek Sanctions Against Sexual Assault', *CP* 79 (1984), 97–113

Colin, G. *Rome et la Grece de 200 a 146 BC avant JC* (Paris: 1905) 'Luxe Oriental et Parfums Masculins dans la Rome Alexandrine', *RBPH 33* (1935), 5–19

Collins, D. (ed.) *Magic in the Ancient Greek World* (Oxford: 2008)

Colton, R. E. 'Juvenal and Martial on Women who Ape Greek Ways', *CB 50* (1973), 42–44

Compton, L. '"An Army of Lovers" – The Sacred Band of Thebes'. *History Today* 44 (1994), 23–29

Connelly, J. B. *Portrait of a Priestess: Women and Ritual in Ancient Greece* (Princeton: 2009)

Cooper, K. *The Virgin and the Bride: Idealized Womanhood in Late Antiquity* (Cambridge, MA: 1996)

Corbeil, A. *Sexing the World: Grammatical Gender and Biological Sex in Ancient Rome* (Princeton, NJ: 2015)

Corbier, M., 'Male Power and Legitimacy through Women', in Hawley (1995), 178–93
'Child Exposure and Abandonment', in Dixon (ed.), *Childhood, Class and Kin in the Roman World* (London: 2001) 52–73

Cox, C. A. *Household Interests: Property, Marriage Strategies, and Family Dynamics in Ancient Athens* (Princeton, NJ: 2014)

Csapo, E. 'Riding the Phallus for Dionysus: Iconology, Ritual, and Gender-Role De/Construction'. *Phoenix* 51 (1997), 260ff

Curran, Leo C. 'The Mythology of Rape', *Classical World* 72 (1978), 97–98

Cyrino, M. S. *Screening Love and Sex in the Ancient World* (London: 2013)

Dalby, A. *Empires of Pleasures: Luxury and Indulgence in the Roman World* (London: 2000)

Dasen, V. 'Multiple Births in Ancient Medical Texts', *Gesnerus* 55 (1998) 183–204
'Multiple Births in Graeco-Roman Antiquity', *Oxford Journal of Archaeology* 16, (1997), 61ff

Dauphin, C. M. 'Brothels, Baths and Babes: Prostitution in the Byzantine Holy Land', *Classics Ireland* 3 (1996), 47–72

Davidson, J. *The Greeks and Greek Love* (London: 2007)
Courtesans and Fishcakes: The Consuming Passions of Classical Athens (London: 1997)

Dayton, L. 'The Fat, Hairy Women of Pompeii', *New Scientist* 1944 24 September 1994

Deacy, S. (ed.) *Rape in Antiquity* (London: 1997)

'From "Flowery Tales" to "Heroic Rapes": Virginal Subjectivity in the Mythological Meadow', *Arethusa* 46 (2013), 395–413

'Uxoricide in Pregnancy: Ancient Greek Domestic Violence in Evolutionary Perspective', *Evolutionary Psychology* 11, 994–1010

Athena, Oxford Bibliographies (2015)

Dean-Jones, L. *Women's Bodies in Classical Greek Science* (Oxford: 1994)

DeBrohun, J. 'Fashion and Dress: Power Dressing in Ancient Greece and Rome', *History Today* 51 (2001)

Dean-Jones, L. 'The Politics of Pleasure: Female Sexual Appetite in the Hippocratic Corpus' in Stanton 1992, *Discourses* 48–77

'Medicine: The 'Proof' of Anatomy', in Fantham, *Women in the Classical World* (1994), 183–215

Women's Bodies in Classical Greek Science (Oxford: 1994)

DeBois, P. *Centaurs and Amazons: Women and the Pre-history of the Great Chain of Being* (Ann Arbor: 1993)

Delaney, J. *Curse: A Cultural History of Menstruation* (Champaign, IL: 1988)

Demand, N. *Birth, Death, and Motherhood in Classical Greece* (Baltimore: 2004)

'Women and Slaves as Hippocratic Patients', in Joshel, *Women* (1998), 69–84

Deslauriers, M. 'Women, Education and Philosophy', in James, *Companion* (2012), 343–353

Detel, W. *Foucault and Classical Antiquity Power: Ethics and Knowledge.* (Cambridge: 2005)

Detienne, M., 'The Violence of Well-born Ladies: Women in the Thesmophoria', in M. Detienne (ed.) *The Cuisine of Sacrifice among the Greeks* (London: 1989)

DeVoto, J. G. 'The Theban Sacred Band', *The Ancient World* 23 (1992), 3–19

Dewald, C. 'Biology and Politics: Women in Herodotus' Histories', *Pacific Coast Philology* 15 (1980), 11–18

'Women and Culture in Herodotus' Histories', *Women's Studies* 8 (1981), 93–127

De Wit-Tak, T. M. 'The Function of Obscenity in Aristophanes' "Thesmophoriazusae" and "Ecclesiazusae"'. *Mnemosyne* 21 (1968), 357–365

Dickason, A. 'Anatomy and Destiny: The Role of Biology in Plato's Views of Women', in *Gould* (ed.), *Women and Philosophy: Toward a Theory of Liberation* (New York: 1976)

Dickie, M. W. 'Who Practised Love-magic in Classical Antiquity and in the Late Roman World?', *CQ* 50 (2000), 563–583
Magic and Magicians in the Graeco-Roman World (London: 2001)

Dickison, S. 'Abortion in Antiquity', *Arethusa* 6 (1973), 158–166

Dillon, M. 'Were Spartan Women Who Died in Childbirth Honoured with Grave Inscriptions?', *Hermes* 135 (2007)
Girls and Women in Classical Greek Religion (London: 2002)

Dodd, D.B. 'Athenian Ideas about Cretan Pederasty', in T. Hubbard (ed.), *Greek Love Reconsidered* (New York: 2000), 33–41

Doherty, L. E. 'Putting the Women Back into the Hesiodic Catalogue of Women', in M. Leonard, *Laughing at Medusa: Classical Myth and Feminist Thought*, (Oxford: 2006), 297–325
Siren's Songs: Gender, Audiences, and Narrators in the Odyssey (Ann Arbor, TX: 1995)

Donahue, J. *The Study of Women and Gender in the Ancient World* (Portland, OH: 1997)

Doniger, W. *Splitting the Difference: Gender and Myth in Ancient Greece and India 2nd edition* (Chicago: 1999)

Dossey, L. 'Wife-beating and Manliness in Late Antiquity', *Past & Present* 199 (2008), 3–40

Doumanis, M. *Mothering in Greece: From Collectivism to Individualism* (New York: 1983)

Dover, K. J. *Greek Homosexuality* (London: 1978)
'Greek Homosexuality and Initiation', in *Que(e)rying Religion: A Critical Anthology* (London: 1997), 19–38
'Classical Greek Attitudes to Sexual Behavior', in Golden, *Sex and Difference*, 114–125
'Aristophanes' Speech in Plato's Symposium', *JHS* 86 (1966), 41–50

Driessen, J. Chercher la Femme: Minoan Gendered Architecture http://www.digitalancienthistory.com/gender-in-minoan-culture.html

Du Bois, P. *Sowing the Body: Psychoanalysis and Ancient Representations of Women* (Chicago: 1988)
Centaurs and Amazons (Ann Arbor: 1982)

Ducat, J. *Spartan Education: Youth and Society in the Classical Period*, (Swansea: 2006)

Duff, T. *Plutarch's Lives: Exploring Virtue and Vice* (Oxford: 1999), 17–25

Dunn, P. M. 'Aristotle: Philosopher and Scientist of Ancient Greece', *Archives of Disease in Childhood Fetal and Neonatal Edition* 91 (2006)

Dutsch, D. (ed.) *Ancient Obscenities: Their Nature and Use in the Ancient Greek and Roman Worlds* (Ann Arbor: 2015)

Easterling, P. E. The Infanticide in Euripides' Medea' in Mossman, J. (ed.) *Euripides* (Oxford)
Greek and Roman Actors (Cambridge: 2002)
Women in Tragic Space, *BICS* 34 (1988), 15–26

Edmonds, R. G. 'Bewitched, Bothered, Bewildered: Erotic Magic in the Greco-Roman World', in Hubbard T. K. (ed.) *A Companion to Greek and Roman Sexualities* (Chichester: 2014), 282–296

Elia, J. P. 'History, Etymology, and Fallacy: Attitudes Toward Male Masturbation in the Ancient Western World'. *Journal of Homosexuality,* 14 (1987) 1–19

Elia, O. *Pitture Murali e Mosaici nel Musea Nazionale di Napoli* (Rome: 1932)

Ellinger, T. H. *Hippocrates on Intercourse and Pregnancy* (New York: 1952)

Ellis, H. *Studies in the Psychology of Sex*, vol. 2: Sexual Inversion. Project Gutenberg text

El Nahas, A., 'Legal Status of Women In Menander', *Bulletin of the Faculty of Arts Cairo University* 63 (2003) 305–348

Elshtain, J. *Women and War* (Chicago: 1995).

Elsom, H. E. 'Callirhoe: Displaying the Phallic Woman', in Richlin, *Pornography* (1992)

Engel, D. M. 'Women's Role in the Home and the State', *History of Political Thought* 101 (2003), 267–288

Engels, D. 'The Problem of Female Infanticide in the Greco-Roman World', *CP* 75 (1980), 112–120

Evans-Grubbs, J. 'Abduction Marriage in Antiquity: A Law of Constantine (*CTh* IX.24.I) and its Social context', *JRS* 79 (1989), 59–83

Ewing, E. *Underwear: A History* (New York: 1976)

Eyben, E. Antiquity's View of Puberty, *Latomus* 31 (1972), 677–697
'Family Planning in Graeco-Roman Antiquity', *Anc.Soc* 11-12 (1980), 5–82

Fabre-Serris, J. (ed.) *Women and War in Antiquity* (Baltimore: 2015)

Famin, S.M.C. *Musée Royal de Naples; Peintures, Bronzes et Statues Erotiques du Cabinet Secret, avec leur Explication (Paris: 1861)*

Fantham, E. 'Women in the Classical World: Image and Text (New York, 1994) Sexual Comedy in Ovid's Fasti: Sources and Motivation', *HSCP* 87 (1983), 185ff

Faraone, C. 'Magical and Medical Approaches to the Wandering Womb in the Ancient Greek World', *Cl Ant* 30 (2011), 1–31
  Prostitutes and Courtesans in the Ancient World (Madison, WI: 2006)
  Ancient Greek Love Magic (Harvard: 2001)
  'Agents and Victims: Constructions of Gender and Desire in Ancient Greek Love Magic', in *The Sleep of Reason*, 410
Farnell, L. *The Cults of the Greek States Vol. IV* (1907)
Faulkner, T. M. (ed.) *Contextualizing Classics: Ideology, Performance, Dialogue* (Lanham, MD: 1999)
Feinberg, L. *Transgender Warriors.* (Beacon Press, 1996)
Felson-Rubin, N. *Regarding Penelope: From Character to Poetics* (Princeton, NJ: 1993)
Field, P. *Is Divinity a Gender Issue? The Case of the Minoan 'Goddess'.* (Masters Thesis in Archaeology, Department of Archaeology, Conservation and Historical Studies Faculty of Humanities University of Oslo 2007)
Filbee, M. *A Woman's Place* (London: 1980)
Fildes, V. *Breasts, Bottles and Babies: A History of Infant Feeding* (Edinburgh: 1987)
  Wet Nursing: A History from Antiquity to the Present (Oxford: 1998)
Finley, M. I. *Aspects of Antiquity* (Harmondsworth: 1972)
  Studies in Ancient Society (London: 1974)
Firebaugh W. C. *The Inns of Greece and Rome: And a History of Hospitality from the Dawn of Time to the Middle Ages* (2012)
Fisher, N. 'Athletics and Sexuality', in Hubbard (2014), 244–264
Fitzpatrick, D. 'Reconstructing a Fragmentary Tragedy 2: Sophocles' *Tereus*', *Practitioners' Voices in Classical Reception Studies* 1 (2007)
Flaceliere, R. *Love in Ancient Greece* (Westport, CT: 1973)
  'Les Epicureans et L'Amour', *Revue des Etudes Grecques* 70 (1969), 3–43
Flemming, R. *Medicine and the Making of Roman Women* (Oxford: 2000)
  'Women, Writing and Medicine in the Classical World', *CQ* 57 (2007), 257–279
Florence, M. 'The Body Politic: Sexuality in Greek and Roman Comedy and Mime', in Hubbard (2014), 366–380
Fogen, T. *Bodies and Boundaries in Graeco- Roman Antiquity* (Amsterdam: 2009)
Foley, H. P. *The Homeric Hymn to Demeter: Translation, Commentary, and Interpretive Essays* (Princeton, NJ: 1994)

'Reverse Similes and Sex Roles in the Odyssey'. in Peradotto (ed.) *Women in the Ancient World, The Arethusa Papers* (New York: 1984), 59–78

(ed) *Reflections of Women in Antiquity* (London: 1981)

'Women in Ancient Epic', in Foley, J.M. (ed.) *A Companion to Ancient Epic* (Chichester 2008), 105–118

'The Conception of Women in Athenian Drama', in H. Foley (ed.), *Reflections of Women In Antiquity* (New York: 1981), 127–68

'The Politics of Tragic Lamentation'. in A. Sommerstein (eds), *Tragedy Comedy and the Polis* (Bari: 1992), 102–4.

'Tragedy and Democratic Ideology' in B. Goff (ed.), *History, Tragedy, Theory* (Austin, TX: 1995), 131–50

'Antigone as Moral Agent', in M.S. Silk (ed.), *Tragedy and the Tragic* (London: 1996), 49–73

'The *"Female Intruder"* Reconsidered in Women in Aristophanes' Lysistrata and Ecclesiazusae', *CP*, 77 (1982), 1–21

Forberg, F. K. *De figuris Veneris* (1824) trans. into English as *Manual of Classical Erotology* by Viscount Julian Smithson, and printed privately in 1884 in Manchester; repr. in 1966 (New York: 1966)

Foucault, M. *The History of Sexuality: The Care of the Self* (New York: 1988)

Foxhall, L. *Studying Gender in Classical Antiquity* (Cambridge: 2013)

(ed.) *Thinking Men: Masculinity and Self-presentation in the Classical Tradition* (London: 1998)

Franco, C. *Shameless: The Canine and the Feminine in Ancient Greece* (Berkeley: 2014)

Freisenbruch. A. *The First Ladies of Rome* (London: 2010)

French, R. (ed.) *Science in the Early Roman Empire* (London: 1986)

Friedman, M. *A Mind of Its Own: A Cultural History of the Penis* (New York: 2003)

Furst, L. R. (ed.) *Women Physicians and Healers* (Lexington: 1997)

Gaca, K. L. *The Making of Fornication: Eros, Ethics and Political Reform in Greek Philosophy and Early Christianity.* (Berkeley: 2003)

'Girls, Women, and the Significance of Sexual Violence in Ancient Warfare', in Heineman, E. D. *Sexual Violence in Conflict Zones: From the Ancient World to the Era of Human Rights* (Philadelphia: 2011), 73–88

'Ancient Warfare and the Ravaging Martial Rape of Girls and Women: Evidence from Homeric Epic and Greek Drama', in Masterson, M. *Sex in Antiquity: Exploring Gender and Sexuality in the Ancient World* (New York: 2015)

Gage, J. 'Matronalia', *Latomus* 60 (1963)

Gager, J. *Curse Tablets and Binding Spells from the Ancient World* (New York: 1992)

Gaimster, D. 'Sex and Sensibility at the Art Museum', *History Today*, 50 (2000), 10–15

Gardner, H.H. 'Ventriloquizing Rape in Menander's Epitrepontes', *Helios* 39 (2012), 121–143

Garland, R. *Celebrity in Antiquity* (London: 2006)
'Deformity and Disfigurement in the Graeco-Roman World', *History Today* 42 (1992)
The Eye of the Beholder: Deformity and Disability in the Graeco-Roman World (Bristol: 2010)

Garlick, B. (ed.) *Stereotypes of Women in Power* (New York: 1992)

Garrison, D.H. *A Cultural History of the Human Body in Antiquity* (London: 2014)
Sexual Culture in Ancient Greece (Norman, OK: 2000)

Gates, C. 'Why Are There No Scenes of Warfare in Minoan Art?' in Laffineur, Robert, ed. Polemos, *Universite de Liege, Histoire de l'art d'archeologie de la Grece antique* (1999), 277–0284

Georgiou, I. E. *Women in Herodotus' Histories* (Swansea: 2002)

Gibbs-Wichrowska, L. 'The Witch and the Wife: A Comparative Study of Theocritus Idyll 2, Simonides Idyll 15 and Fatal Attraction', in Archer, *Women in Ancient Societies* (1994), 252–68

Gilbert, A. N. 'Conceptions of Homosexuality and Sodomy in Western History', in Golden (ed.), *A Cultural History of Sexuality Volume I In The Classical World*, 57–68

Gilman, S. *Hysteria Beyond Freud* (Berkeley: 1993)

Glazebrook, A. 'Greek and Roman Marriage', in Hubbard (2014), 69–82
'Sexual Rhetoric from Athens to Rome', in Hubbard (2014), 431–445
'Cosmetics and Sôphrosunê: Ischomachos' Wife in Xenophon's Oikonomikos', *CW* 102(2009), 233–248
'The Making of a Prostitute: Apollodoros's Portrait of Neaera', *Arethusa* 38.2 (2005), 161–87
(ed) *Greek Prostitutes in the Ancient Mediterranean, 800 BCE–200CE* (Wisconsin: 2011)

Glendinning, E. 'Reinventing Lucretia: Rape, Suicide and Redemption from Classical Antiquity to the Medieval Era', *International Journal of the Classical Tradition* (2013)

Glenn, C. *Locating Aspasia on the Rhetorical Map. Listening to Their Voices* (Columbia, SC: 1997)

'Sex, Lies, and Manuscript: Refiguring Aspasia in the History of Rhetoric', *Composition and Communication* 45, 180–199

Goebel, G. A., 'Andromache 192–204: The Pattern of Argument', *CP* 84, (1989) 32–35

Goff, B. *Citizen Bacchae: Women's Ritual Practice in Ancient Greece* (Berkeley: 2004)

'The Priestess of Athena Grows a Beard: Latent Citizenship in Ancient Greek Women's Ritual Practice', in G. Polock, *The Sacred and the Feminine. Imagination and Sexual Difference,* (London: 2007), 49–60

Goldberg, S. 'Comedy and Society from Menander to Terence', in Mc Donald, M. (ed.) *Cambridge Companion to Greek and Roman Theatre* (Cambridge: 2007), 124–138

Golden, M. 'Did the Ancients Care When their Children Died?' *G&R* 35 (1988), 152–163

Sex and Difference in Ancient Greece and Rome (Edinburgh: 2008)

'Donatus and Athenian Phratries', *CQ* 35 (1985), 9–13

'Slavery and Homosexuality at Athens', *Phoenix* 38 (1984), 308–24

(ed.) *A Cultural History of Sexuality Volume I In The Classical World* (Oxford: 2011)

'Demography and the Exposure of Girls at Athens', *Phoenix* 35, (1981) 316–31

Children And Childhood In Classical Athens (Baltimore: 1990)

Goldhill, S. *Foucault's Virginity: Ancient Erotic Fiction and the History of Sexuality* (Cambridge: 1995)

Gomme, A. 'The Position of Women in Athens in the Fifth and Fourth Centuries', *CP* 1925, 1–25

Gonzalez-Reigosa, F. 'Greek Homosexuality, Greek Narcissism, Greek Culture: the Invention of Apollo', *Psychohistory Review* 17 (1989), 149–181

Gould, J. 'Law, Custom and Myth: Aspects of the Social Position of Women in Classical Athens', *JHS* 100 (1980), 38–59

Gordon, R. L. 'Aelian's Peony: The Location of Magic in Graeco-Roman Tradition', *Comparative Criticism* 9 (1987), 59–95

'Imagining Greek and Roman Magic', in Ankerloo, B. (ed) *Magic and Witchcraft in Europe: Greece and Rome* (Philadelphia PA 1999)

Studies in Honour of H. S. Versnel (Leiden: 2002)

Gourevitch, D. 'Women Who Suffer from a Man's Disease', in Hawley, *Women* (1995), 149–165

'Quelques Fantasmees Erotiques et Perversions d'Objets dans la Literature Greco-Romaine' in *Melanges de l'Ecole Francaise de Rome, Antiquite* 94, 823–42

Graf, F. *Magic in the Ancient World* (Cambridge, MA: 1999)

Grant, M. *Eros in Pompeii: The Erotic Art Collection of the Museum of Naples* (New York: 1997)

Graves, F. P, *The Burial Customs of the Ancient Greeks* (repr. 2015)

Green, M. H. *Making Women's Medicine Masculine: The Rise of Male Authority in Pre-Modern Gynaecology* (Oxford: 2008)

Geene, E. *Re-Reading Sappho: Reception and Transmission* (Berkeley: 1998)

Griffith, M. *Sophocles' Antigone* (Oxford: 1998)

Grmek, M. *Les Maladies a l'Aube de la Civilisation Occidentale* (Paris 1983) *Diseases in the Ancient Greek World* (Baltimore: 1989)

Groneman, C. *Nymphomania.* (London: 2000)

Grubbs, J.E. 'The Dynamics of Infant Abandonment: Motives, Attitudes and (unintended) Consequences', in K. Mustakallio (ed.) *The Dark Side of Childhood in Late Antiquity and the Middle Ages. Unwanted, Disabled and Lost* (Oxford: 2011), 21–37

Gruber, H. *The Women of Greek Declamation and the Reception of Comic Stereotypes* (PhD diss. University of Iowa)

Gusman, P. *Pompeii: The City, Its Life and Art* (London: 1910)

Haas, N. 'Hairstyles in the Art of Greek and Roman Antiquity', *Jnl of Investigative Dermatology Proceedings* 10 (2005), 298–300

Habinek, T. 'The Invention of Sexuality in the World-City of Rome', in Habinek, T. *The Roman Cultural Revolution,* (Cambridge: 2004)

Hackworth Petersen, L. *Mothering And Motherhood In Ancient Greece And Rome* (Austin, TX: 2013)

Haley, H. W. *The Social and Domestic Position of Women in Aristophanes, HSCP* 1 (1890), 159–186

Halliwell, S. 'Aristophanic Sex: The Erotics of Shamelessness', in Nussbaum, M.C. *The Sleep of Reason* (2002), 120–42

Halperin, D. M. *One Hundred Years of Homosexuality and Other Essays on Greek Love* (New York: 1990)

'Plato and the Metaphysics of Desire', in J. Cleary (ed) *Proceedings of the Boston Area Colloquium in Ancient Philosophy* Vol. 5, Lanham, 27–52

Hame, K. J. 'All in the Family: Funeral Rites and the Health of the *oikos* in Aeschylus' Oresteia', *AJP* 125, (2004), 513–538

Hamel, D. *Trying Neaera: The True Story of a Courtesan's Scandalous Life in Ancient Greece* (Yale, 2005)

Hamilton, G. 'Society Women Before Christ', *North American Review* 151 (1896)

Hammond, N. G. L. (ed) *The Oxford Classical Dictionary (2nd ed.)* (Oxford: 1970)

Hansen, M. H. *The Shotgun Method: The Demography of the Ancient Greek City-State Culture* (University of Missouri Press, 2006)

Hanson, A. E. 'The Restructuring of Female Physiology at Rome', in *Les Ecoles Médicales à Rome* (Nantes, 1991), 267ff.

'The Medical Writers' Woman', in Halperin, *Before Sexuality* (1990), 309–338

'The Eight Months' Child and the Etiquette of Birth: *obsit omen!*', *BHM* 61 (1987), 589–602

Harris, E. M. 'Did Rape Exist in Classical Athens? Further Thoughts on the Laws about Sexual Violence', *Dike* 4 (2004) 41–83

Harris, W. V. 'The Theoretical Possibility of Extensive Female Infanticide in the Graeco-Roman World', *CQ* 32 (1982), 114–116 *Ancient Literacy* (Cambridge, Mass: 1989)

Harrison, T. 'Herodotus and the Ancient Greek Idea of Rape', in Deacy (1997), 185–208

Hart, G. D. *Asclepius: the God of Medicine* (London: 2001)

Harvey, F. D. 'The Wicked Wife of Ischomachus', *EMC* 3 (1984)

Hasan, A. 'Plato's Antifeminism: A New Dualistic Approach', *E-Logos Electronic Journal for Philosophy* 22 (2012) http://nb.vse.cz/kfil/elogos/ethics/hasan12.pdf

Havelock, C. M. *The Aphrodite of Knidos and Her Successors: A Historical Review of the Female Nude in Greek Art* (Ann Arbor, TX: 2010)

Haward, A. *Penelope to Poppaea* (Bristol: 1990)

Hawley, R. 'The Problem of Women Philosophers in Ancient Greece', in Archer, *Women in Ancient Societies: An Illusion of the Night* (1994), 70–87

Hawley R. (ed.) *Women in Antiquity: New Assessments* (London: 1995)
'Ancient Collections of Women's Sayings', *BICS* 50 (2007), 161–169
'"Give Me a Thousand Kisses": The Kiss, Identity, and Power in Greek and Roman Antiquity', *Leeds International Classical Studies* 6 (2007)
Hays, M. *Female Biography or Memoirs of Illustrious and Celebrated Women of all Ages and Countries 6 volumes* (London: 1803)
Hazewindus, M. W. *When Women Interfere: Studies in the Role of Women in Herodotus' Histories* (Amsterdam: 2004)
Heckel, W. *Who's Who in the Age of Alexander the Great: Prosopography of Alexander's Empire*, (Chichester: 2006)
Henderson, J. *The Maculate Muse: Obscene Language in Attic Comedy 2nd Edition* (Oxford: 1991)
'Women in the Athenian Dramatic Festivals', *TAPA*, 121 (1991), 133–47
'Greek Attitudes towards Sex', in Grant, M. (ed.) *Civilisation of the Ancient Mediterranean: Greece and Rome Vol 2* (New York: 1988)
'Older Women in Attic Old Comedy', *TAPA* 117 (1987), 105–29
Henry, M. M. *Prisoner of History: Aspasia of Miletus and Her Biographical Tradition* (Oxford: 1997)
Heyob, S. K. *The Cult of Isis Amongst Women of the Graeco-Roman World* (Leiden: 1975)
Himes, N. *Medical History of Contraception.* (London: 1970)
Hodges, F. M. 'The Ideal Prepuce in Ancient Greece and Rome: Male Genital Aesthetics and their Relationship to Lipodermos, Circumcision, Foreskin Restoration, and the *Kynodesme*', *BHM* 75 (2001), 375–405
Hodkinson, O. 'Epistolography', in Hubbard, T. K. (ed) *Companion to Greek and Roman Sexualities*, Chichester: 2014), 463–478
Hodkinson, S. *Property and Wealth in Classical Sparta*, (Swansea: 2000)
Holland, L. B. 'The Mantic Mechanism at Delphi', *American Journal of Archaeology* 37 (1933), 201–214
Holmberg, I. E. 'Sex in Ancient Greek and Roman Epic', in Hubbard, (2014), 314334
Holst-Warhaft, G. *Dangerous Voices: Women's Laments and Greek Literature* (New York: 1992)

Holt, F. L. 'Alexander the Great's Little Star', *History Today* 38 (1988)

Hong, Y. 'Talking About Rape in the Classics Classroom', *CW* 106 (2013), 669675

Hornblower, S. (ed.) *The Oxford Classical Dictionary, third edition.* (Oxford: 1996)

Hubbard, T. K. (ed.) *Companion to Greek and Roman Sexualities,* (Chichester: 2014)
    (ed.) *Homosexuality in Greece and Rome: A Sourcebook of Basic Documents* (Berkeley: 2003)
    (ed.) *Greek Love Reconsidered,* (New York: 2000)

Hufnagel, G. L. *A History of Women's Menstruation from Ancient Greece to the Twenty-first-century: Psychological, Social, Medical, Religious, and Educational Issues* (New York: 2012)

Hughes, B. *Helen of Troy: Goddess, Princess, Whore* (London: 2005)

Hunter, V. J. 'Gossip and the Politics of Reputation in Classical Athens', *Phoenix* 44 (1990), 299–325

Hyde, H.M. *A History of Pornography* (London: 1969)

ICD: *International Classification of Diseases (10 version,* Geneva: 2010) [see WHO]

Ireland, S. *Menander: Dyskolos, Samia and Other Plays* (Bristol: 1992)

Isager, S. 'Gynaikonitis – The Women Quarters', *Museum Tusculanum* 33 (1978), 39ff.

Jackson, R. *Doctors and Diseases in the Roman Empire* (London: 1988)

James, S. L. *Companion to Women in the Ancient World* (Chichester: 2012)

Johansson, L. 'The Roman Wedding and the Household Gods', in Loven, L. L. (ed.), *Ancient Marriage in Myth and Reality* (Newcastle: 2010), 136–149

Johns, C. *Sex or Symbol: Erotic Images of Greece and Rome* (London: 1982)

Johnson, M. *Sexuality in Greek and Roman Society and Literature: A Sourcebook* (London: 2005)

Johnson, M. *Ancient Greek Dress* (Chicago: 1964)

Johnson, S. I. *Restless Dead: Encounters Between the Living and the Dead in Ancient Greece* (Berkeley: 2013)

Jones, R. 'Ariadne's Threads : the Construction and Significance of Clothes in the Aegean Bronze Age', *Aegaeum : Annales liégeoises et PASPiennes d'archéologie égéenne* 38 (Liège, 2015)

Jones, C.P. 'Stigma: Tattooing and Branding in Graeco-Roman Antiquity', *JRS* 77 (1987), 139–155

Jope, J. 'Stoic and Epicurean Sexual Ethics', in Hubbard, (2014), 417430

Joplin, P. K. 'The Voice of the Shuttle Is Ours' in Higgins, L. A. *Rape and Representation* (New York: 1991), 35–64

Joshel, S. R *Women and Slaves in Graeco-Roman Culture* (London: 1998)

Joy, M. *Women and the Gift: Beyond the Given and All-Giving* (Bloomington, IN: 2013)

Joyce, R. A. *Ancient Bodies, Ancient Lives: Sex, Gender and Archaeology* (London: 2008)

Just, R. *Women in Athenian Law and Life* (London: 1989)

Kallet-Marx, L. 'Thucydides 2.45.2 and the Status of War Widows in Periclean Athens', *in Nomodeiktes: Greek Studies in Honor of Martin Ostwald, edited by Ralph M. Rosen* (1993), 133–143

Kampen, N. (ed.) *Sexuality in Ancient Art: Near East, Egypt, Greece, and Italy* (Cambridge: 1996)

Kampouroglou, G. 'Hypospadias Pathophysiology and Treatment Principles, Not as Recent as We Think', *General Health and Medical Sciences* 1 (2014), 1–2

Kapparis, K. A. *Abortion in Antiquity* (London: 2002)

Karanika, A. *Voices at Work: Women, Performance, and Labor in Ancient Greece* (Baltimore: 2014)

Karras, R. M. Active/Passive, Acts/Passions: Greek and Roman Sexualities, *American Historical Review* 105 (2000), 1250–1265

Katz, M. 'Women and Democracy in Ancient Greece', in Faulkner T. M. *Contextualizing Classics*

'Ideology and The Status of Women In Ancient Greece', *History & Theory* 31 (1992)

Penelope's Renown: Meaning and Indeterminacy in the Odyssey (Princeton, NJ: 1991)

Keesling, C. 'Heavenly Bodies: Monuments to Prostitutes in Greek Sanctuaries', in Faraone, C. A. *Prostitutes and Courtesans in the Ancient World* (Madison, WI: 2006)

Kennedy, R. 'Herodotus, Nitocris, and Harmonizing Extraordinary Ancient Women Into History', *Historically Speaking*, 6 (2005), 9–10

Kennell, N. M. *The Gymnasium of Virtue: Education and Culture in Ancient Sparta* (Chapel Hill, NC: 1995)

Kersey, E. M. *Women Philosophers: A Bio-critical Source Book* (New York: 1989)

Keuls, E. C. *The Reign of the Phallus: Sexual Politics in Ancient Athens* (Berkeley: 1993)

King, H. 'Sowing the Field: Greek and Roman Sexology', in Porter, R. *Sexual Knowledge, Sexual Science: The History of Attitudes to Sexuality* (Cambridge: 1994), 38ff

'Producing Woman: Hippocratic Gynecology', in Archer, *Women in Ancient Societies* (1994), 102–114

'Once upon a Text: Hysteria from Hippocrates', in Gilman, S. *Hysteria Beyond Freud* (1993), 3–90

'Self-help, Self-knowledge: in Search of the Patient in Hippocratic Gynaecology', in Hawley (1995), 135–148

Women and Goddess Traditions (Minneapolis, MN: 1997)

Hippocrates' Woman: Reading the Female Body in Ancient Greece (London: 1998)

Greek and Roman Medicine (London: 2003)

The Disease of Virgins: Green Sickness, Chlorosis and the Problems of Puberty (New York: 2004)

'Healthy, Wealthy and – Dead?' *Ad Familiares* 33 (2007), 3–4

The One-Sex Body on Trial: The Classical and Early Modern Evidence (London: 2013)

'Sex and Gender: the Hippocratic Case of Phaethousa and her Beard', *Journal on Gender Studies in Antiquity*, 3 (2013), 124–142

Knight, R. P. *A Discourse on the Worship of Priapus* (London: 1786)

Knox, B. M. 'Elegy and Iambus: Hipponax'. in *The Cambridge History of Classical Literature: Greek Literature*, P. Easterling (ed.), (Cambridge: 1985), 163

Konstan, D. (ed.) *Envy, Spite and Jealousy: The Rivalrous Emotions in Ancient Greece* (Edinburgh: 2003)

'Between Courtesan and Wife: Menander's Perikeiromene', *Phoenix* 41 (1987) 122–39, Reprinted in *Greek Comedy and Ideology* (New York: 1995)

Koortbojian, M. 'In Commemorationem Mortuorum: Text and Image Along the Street of Tombs', in Elsner, 210–233

Kraemer, R. S. *Maenads, Martyrs, Matrons, Monastics* (Philadelphia, PA: 1988)

Women's Religions in the Greco-Roman World: A Sourcebook (New York: 2004)

'Ecstasy and Possession: The Attraction of Women to the Cult of Dionysus', *Harvard Theological Review* 72 (1979)

Krafft-Ebing, R. von *Psychopathia Sexualis, with Special Reference to the Antipathic Sexual Instinct: A Medico-Forensic Study* (Cornell, 1906)

Krenkel, W. A. *Fellatio* and *Irrumatio*, *W.Z. Rostock* 29 (1980), 77–88

'Tonguing', *W. Z. Rostock* 30 (1981), 37–54

Kruger, K. S. *Weaving the Word: the Metaphorics of Weaving and Female Textual Production* (Selinsgrove: Susquehanna University Press, 2001)

Krzszkowska, O, 'So Where's the Loot? The Spoils of War and the Archaeological Record', in Laffineur, Robert, ed., *Polemos: Le Contexte Guerrier en Egee a L'Age du Bronze. Actes de la 7e Rencontre egeenne internationale Universite de Liege, 1998, Universite de Liege Histoire de l'art d'archeologie de la Grece antique* (1999), 489–498

Kudlien, F. 'Medical Education in Classical Antiquity', in O'Malley, *The History of Medical Education* (1970), 3–37

Kuhrt, A. 'Non-Royal Women in the Late Babylonian Period: A Survey', ed. Barbara S. Lesko, in *Women's Earliest Records: From Ancient Egypt and Western Asia*, (Atlanta, GA: 1989)

Kurke, L. 'Inventing the "Hetaira": Sex, Politics, and Discursive Conflict in Archaic Greece', *Classical Antiquity* 16 (1997), 107–108

Kuttner, A. L. 'Culture and History at Pompey's Museum', *TAPA* 129 (1999), 343

Lacey, W. K. *The Family in Classical Greece* (Ithaca, NY: 1968)

Laes, C. (ed.) *Children and Family in Late Antiquity: Life, Death and Interaction* (Leuven: 2015)

'When Classicists Need to Speak up: Antiquity and Present Day Pedophilia', *Aeternitas Antiquitatis: Proceedings of the Symposium Held in Skopje, August 28. As Part of the 2009 Annual Conference of Euroclassica.*

Laios, K. 'Hypospadias and Sex Change in Ancient Greece', *Journal of Sexual Medicine* 11 (2014), 1343–1344

'Peyronie's Disease in Minoan Art', *Journal of Sexual Medicine* 10 (2013), 3144–3145

'A Unique Representation of Hypospadias in Ancient Greek Art', *Can Urol Assoc J* 6 (2012)

Laiou, A. E. *Consent and Coercion to Sex and Marriage in Ancient and Medieval Societies* (Washington DC: 1993)

Lambert, R. *Beloved and God: The Story of Hadrian and Antinous* (London: 1984)

Lambropoulou, V. 'Some Pythagorean Female Virtues', in Hawley, R. *Women in Antiquity* (London: 1995)

Lape, S. *Reproducing Athens: Menander's Comedy, Democratic Culture, and the Hellenistic City* (Princeton, 2003)

'Solon and the Institution of the "Democratic" Family Form', *Classical Journal* 98 (2002), 117–139

'Democratic Ideology and the Poetics of Rape in Menandrian Comedy', *Classical Antiquity* 20 (2001), 79–119

Laqueur, T. *Making Sex: Body and Gender from the Greeks to Freud*, (Cambridge, MA: 1990)

Lardinois, A. (ed.) *Making Silence Speak: Women's Voices in Greek Literature and Society* (Princeton, 2001)

Larson, J. *Greek and Roman Sexualities: A Sourcebook* (London: 2012)

'Sexuality in Greek and Roman Religion', in Hubbard (2014), 214–229

Larson, S. 'Kanduales' Wife, Masistes' Wife: Herodotus' Narrative Strategy in Suppressing Names of Women (Hdt. 1.8-12 and 9.108-13)', *CJ* 101 (2006), 225–244

Larsson, L. L. (ed.) *Aspects of Women in Antiquity* (1997)

'Lanam fecit: Woolmaking and Female Virtue' in Larsson, *Aspects* (1997), 85–95

Laurence, R. (ed.) *Families in the Greco-Roman World* (London: 2011)

Roman Passions (London: 2009)

Lawler, L. B. *The Dance in Ancient Greece* (1964)

Lear, A. 'Ancient Pederasty: An Introduction', in Hubbard (2014), 102–127

Images of Ancient Greek Pederasty: Boys Were Their Gods (London: 2008)

Lee, M. M. *Body, Dress, and Identity in Ancient Greece* (Cambridge: 2015)

Lefkowitz, M. R. *Women in Greek Myth* (London: 2007)

Heroines and Hysterics (London: 1981)

Women's Life in Greece & Rome 3rd Ed. (London: 2005)

'Wives and husbands', in I. McAuslan (ed), *Women in Antiquity* (Oxford: 1996), 67–82

Leigh, M. 'Funny Clones: "Greek" Comedies on the Roman Stage', *Omnibus* 54 (2007), 26–28

Leisner-Jensen, M. '"Vis comica": Consummated Rape in Greek and Roman New Comedy', *C&M* 53 (2002), 173–196

Leitao, D. D. 'Sexuality in Greek and Roman Military Contexts', in Hubbard (2014), 230–243

The Pregnant Male as Myth and Metaphor in Classical Greek Literature, (Cambridge: 2012)

Leon, V. *The Joy of Sexus: Lust, Love, and Longing in the Ancient World* (2013)

Lesko, B. 'Women and Religion in Ancient Egypt', in *Diotima* http://www/stao.org

Leunissen, M. 'Physiognomy in Ancient Science and Medicine', https://mleunissen.files.wordpress.com/ ... /leunissen-physiognomy (2012)

Lewis, N. *The Interpretation of Dreams & Portents in Antiquity.* (Bolchazy-Carducci Publishing, 1999)

Licht, H. *Sexual Life in Ancient Greece* (London: 1994)

LiDonnici, L. 'Burning for It: Erotic Spells for Fever and Compulsion in the Ancient Mediterranean World', *GRBS* 39 (1998), 63-98

Lidov, J. B. 'Sappho, Herodotus, and the Hetaira', *CP* 97 (2002), 21

Lightman, M. *A to Z of Ancient Greek and Roman Women* (New York: 2008)

Lipking, D. *Abandoned Women and Poetic Tradition* (Chicago: 1988)

Lloyd-Jones, H. *Females of the Species: Semonides on Women* (London: 1975)

Llewellyn-Jones, L. 'Veiling the Spartan Woman', in M. Harlow (ed.), *Dress and Identity* (Oxford: 2011), 19–38

'Dress, Textiles, Hair and Hairstyles', in *Homer Encyclopedia*, ed. M. Inkelberg (Oxford: 2011)

'Domestic Violence in Ancient Greece', in *Sociable Man: Essays in Greek Social Behaviour in Honour of Nick Fisher*, ed. S Lambert, (Swansea: 2011), 231–266

'The Big and Beautiful Women of Asia: Picturing Female Sexuality in Greco-Persian Seals', in *The World of AchaemenidPersia*, ed. S. Simpson, (London: 2010), 165–176

'Prostitution', in *Oxford Encyclopedia of Greece and Rome*, ed. M Gargarin (Oxford: 2010)

'Orientalism in Western Dress and Stage Costume', in *Berg Encyclopedia of World Dress – The Middle East and Central Asia* ed. G Vogelsang- Eastwood, (2010) 321–22

'House and Veil in Ancient Greece', in N Fisher (ed.) *BuildingCommunities: House, Settlement and Society in the Aegean and Beyond* (Athens: 2007)

'Athens' Lady Boys? Gesture and the Male Performance of Women in Athenian tragedy', in D. L. Cairns (ed.), *Gesture and Non-Verbal Communication in Classical Antiquity* (London: 2005)

'A woman's view? Dress, Eroticism, and the Ideal Female Body in Athenian Art', in L. Llewellyn-Jones (ed.), *Women's Dress in the Ancient Greek World* (Swansea: 2002), 171–202

'Sexy Athena: the Dress and Erotic Representation of a Virgin War Goddess', in S. Deacy (ed.), *Athena in the Classical World* (Leiden: 2001), 233–57

Greek and Roman Dress from A to Z (The Ancient World from A To Z) (London: 2007)

Aphrodite's Tortoise: The Veiled Woman of Ancient Greece (London: 2003)

Eunuchs in Antiquity and Beyond (Swansea: 2002)

Lloyd, G. E. R. (ed.) *Hippocratic Writings* (Harmondsworth, 1978)

Magic, Reason and Experience (Cambridge: 1979)

Long, A. A. 'The Socratic Tradition: Diogenes, Crates, and Hellenistic Ethics', in Bracht Branham, R. *The Cynics: The Cynic Movement in Antiquity and Its Legacy*, (Berkeley: 1996)

Longrigg, J. *Greek Rational Medicine* (London: 1993)

Greek Medicine: From the Heroic to the Hellenistic Age A Source Book (London: 1998)

Loraux, N. *Aspasie, l'étrangère, l'intellectuelle.* La Grèce au Féminin (Paris: 2003)

The Children of Athena: Athenian Ideas about Citizenship and the Division Between the Sexes (Princeton, NJ: 1994)

Tragic Ways of Killing a Woman (Cambridge, MA: 1987)

Lovibond, S. 'An Ancient Theory of Gender: Plato and the Pythagorean Table', in Archer, *Women in Ancient Societies* (1994), 88–101

Lowe, J. E. *Magic in Greek and Latin Literature* (Oxford: 1929)

Luck, G. *Arcana Mundi: Magic and the Occult in the Greek and Roman Worlds* (Baltimore: 1985)

Luntz L. L. 'History of Forensic Dentistry', *Dent Clin. North Am.* 21 (1997), 7–17

Luschnig, C. *Granddaughter of the Sun A Study of Euripides' Medea* (Leiden: 2007)

Lyons, D. 'Dangerous Gifts: Ideologies of Marriage and Exchange in Ancient Greece', *Classical Antiquity* 22, 93–134

Macdowell, D. M. 'Love versus the Law: An Essay on Menander's Aspis', *G&R* 29 (1982), 42–5

Maclachlan, B, *Women in Ancient Greece: A Sourcebook* (New York: 2012)

Maines, R. P. *The Technology of Orgasm: 'Hysteria', the Vibrator, and Women's Sexual Satisfaction* (Baltimore: 1998)

Maiuri, A. *Pompeii* (Rome: 1934)

Maloney, L. M. 'The Arguments for Women's Difference in Classical Philosophy and Early Christianity', *Concilium: International Journal for Theology* (1991)

Manniche, L. *Sexual Life in Ancient Egypt* (London: 1987)

Mantle, I. *Violentissimae et Singulares Mortes*, CA News 39 (2008), 1–2

'Women of the Bardo', *Omnibus* 65, January 2013, 4–6

Mantos, K. 'Women and Athletics in the Roman East', *Nikephoros* 8 (1995), 125–144

Marquardt, P. A. 'Hesiod's Ambiguous View of Women', *CP* 77 (1982), 283–91

Marshall, A. J. 'Roman Women and the Provinces', *Anc Soc* 6 (1975), 109–129

Martin, M. *Magie et Magiciens dans le Monde Gréco-romain* (Paris: 2005)

Sois maudit!: Malédictions et Envoûtements dans l'Antiquité (Paris: 2010)

La Magie dans l'Antiquité (Paris: 2012)

Mason, M. K. *Ancient Athenian Women of the Classical Period* www.moyak.com/papers/athenian-women.html

Annotated Bibliography of Women in Classical Mythology http://www.moyak.com/papers/women-classical-mythology.html

Massey, M. *Women in Ancient Greece and Rome* (Cambridge: 1988)

Masterson, M. *Sex in Antiquity Exploring Gender and Sexuality in the Ancient World* (London: 2015)

'Studies in Ancient Masculinity', in Hubbard (2014), 17–30

Exploring Gender and Sexuality in the Ancient World (2014)

Matz, D. *Voices of Ancient Greece and Rome: Contemporary Accounts of Daily Life* (New York: 2012)

Maurizio, L. The Voice at the Centre of the World: The Pythia's Ambiguity and

'Authority', in Lardinois, A. (ed.) *Making Silence Speak: Women's Voices in Greek Literature and Society*, (Princeton, NJ: 2001)

Mayor, A. *The Amazons: Lives and Legends of Warrior Women across the Ancient World* (Princeton, NJ: 2014)

Greek Fire, Poison Arrows, and Scorpion Bombs: Biological and Chemical Warfare in the Ancient World (New York: 2003)

McAuslan, I. (ed.) *Women in Antiquity* (Oxford: 1996)

McBrown, P. G. 'Love and Marriage in Greek New Comedy', *CQ* 43, (1993), 189–205

McClure, L. K. *Courtesans at Table: Gender and Greek Literary Culture in Athenaeus* (New York: 2003)

'Subversive Laughter: The Sayings of Courtesans in Book 13 of Athenaeus' Deipnosophistae', *AJP* 124 (2003), 268ff.

Sexuality and Gender in the Classical World (Chichester: 2002)

Spoken Like a Woman: Speech and Gender in Athenian Drama (Princeton, 1993)

McDermott, E. *Euripides' Medea: The Incarnation of Disorder* (University Park, PA: 1985)

McHardy, F. (ed.) *Women's Influence on Classical Civilisation* (London: 2004)

McKeown, J. C. *The Cabinet of Greek Curiosities: Strange Tales and Surprising Facts from the Cradle of Western Civilization* (Oxford: 2013)

McLaren, A. *History of Contraception: From Antiquity to the Present Day* (Chichester: 1992)

McLees, H. *A Study of Women in Attic Inscriptions* (New York: 1920)

McLeod, G. *Virtue and Venom: Catalogs of Women from Antiquity to the Renaissance* (Ann Arbor, TX: 1991)

McManus, B. *Classics and Feminism: Gendering the Classics* (New York: 1997)

McMullen, R. 'Roman Attitudes Toward Greek Love', *Historia* 31 (1982), 484–502

Meyer, J. C. *Women in Classical Athens in the Shadow of North-West Europe or in the Light from Istanbul* http://www.hist.uib.no/antikk/antres/womens%20life.htm

Miles, C. *Love in the Ancient World* (London: 1997)

Miner, J. 'Courtesan, Concubine, Whore: Apollodorus' Deliberate Use of Terms for Prostitutes', *AJP* 124 (2003), 19–37

Minois, G. *A History of Old Age* (Chichester: 2012)

Molloy, B. P. C. 'Martial Minoans? War as Social Process, Practice and Event in Bronze Age Crete', *The Annual of the British School at Athens* (2012), 107

Montserrat, D. *Changing Bodies, Changing Meanings: Studies on the Human Body in Antiquity* (London: 2011)

Moog, F. P. 'Between Horror and Hope: Gladiator's Blood as a Cure for Epileptics in Ancient Medicine', *Journal of the History of the Neurosciences* 12 (2003), 137–43

Morales, H. 'Fantasising Phryne: The Psychology and Ethics of Ekphrasis', *Cambridge Classical Journal* 57 (2011), 71–104

Morgan, T. 'The Wisdom of Semonides Fragment 7', *Cambridge Classical Journal* 51 (2005), 72–85

Morton, R. S. 'Sexual Attitudes, Preferences and Infections in Ancient Greece: Has Antiquity Anything Useful For Us Today?' *Genitourinary Medicine* 67 (1991), 59–66

Munson, R. 'Artemisia in Herodotus', *CA* 7 (1988), 91–106

Murnaghan, S.,'Women in Tragedy' in R. Bushnell (ed.) *A Companion to Tragedy*, (Oxford: 2005), 234–251

Mustakallio, K. *Hoping for Continuity: Childhood Education and Death in Antiquity* (Helsinki: 2005)

Nais, D. 'The Shrewish Wife of Socrates', *EMC* 4 (1985), 97–9

Nardo, D. *Women of Ancient Greece* (San Diego: 2000)

National Theatre: http://www.nationaltheatre.org.uk/video/women-in-greek-theatre-1

Neils, J. *Women in the Ancient World* (London: 2011)

Neilson III, H. R. A 'Terracotta Phallus from Pisa Ship E: More Evidence for the Priapus Deity as Protector of Greek and Roman Navigators', *International Journal of Nautical Archaeology* 31 (2002), 248–253

Nelson, M. 'A Note on the ὄλισβος', *Glotta* 76 (2000), 75–82

Neuburg, M. 'How Like A Woman: Antigone's "Inconsistency"', *CQ* 40 (1990), 54–76

Nevett, L. C. *House and Society in the Ancient Greek World* (Cambridge: 2001)

Nikolaidis, A. G. 'Plutarch on Women and Marriage', *WS* 110 (1997), 27–88

Nikoloutsos, K. P. (ed.) *Ancient Greek Women in Film* (Oxford: 2013)

'Beyond Sex: The Poetics and Politics of Pederasty in Tibullus 1.4', *Phoenix* 61 (2007), 55–82

North, H. 'The Mare, the Vixen, and the Bee: Sophrosyne as the Virtue of Women in Antiquity', *Illinois Classical Studies* 2 (1977)

Nussbaum, M. C. 'The Incomplete Feminism of Musonius Rufus, Platonist, Stoic, and Roman', in Nussbaum *The Sleep of Reason: Erotic Experience and Sexual Ethics in Ancient Greece and Rome* (2002), p. 305f

Same–Sex Desire and Love in Greco-Roman Antiquity and in the Classical Tradition of the West (Binghamton, NY: 2005)

Nutton, V. *Ancient Medicine 2/e* (London 2013)

'Galen and Medical Autobiography', *PCPS* 18 (1972), 50f

'The Drug Trade in Antiquity', *Jnl of the Royal Society of Medicine* 78 (1985), 138–145

Murders and Miracles: Lay Attitudes to Medicine in Antiquity (1985) in Porter: *Patients and Practitioners* 25–53

'The Seeds of Disease: An Explanation of Contagion and Infection from the Greeks to the Renaissance', *Medical History* 27 (1983), 1–34

Oakley, J. H. *The Wedding in Ancient Athens* (Madison, WI: 1993)

Ogden, D. *Magic, Witchcraft and Ghosts in the Greek and Roman Worlds* (Oxford: 2002)

Greek and Roman Necromancy (Princeton, NJ: 2004)

Night's Black Agents: Witches Wizards and the Dead in the Ancient World (London: 2008)

Polygamy, Prostitutes and Death: The Hellenistic Dynasties (Swansea: 2010)

'Homosexuality and Warfare in Ancient Greece', in *Battle in Antiquity* (Swansea: 2009)

Gendering Magic', *CR* 50 (2000), 476–78

'Rape, Adultery and the Protection of Bloodlines in Classical Athens', in S. Deacy (ed.) *Rape in Antiquity: Sexual Violence in the Greek and Roman Worlds* (Swansea: 1997), 25–41

Ogilvie, M. (ed.) *Biographical Dictionary of Women in Science: Pioneering Lives From Ancient Times to the Mid-20th Century* (New York: 2000)

Women in Science: A Biographical Dictionary with Annotated Bibliography (Cambridge, MA: 1990)

O'Higgins, L. *Women and Humor in Classical Greece* (Cambridge: 2003)

Olsen, B. A. *Women in Mycenaean Greece: The Linear B Tablets from Pylos and Knossos* (Hoboken, NJ: 2004)

'Women, Children and the Family in the Late Aegean Bronze Age: Differences in Minoan and Mycenaean Constructions of Gender', *Intimate Relations* (1998), 380–392

Olson, J. S. *Bathsheba's Breast: Women, Cancer, and History* (Baltimore, MD: 2002)

O'Malley, C. D. (ed.) *The History of Medical Education* (Berkeley, CA: 1970)

Omitowoju, R. *Rape and the Politics of Consent in Classical Athens* (Cambridge: 2002)

O'Neal, W. J. 'The Status of Women in Ancient Athens', *International Social Science Review* 68 (1993)

Onq, R. 'Aspasia: Rhetoric, Gender, and Colonial Ideology', in Lunsford, A. A. *Reclaiming Rhetorica* (Pittsburgh, PA: 1995)

O'Pry, K. 'Social and Political Roles of Women in Athens and Sparta', *Saber and Scroll*, 1 (2012), 7–14

Ormand, K. *Controlling Desires: Sexuality in Ancient Greece and Rome* (New York: 2008)

'Marriage, Identity, and the Tale of Mestra in the Hesiodic Catalogue of Women', *AJP* 125 (2004) 303–338

Orrells, D. *Sex: Antiquity and its Legacy* (London: 2015)

Osborne, M. L. (ed.) *Woman in Western Thought* (New York: 1979)

Osborne, R. 'The Use of Abuse: Semonides 7', *Cambridge Classical Journal* 47 (2001), 47–64

O'Toole, C. *Aegean Gender: Minoans, Mycenaeans, and Classical Greeks* www.chelsea-otoole.wikispaces.com

Padel, R. 'Women: Model for Possession by Greek Daemons', in Cameron A. *Images of Women in Antiquity* (Canberra, 1986), 3–19

Pantel, P. S. *A History of Women from Ancient Goddesses to Christian Saints* (Cambridge, MA: 1992)

Papadopoulos I. 'Priapus and Priapism: From Mythology to Medicine'.*Urology* 32 (1988), 385–386

Papadopoulou, M. 'The Woman in Ancient Sparta: The Dialogue between the Divine and Human', *Sparta*, 6. 2 (2010), 5–10 Alcman, *Sparta*, 6. 1 (2010), 1–11

Papagrigorakisa, M. J. 'Facial Reconstruction of an 11-year-old Female Resident of 430 BC Athens', *Angle Orthodontist* 81 (2011)

Parca, M. *Finding Persephone: Women's Rituals in the Ancient Mediterranean* (Urbana-Champaign, IL: 2007)

Parke, H. W. *Sibylls and Sibylline Prophecy in Classical Antiquity* (London: 1998)

Parker, D. 'The Congresswomen of Aristophanes', *Arion* 6, (1967), 23–37

Parker, H. N. 'Love's Body Anatomized: The Ancient Erotic Handbooks and "Rhetoric of Sexuality"', in Richlin, *Pornography* (1992)
'The Myth of the Heterosexual: Anthropology and Sexuality for Classicists', *Arethusa* 34 (2001), 313–362
'Women Physicians in Greece, Rome and the Byzantine Empire', in *Furst* (2004), 134–150
'Women and Medicine', in James, *Companion* (2012), 107–124

Parsons, B. A. 'Aristotle On Women', in *Women's Studies Encyclopedia*, ed. Helen Tierney (Greenwood Press, 2002)

Patterson, C. B. 'Not Worth the Rearing: The Causes of Infant Exposure in Ancient Greece', *TAPA* 115 (1985), 103–23
The Family in Greek History (Cambridge, MA: 1998)

Pellauer, M. 'Augustine on Rape', in Adams, C. J. *Violence Against Women and Children: A Christian Theological Sourcebook* (New York: 1998), 207–241

Pembroke, S. 'Women in Charge: The Function of Alternatives in Early Greek Tradition and the Idea of Matriarchy', *Journal of the Warburg and Courtauld Institutes* 30 (1967), 1–35

Pequigney, J. *Classical Mythology: Achilles, Patroclus, and the Love of Heroes* (2002), 5

Peradotto, J. (ed.) *Women in the Ancient World: The Arethusa Papers* (Albany, NY: 1984)

Percy, W. A. *Pederasty and Pedagogy in Archaic Greece* (Chicago: 1996)

Petersen, L. H. *Mothering and Motherhood in Ancient Greece and Rome* (Austin, TX: 2013)

Phillips, E. D. 'Doctor and Patient in Classical Greece', *G&R* (1953), 70–81

Phillips, K. M. *Sex Before Sexuality: A Premodern History* (Cambridge: 2011)

Pierce, K. F. 'The Portrayal of Rape in New Comedy', in Deacy, S. *Rape in Antiquity* (London: 1997), 163–184

Pinault, J. R. 'The Medical Case for Virginity in the Early 2nd Century CE: Soranus', *Helios* 19, 123–39

Plant, I. M. *Women Writers of Ancient Greece and Rome: An Anthology,* (Norman, OK: 2004)

Pomeroy, S. B. *Ancient Greece: A Political, Social, and Cultural History* (New York: 2011)

    'Selected Bibliography on Women in Antiquity', *Arethusa* 6(1973), 125–157

    Women in Roman Egypt: A Preliminary Study Based on Papyri Foley 301–322

    (ed.) *Women's History and Ancient History* (Chapel Hill: 1991)

    Goddesses, Whores, Wives and Slaves (New York: 1995)

    Spartan Women (Oxford: 2002)

    The Murder of Regilla: A Case of Domestic Violence in Antiquity (Cambridge: 2007)

    Families in Classical and Hellenistic Greece (Oxford: 1997)

Porter, A. J. 'The Temple of Asclepius at Corinth', in Stahnisch, 295ff

Porter, R. (ed.) *Sexual Knowledge, Sexual Science: The History of the Attitudes to Sexuality* (Cambridge: 1994)

    (ed.) *Patients and Practitioners* (Cambridge: 1985)

Post, L. 'A. Woman's Place in Menander's Athens', *TAPA* 71 (1940), 420–459

Powell, A. 'Sparta: A Modern Woman Imagines', *CR* 54 (2004), 465–467

    Athens and Sparta: Constructing Greek Political and Social History from 478 BC 2nd edition (London: 2016)

    'Athens' Pretty Face: Anti-feminine Rhetoric and Fifth-century Controversy over the Parthenon'. in *The Greek World* (London: 1995)

Euripides, Women, and Sexuality. (London: 1990)

Pressfield, S. *Last of the Amazons* (New York: 2002)

Prince, M. 'Medea and the Inefficacy of Love Magic', *CB* 79 (2003), 205–218

Puschmann, T. (ed.) *Alexander of Tralles, Twelve Books on Medicine* (1878)

Queenan, E. 'Patron Goddesses of Sparta: Athena's and Artemis' Significance to Ancient Spartan Society', *Sparta* 7 (2011), 12–17
'Entertainment: Spartan Style', *Sparta,* 5 (2009), 4–10

Qviller, B. *Reconstructing the Spartan Partheniai* (1996)

Rabinowitz, N. S. *Among Women: From the Homosocial to the Homoerotic in the Ancient World* (Austin, TX: 2002)
(ed.) *Feminist Theory and the Classics* (New York: 1993)

Rawles, R. 'Erotic Lyric', in Hubbard, (2014), 335–351

Redfield, J. 'The Women of Sparta', *CJ* 73 (1978)

Reeder, E. (ed.) *Pandora: Women in Classical Greece* (Princeton, NJ: 1996)

Rees, O. 'Musings on Sparta's Muses', *Sparta* 5, 2 (2009), 24–26

Rehm, R. *Marriage to Death: the Conflation of Wedding and Funeral Rituals in Greek Tragedy* (Princeton, NJ: 1994)

Reinhold, M. 'The Generation Gap in Antiquity', in Bertman, 15–54

Rempelakos L. 'Penile Representations in Ancient Greek Art', *Archivos Españoles de Urología* 66 (2013), 911–6

Ricci, J. V, *The Development of Gynaecological Surgery and Instruments* (Philadelphia: 1949)

Richlin, A. (ed.) *Pornography and Representation in Greece and Rome* (Oxford: 1992)
'Reading Boy-love and Child-love in the Greco-Roman World', in Masterson, M. *Sex in Antiquity (*New York: 2015)

Riddle, J. M. *Contraception and Abortion from the Ancient World to the Renaissance* (Cambridge, MA: 1992)

Rinaldo, M. 'Women, Culture and Society', in Blok, J. *Sexual Assymetry* (Amsterdam: 1987), 17–42

Rist, J. M. 'Hypatia', *Phoenix* 19 (1965), 214–225

Robb, J. *The Body in History: Europe from the Palaeolithic to the Future* (Cambridge: 2015)

Roberts, J. T. *Herodotus: A Very Short Introduction* especially chapter 5, 'Women in History – Women in the 'Histories' (Oxford: 2011)
Athens on Trial: The Antidemocratic Tradition in Western Thought (Princeton: 1994)

Robson, J. 'Beauty and Sex Appeal in Aristophanes', *Eugesta Recherche* 3 (2013)

Aristophanes: An Introduction, especially chapter 7 'Talking Dirty: Aristophanic Obscenity' (London: 2009)

Humour, Obscenity and Aristophanes. (Tubingen: 2006)

Roice, Philip. *Ancient Greek Education* (Portland: 1997)

Roisman, H. M. 'Greek and Roman Ethnosexuality', in Hubbard (2014), 398–416

Rose, M. L. 'Demosthenes' Stutter: Overcoming Impairment', in *The Staff of Oedipus* (Michigan: 2003)

Rosen, R. M. 'Greco-roman Satirical Poetry', in Hubbard (2014), 381–397

Rosivach, V. J. *When a Young Man Falls in Love: The Sexual Exploitation of Womenin New Comedy* (London: 1998)

Rossellini, M. 'Usages de femmes et autres nomoi chez les 'sauvages' d' Hérodote: Essai de lecture structurale', *Annali della scuola normale superiore di Pisa* 8 (1978), 949–1005

Rouselle, A. *Porneia: On Desire and the Body In Antiquity* (Oxford: 1993)

Rowlandson, J. *Women and Society in Greek and Roman Egypt: A Sourcebook* (Cambridge: 1998)

Roy, J. 'Polis and Oikos in Classical Athens', *G&R* 46 (1999), 1–18

'An Alternative Sexual Morality for Classical Athenians', *G&R* 44 (1997), 11–22

Rudd, N. 'Romantic Love in Classical Times?' *Ramus* 10 (1981), 140–158

Sabetai, V. *Women and the Cycle of Life* (2008) https://www.academia.edu/480969/Women_and_the_Cycle_of_Life

Sancisi-Weerdenburg, H. 'Exit Atossa: Images of Women in Greek Historiography on Persia', in A. Cameron (ed.), *Images of Women in Antiquity* (Detroit: 1983), 23ff

Saxonhouse, A. W. 'Another Antigone: the Emergence of the Female Political actor in Euripides' Phoenician Women', *Political Theory,* 33 (2005), 472–94

Scanlon, T. F. *Eros and Greek Athletics* (Oxford: 2002)

Schapira, L. L. *The Cassandra Complex: Living with Disbelief – A Modern Perspective on Hysteria* (Toronto: 1988)

Schaps, D. M. 'What was Free about a Free Athenian Woman?', *TAPA* 128 (1998), 161–188

'Women in Greek Inheritance Law', *CQ* 25 (1975), 53–57

Economic Rights of Women in Ancient Greece (Edinburgh: 1979)

Scheid, J. *The Craft of Zeus: Myths of Weaving and Fabric* (trans. Carol Volk) (Cambridge, MA: 1996)

Scheidel, W. 'The Most Silent Women of Greece and Rome: Rural Labour and Women's Life', *G&R* 42/43 (1995/1996), 202–17; 1–10
'Libitina's Bitter Gains: Seasonal Mortality and Endemic Disease', *Ancient Society* 25 (1994), 151–175
The Cambridge Economic History of the Greco-Roman World (Cambridge: 2007)

Schmitt, J-C. 'Prostituées, Lépreux, Hérétiques: les Rayures de l'infamie', *L'Histoire* 148 (1991), 89

Scholz, P. *Eunuchs and Castrati.* (Markus Weiner Publishers, 2001)

Schrader, H. P. 'Sons and Mothers', *Sparta: Journal of Ancient Sparta and Greek History* 7 (2011), 24–26
'Scenes from a Spartan Marriage', *Sparta* 6 (2010), 46–9

Schultheiss, D. 'Preputial Infibulation: From Ancient Medicine to Modern Genital Piercing', *BJU Int.* 92 (2003), 758–63

Scurlock, J. A. 'Baby-snatching Demons, Restless Souls and the Dangers of Childbirth', *Incognita* 2 (1991), 135–183

Sealey, R. *The Justice of the Greeks* (Ann Arbor, MI: 1994)
Women and Law in Classical Greece (Chapel Hill, NC: 1990)

Seidensticker, B. 'Women on the Tragic Stage', in Goff, B. (ed.), *History, Tragedy, Theory* (Austin, TX: 1995), 151–73

Seller, R. *The Family and Society* in Bodel (2001), 95–117

Seltman, C. 'The Status of Women in Athens', *G&R* Vol. 2 (1955), 119–124
Women in Antiquity (London: 1956)
'Life in Ancient Crete II: Atlantis', *History Today* 2 (1952)

Sharrock, A. R. 'Womanufacture,' *JRS* 81 (1991), 36–49

Shaw, M. 'The Female Intruder: Women in Fifth-century Drama', *CP* 70 (1975) 255–66

Shepherd, G. 'Women in Magna Graecia', in James, *Companion* (2012), 215–228

Simon, B, *Mind and Madness in Ancient Greece* (Ithaca, NY: 1978)

Sissa, J. *Sex and Sensuality in the Ancient World* (London: 2008)
Le Corps Virginal: La Virginite Feminine en Grece Ancienne (Paris: 1987)

Skinner, M. B. *Sexuality in Greek and Roman Culture, 2nd Edition* (Chichester: 2014)
'Aphrodite Garlanded: Erôs and Poetic Creativity in Sappho and Nossi', in Rabinowitz, *Among Women: From the Homosocial to the Homoerotic in the Ancient World Corinna of Tanagra and Her Audience* (Tulsa, OK: 1983)

Slater, P. *The Glory of Hera: Greek Mythology and the Greek Family* (Princeton, NJ: 1992)

Smith, N. D. 'Plato and Aristotle on the Nature of Women', *Journal of the History of Philosophy* 21 (1983), 467–478

Snyder, J. M. 'Korinna's Glorious Songs of Heroes', *Eranos* 82 (1984), 1–10

The Woman and the Lyre: Women Writers in Classical Greece and Rome (Illinois: 1989)

Sobol, D. *The Amazons of Greek Mythology* (South Brunswick: 1972)

Sourvinou-Inwood, C. 'Assumptions and the Creation of Meaning: Reading Sophocles' Antigone', *JHS* 109 (1989), 134–48

Spacks, P. M. *Gossip* (New York: 1985)

Spaeth, B. S. *The Roman Goddess Ceres* (Austin, TX: 1993)

Squire, M. *The Art of the Body: Antiquity and its Legacy* (London: 2011)

Staden, H. von, 'Women, Dirt and Exotica in the Hippocratic Corpus', *Helios* 19 (1992), 7–30

Stahnisch, F. W. (ed.) *The Proceedings of the 18th Annual History of Medicine Day Conference 2009: The University of Calgary Faculty of Medicine, Alberta, Canada* (Cambridge Scholars Publishing, 2012)

Stallsmith, A. 'Interpreting the Athenian Thesmophoria', *CB* 84 (2009)

Stannard, J. 'Marcellus of Bordeaux and the Beginnings of the Medieval Materia Medica', *Pharmacy in History* 15 (1973), 48

Stanton, D. C. (ed.) *Discourses of Sexuality: From Aristotle to Aids* (Ann Arbor, MI: 1992)

Stauffer, D. 'Aristotle's Account of the Subjection of Women', *Journal of Politics* 70 (2008), 929–941

Stavrakakis, Y. 'Thessaloniki Brothel', *Archaeology Archive* 51 (1998) archive.archaeology.org/9805/newsbriefs/brothel.html

Stehle, E. *Performance and Gender in Ancient Greece: Nondramatic Poetry in its Settings* (Princeton: 1997)

Stengers, J. *Masturbation: The History of a Great Terror* (London: 2001)

Stewart, S. *Cosmetics & Perfumes in the Roman World* (Stroud: 2007)

Storey, I. C. 'Domestic Disharmony in Euripides' Andromache', *G&R* 36, (1989) 16–20

Stratton, K.B. (ed.) *Daughters of Hecate: Women and Magic in the Ancient World* Oxford 2014)

Naming the Witch: Magic, Ideology and Stereotype in the Ancient World (Columbus, OH: 2007)

Stromberg, A. *The Family in the Graeco-Roman World* (New York: 2011)

Strong, R. A. *The Most Shameful Practice: Temple Prostitution in the Ancient Greek World* (Berkeley: 1997)

Suda online: http://www.stoa.org/sol/

Sutton, R. F. 'Nuptial Eros: The Visual Discourse of Marriage in Classical Athens', *JWAG* 55-56 (1998), 27–48

Swain, S. (ed.) *Seeing the Face, Seeing the Soul: Polemon's Physiognomy from Classical Antiquity to Medieval Islam* (Oxford: 2007)

Swancutt, D. M. 'Still before Sexuality: "Greek" Androgyny, the Roman Imperial Politics of Masculinity and the Roman Invention of the *tribas*', in *Mapping Gender in Ancient Religious Discourses*, 22ff

Swift, L. A. 'Sexual and Familial Distortion in Euripides' Phoenissae', *TAPA* 139 (2009), 53–87

Symonds, J. A. *A Problem in Greek Ethics* (1901) http://www.sacred-texts.com/lgbt/pge/pge21.htm

Syropoulos, S. 'An exemplary Oikos. Domestic Role-models in Euripides' Alcestis', *Eirene* 37 (2001), 5–18
    Gender and the Social Function of Athenian Tragedy (Oxford: 2003)
    'Women vs Women: The Denunciation of Female Sex by Female Characters in Drama', *Ágora. Estudos Clássicos em Debate* 14 (2012)

Tacaks, S. *Vestal Virgins, Sibyls, and Matrons* (Austin, TX: 2008)

Tannery, A. *A History of the Pregnancy Test or Is the Rabbit in Heat?* (2007)

Taylor, C. C. W. 'The Role Of Women In Plato's Republic', in Kamtekar, R. (ed.) *Virtue and Happiness: Essays in Honour of Julia Annas* (2012)

Taylor, T. *The Prehistory of Sex: Four Million Years of Human Sexual Culture* (London: 1996)

Temkin, O. *Soranus' Gynecology* (Baltimore, MD: 1956)

Tetlow, E. M. Women, *Crime and Punishment in Ancient Law and Society: Volume 2: Ancient Greece* (1995)

Thorndike, L. *The Place of Magic in the Intellectual History of Europe* (New York: 1905)
    History of Magic and Experimental Science (Columbia, OH: 1923)

Thornton, B. S. *Eros: The Myth of Ancient Greek Sexuality* (Boulder, CO: 1997)

Toohey, P. 'Death and Burial in the Ancient World', in *The Oxford Encyclopedia of Ancient Greece and Rome*, vol. 1 (Oxford 2010), 364ff

Totelin, L. 'Sex and Vegetables in the Hippocratic Gynecological Treatises', *SHPBBS* 38 (2007), 531–540

Tourraix, A. 'La femme et le pouvoir chez Hérodote', *Dialogues d' Histoire Ancienne* 2 (1976), 369–386

Traill, A. *Women and the Comic Plot in Menander* (Cambridge: 2012)

Treggiari, S. 'Concubinae', *PBSR* 49 (1981), 59–81

Tsang, G. 'Gladiators: How Bloodshed Gave Rise to Western Medicine', in Stahnisch, 302ff

Tyrrell, W. B. *Amazons: A Study in Athenian Mythmaking* (Baltimore: 1989)

Ucko, P. J. 'Penis Sheaths: A Comparative Study', in Buchli, V. *Material Culture Critical Concepts in the Social Sciences* (London: 2004), 260

Ungaretti J. R. 'Pederasty, Heroism, and the Family in Classical Greece', *Journal of Homosexuality* 3 (1978), 291–300

Valeva, (ed.) *A Companion to Ancient Thrace* (Chichester: 2015)

Van der Gracht, S. 'Setting Aside the Loom: Hermaphroditism in Ancient Medicine' in Stahnisch, 247ff

Vanggard, T. *Phallos: A Symbol and Its History in the Male World* (New York: 1972)

van Hook, La Rue 'The Exposure of Infants at Athens', *TAPA* 51 (1920) 134–45

van Nievelt, A. 'In Love with the Impossible: The Defeat of Androgyny in Killing and Dying', *Helicon* 2012

Verstraete, B. *Same-Sex Desire and Love in Greco-Roman Antiquity and In the Classical Tradition of the West* (Harrington Park Press, 2005)

Vidal F. 'The School of Alexandria, Cradle of Anatomy and Physiology'. *Chir Dent Fr.* 18 (1985), 35–9

Vout, C. *Sex on Show: Seeing the Erotic in Greece and Rome* (London: 2013)

Wagner-Hasel, S. 'Women's Life in Oriental Seclusion? On the History and Use of a Topos', in *Golden: Sex and Difference in Ancient Greece and Rome* (2003)

Waithe, M. E. *A History of Women Philosophers: Ancient Women Philosophers Vol 1 600 BC–AD 500* (Dordrecht: 1987)

Walcot, P. 'Plutarch on Sex', *G&R* 45 (1998), 166–187

'On Widows and their Reputation in Antiquity', *SO* 66 (1991) 5–26

'Herodotus on Rape', *Arethusa* 11 (1978), 137–147

Walker, S. 'Women and Housing in Classical Greece: The Archaeological Evidence', in Cameron, A. *Images of Women in Antiquity* (1983) 81ff

Walter, K. *The Secret Museum: Pornography in Modern Culture* (Berkeley, CA: 1996)

Watson, P. A. 'Ancient Stepmothers', *Mnemosyne* 143 (1995)

West, M. L. 'Corinna', *CQ* 29 (1970), 277–287

Whitbeck, C. 'Theories of Sex Difference', in Gould (ed.), *Women and Philosophy*, (New York: 1976), 54–80

White, M. J. 'The Statue Syndrome: Perversion? Fantasy? Anecdote?', *Journal of Sex Research* 14 (1978)

Whiteley, R. *Courtesans and Kings: Ancient Greek Perspectives on the Hetairai.* MA Diss, University of Calgary (2000)

Whittaker, T. 'Sex and the Sack of the City', *G&R* 56 (2009), 234–242

WHO *ICD: International Classification of Diseases* (10 version, Geneva 2010)

Wider, K. 'Women Philosophers in the Ancient Greek World: Donning the Mantle', *Hypatia* 1 (1986)

Wiles, D. 'Marriage and Prostitution in Classical New Comedy', in J. Redmond (ed.), *Themes In Drama 11: Women in Theatre* (Cambridge: 1989) 31–48

Wilkinson L. P. 'Classical Approaches: I. Population and Family Planning', *Encounter* 50.4 (1978), 22–32

Will, E. L. 'Women in Pompeii', *Archaeology* 32 (1979), 34–43

Williams, C. A. Greek Love at Rome, *CQ* 45 (1995), 517–38

'Sexual Themes in Greek and Latin Graffiti', in Hubbard (2014), 493–508

Roman Homosexuality: Ideologies of Masculinity in Classical Antiquity (Oxford: 1999)

Winkler, J. J. *The Constraints of Desire: The Anthropology of Sex and Gender in Ancient Greece* (London: 1990)

'Laying Now the Law: The Oversight of Men's Sexual Behavior in Classical Athens', in Halperin, *Before Sexuality*, 171–209

Wohl, V. *Love Among the Ruins: the Erotics of Democracy in Classical Athens* (Princeton, NJ: 2002)

Woman, N. *Abusive Mouths in Classical Athens* (Cambridge: 2008)

Wright, J. 'The White Man's Magic in Homer', *The Scientific Monthly* 9 (1919), 550–560

Yamagata, N. *Homeric Morality* (Leiden: 1998)

Yarnall, J. *Transformations of Circe: The History of an Enchantress* (Chicago: 1994)

Yatromanolakis, D. *Sappho in the Making: The Early Reception* (Cambridge, MA: 2008)

Younger, J. G. *Sex in the Ancient World from A-Z* (London: 2005)

Zampieri N. 'Male Circumcision Through the Ages: the Role of Tradition', *Acta Paediatrica* 97 (2008), 1305–7

Zeitlin, F. 'The Dynamics of Misogyny: Myth and Mythmaking in the Oresteia', in Peradotto J. *Women in the Ancient World: The Arethusa Papers* (1984)

'Playing the Other: Theater, Theatricality and the Feminine in Greek Drama', *Representations* 11 (1985) 63–94

'The Politics of Eros in the Danaid Trilogy of Aeschylus' in R. Hexter (ed.) *Innovations of Antiquity* (New York: 1996), 203–52

Index

foreigners' sexual behaviour,
  perception of   138ff, 157–8,
  158–9, 160
foreskin   163f, 209
funerals   156

Ganymede   16, 23, 6
gender reassignment   82
gender double standards   45, 74
gender selection   79–80, 198
genital mutilation   32, 210
grief for a partner   64, 146, 156
grooming   110
group sex and troilism   111
gunaikonomoi   77
gynaecology *see* obstetrics and
  gynaecology

hate mail   64
Hector   40, 73
'Hector Horse' sexual position   84
Helen of Troy   21, 31, 41, 43, 47,
  73, 140, 167, 181
Hephaestus   73
Hera   12, 17, 19, 21
Hercules   104, 182
Hermai, mutilation of   211–2
hermaphrodites   23, 32, 80–81,
  83, 96–7, 8
Hermaphroditus   20, 23
Hermes   211
Herodas   60, 90–1
Herodotus   138ff
Hesiod   62
hetaerae   86, 109f, 112f, 129,
  170, 21
heterosexuality   40, 66, 176
Hippocratics, The   79–80, 188ff
Hipponax   83, 198–9
Homer
  on marriage   47
homosexuals and
  homosexuality   23, 37, 39,
  40, 66, 93, 96ff, 99, 100–103,
  106, 122, 216–7, 24, 28

homosexuals, admiration for   98
  demonization of   66, 106,
  216–7
  in the military   40, 102
Hyacinth   38
hypersexuality   32–3
hypospadias   81–2
hystera see womb
hysteria   194

impotence   188ff
incest   20–21, 38, 51–3, 83, 94
infanticide   45–6
infertility   193
infibulation female   *see* female
  genital mutilation
infibulation, male   164
in flagrante delicto   74, 77, 98
instantaneous transgender
  transgression   *see* gender
  reassignment
internet abuse of women   64, 155
irrumation   165–6, 17
Ixion   28

Julia, daughter of Augustus   67
Julius Caesar   105

kissing   67–8
kourotrophoi   11

Leda   31, 12
'lesbianism' and 'lesbians'   66,
  97, 106–7
  demonization of   66, 106–7
Leucippe and Clitophon: 68
love   23, 41–4, 45, 58–9, 64f,
  175, 176
  as cause of illness and
  debilitation   69–70
Lupercalia   104

Macedon   126ff
magic, witchcraft and superstition
  67, 178ff